北京外国语大学 | 图史

An Illustrated History of Beijing Foreign Studies University

1941-2014

《北京外国语大学图史》编撰委员会 编

外语教学与研究出版社
FOREIGN LANGUAGE TEACHING AND RESEARCH PRESS
北京 BEIJING

宝塔山苍苍，延河水泱泱。北京外国语大学肇基于陕北延安，其历史可以追溯到一九四一年成立的中国人民抗日军政大学三分校俄文队——中国共产党创办的第一所高等外语教育学府。她在民族解放战争的烽火硝烟中诞生，伴随共和国的成长而发展壮大，峥嵘岁月，英才辈出，为国家的外交、经贸、文教等事业做出了突出贡献。七十余载风雨砥砺，七十余载弦歌不辍。北京外国语大学的光荣传统将永远薪火相传，发扬光大；北外人将永远志存高远，铸造辉煌！

The origin of Beijing Foreign Studies University — the first higher education institution for foreign language learning founded by the Communist Party of China — can be traced back to Yan'an in northern Shaanxi in 1941 when, at the foot of the emerald coloured Pagoda Mountain overlooking the gurgling Yan River, a Russian programme was set up at the Third Campus of the Military and Political University of Chinese People's War of Resistance Against Japanese Aggression. Born during the nation's struggles for liberation, Beijing Foreign Studies University has grown and flourished along with the People's Republic. Over the past decades it has educated generation after generation of brilliant foreign language professionals, making significant contributions to China's diplomatic, economic, cultural and educational endeavors. With a stormy but glorious 70 years of history fit for a ballad, the honourable traditions of Beijing Foreign Studies University will be passed from one generation to the next, never to be forgotten. The people of BFSU will always strive to improve themselves in the pursuit of their lofty ambitions and build on their past achievements for an even more glorious future.

北京外国语大学历史沿革简表

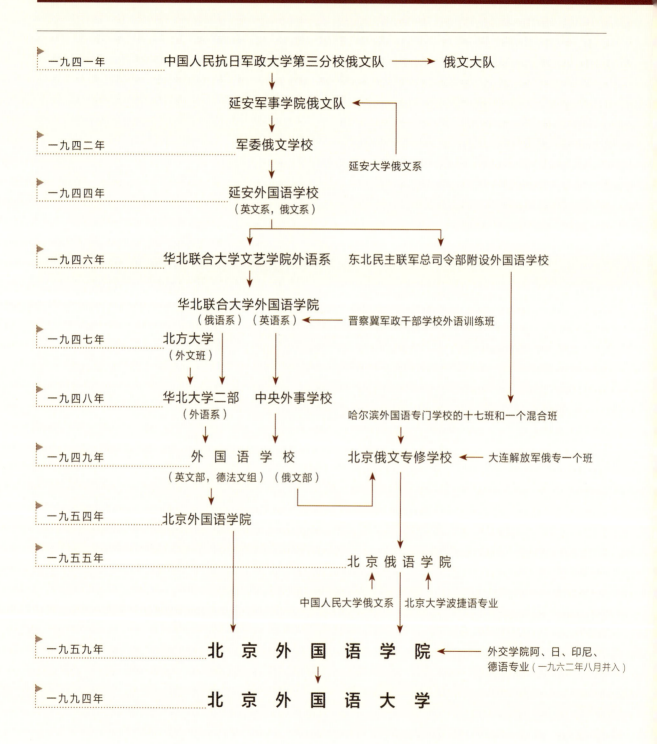

一九四一年　中国人民抗日军政大学第三分校俄文队 ──→ 俄文大队

延安军事学院俄文队 ←── 延安大学俄文系

一九四二年　军委俄文学校

一九四四年　延安外国语学校
（英文系，俄文系）

一九四六年　华北联合大学文艺学院外语系　　东北民主联军总司令部附设外国语学校

华北联合大学外国语学院
（俄语系）（英语系） ←── 晋察冀军政干部学校外语训练班

一九四七年　北方大学
（外文班）

一九四八年　华北大学二部　中央外事学校
（外语系）

哈尔滨外国语专门学校的十七班和一个混合班

一九四九年　外 国 语 学 校　　　北京俄文专修学校 ←── 大连解放军俄专一个班
（英文部，德法文组）（俄文部）

一九五四年　北京外国语学院

一九五五年　北京俄语学院

中国人民大学俄文系　北京大学波捷语专业

一九五九年　**北 京 外 国 语 学 院** ←── 外交学院阿、日、印尼、
德语专业（一九六二年八月并入）

一九九四年　**北 京 外 国 语 大 学**

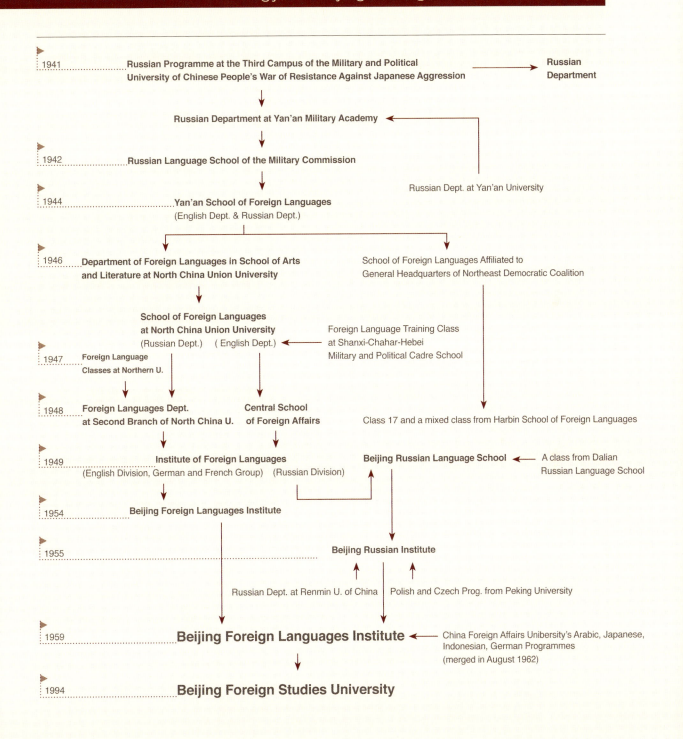

▷ 1941 — Russian Programme at the Third Campus of the Military and Political University of Chinese People's War of Resistance Against Japanese Aggression → **Russian Department**

Russian Department at Yan'an Military Academy ←

▷ 1942 — **Russian Language School of the Military Commission**

Russian Dept. at Yan'an University

▷ 1944 — **Yan'an School of Foreign Languages** (English Dept. & Russian Dept.)

▷ 1946 — **Department of Foreign Languages in School of Arts and Literature at North China Union University**

School of Foreign Languages Affiliated to General Headquarters of Northeast Democratic Coalition

School of Foreign Languages at North China Union University (Russian Dept.) (English Dept.) ← Foreign Language Training Class at Shanxi-Chahar-Hebei Military and Political Cadre School

▷ 1947 — **Foreign Language Classes at Northern U.**

▷ 1948 — **Foreign Languages Dept. at Second Branch of North China U.**   **Central School of Foreign Affairs**

Class 17 and a mixed class from Harbin School of Foreign Languages

▷ 1949 — **Institute of Foreign Languages** (English Division, German and French Group)   (Russian Division)

Beijing Russian Language School ← A class from Dalian Russian Language School

▷ 1954 — **Beijing Foreign Languages Institute**

▷ 1955 — **Beijing Russian Institute**

Russian Dept. at Renmin U. of China │ Polish and Czech Prog. from Peking University

▷ 1959 — **Beijing Foreign Languages Institute** ← China Foreign Affairs Unibersity's Arabic, Japanese, Indonesian, German Programmes (merged in August 1962)

▷ 1994 — **Beijing Foreign Studies University**

目　录

第一章
延安建校　艰苦创业
（1941—1946年）

Chapter One
Starting in Yan'an,
challenging beginnings
(1941–1946)

1941 年 3 月，中国人民抗日军政大学（简称"抗大"）三分校俄文队成立，其后发展演变为俄文大队、延安军事学院俄文队、军委俄文学校，直至 1944 年的延安外国语学校。从抗大俄文队到延安外国语学校，是中国共产党创办外语教育的发轫奠基阶段。

In March 1941, the Russian Programme at the Third Campus of the Military and Political University of Chinese People's War of Resistance Against Japanese Aggression (commonly abbreviated to Kangda) was established. In the following years, the programme first became a department at the University, which was then renamed Russian Department at Yan'an Military Academy, then the department became Russian Language School of the Military Commission, and eventually in 1944 the school was expanded into Yan'an School of Foreign Languages. Its evolution from the Russian Programme at Kangda to Yan'an School of Foreign Languages constituted the initial stage of the Chinese Communist Party's drive for foreign language education.

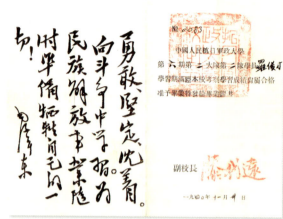

1   2

1. 延安时期的抗大校门

2. 中国人民抗日军政大学毕业证书（罗俊才提供）

1. Kangda's front gate at Yan'an

2. Kangda's Graduation Certificate (provided by Luo Juncai)

1939

　　中国人民抗日军政大学原名抗日红军大学，校址设在延安。1939 年 7 月，抗大总校从延安迁往晋东南太行区时，留下一部分师生组成第三分校。

　　三分校是一所培养中高级军事、政治、技术干部的学校，第一任校长是许光达，后由陈奇涵、郭化若继任。

　　Located in Yan'an, the Military and Political University of Chinese people's War of Resistance Against Japanese Aggression was originally named Red Army University of Resistance Against Japanese Aggression. In July 1939, Kangda's main campus relocated to the district of Taihang in Southeast Jin (present-day Shanxi Province), but left behind some of its staff and students to form its Third Campus.

　　The purpose of the Third Campus was to cultivate middle to high-ranking military, political and technical officers. The first president was Xu Guangda, followed by Chen Qihan and then Guo Huaruo.

常乾坤（1904—1973），山西垣曲人。1925年入黄埔军校学习，同年加入中国共产党。1926年赴苏联，入红军航空学校学习。1941年任抗大三分校俄文大队大队长，1942年任延安军事学院俄文队队长。中华人民共和国成立后，历任中国人民解放军空军副司令员兼训练部部长、中国人民志愿军空军副司令员、中国人民解放军空军副司令员兼空军学院副院长、空军工程学院院长和政治委员、空军军事科研部部长。1955年被授予中将军衔，曾获二级独立自由勋章、一级解放勋章。

Chang Qiankun (1904-1973), born in Yuanqu, Shanxi Province, enrolled in Huangpu Military Academy in 1925 and joined the Communist Party of China in the same year. He went to the Soviet Union in 1926 and studied at the Red Army Air Force Academy. In 1941, he became Head of the Russian Department at the Third Campus of Kangda and later Head of the Russian Department at Yan'an Military Academy. After the founding of the People's Republic of China, he served terms as Deputy Commander of Chinese People's Liberation Army Air Force and Director of its Training Division at the same time, Deputy Commander of the Chinese People's Volunteer Army Air Force, Deputy Commander of the Chinese People's Liberation Army Air Force and Vice President of the Air Force Academy at the same time, President and Political Commissar of the Air Force Engineering College, and Director of the Air Force Military Research Division. He was promoted to Lieutenant General in 1955 and was awarded the Medal of Independence of the Second Order and the Medal of Liberation of the First Oder.

1940

▍抗大三分校俄文队

1940年10月，抗日战争进入战略相持阶段。为了适应抗战形势的发展，培养俄文军事翻译，根据中共中央军委的指示，1941年3月，抗大三分校俄文队正式成立，到1941年7月发展为俄文大队，共有300余人，大队长常乾坤，副大队长何振亚、何辉燕，政治协理员李觉民。常乾坤、王弼、张培成兼任教员，专任教员有卢竞如、李洁民、王玉、李海、陈饪、金涛等。

1941年8月，俄文大队正式上课，当时队址在延安东关黑龙沟，地处清凉山东麓，南临延河，对岸是嘉岭山（即宝塔山），山下是南川河与延河的交汇处。

Russian Department at Kangda's Third Campus

In October 1940, Chinese People's War of Resistance Against Japanese Aggression reached stalemate. In order to adapt to the changing conditions and train Russian translators for military purposes, a Russian programme was established at Kangda's Third Campus in March 1941 at the direction of the CPC Central Military Commission. In July 1941, Russian Department was founded, including more than 300 staff and students. Chang Qiankun was Head of the Department, his deputies He Zhenya and He Huiyan, and Political Assistant Li Juemin. Chang Qiankun, Wang Bi and Zhang Peicheng served as part-time teachers. Full time teachers included Lu Jingru, Li Jiemin, Wang Yu, Li Hai, Chen Ren and Jin Tao.

In August 1941, the Russian Department formally started lessons. At the time the department was located in Heilonggou in Dongguan, Yan'an. The site was on the east side of Qingliang Mountain, bordered in the south by Yan River. On the opposite bank of the river was Jialing Mountain (better known as Pagoda Mountain), which was situated at the confluence of Nanchuan and Yan rivers.

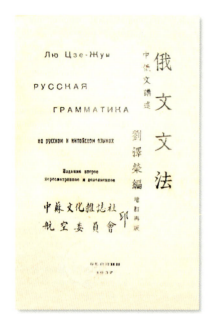

俄文大队使用的教材

Russian Grammar used by the Russian Department

俄文大队组成结构图

Russian Department's organisational chart

俄文一队
Class One
1941 年 5 月底以前入学的学员 100 余人，队长曹慕岳，政治指导员汪涵之。
More than 100 students enrolled before the end of May 1941. Class Leader: Cao Muyue; Political Instructor: Wang Hanzhi.

俄文二队
Class Two
1941 年 6 月以后入学的学员 90 余人，队长白映奎，政治指导员徐继远。
Over 90 students enrolled after June 1941. Class Leader: Bai Yingkui; Political Instructor: Xu Jiyuan.

俄文三队
Class Three
1941 年 7 月安塞工程学校停办后转来的师生，队长陶铁英，政治指导员刘端祥。
Teachers and students were transferred from the disbanded Ansai Engineering School in July 1941. Class Leader: Tao Tieying; Political Instructor: Liu Duanxiang.

中央和军委直属机关

Departments directly under the CPC Central Committee and the Central Military Commission

从三分校毕业生及干部中抽调

Graduates and cadres from the Third Campus

陕甘宁边区政府各部门

Departments of Shaanxi-Gansu-Ningxia Border Area government

俄文队学生来源

Background of students of the Russian Department

地方党政机关

Local party and government departments

八路军后方留守兵团

Red Corps of Eighth Route Army

各根据地前方部队

Various base areas of frontline troops

1941

延安军事学院俄文队

1941 年 12 月，根据中共中央的决定，抗大三分校改为延安军事学院。军事学院直属军委参谋部，院长由朱德兼任，副院长叶剑英，教育长郭化若。下设高干队、特科队、俄文队和参谋训练队。

俄文队有学员近 200 人。原抗大三分校俄文一队、二队合编为一个队，下辖五个区队。工程队（俄文三队）调归工程科。俄文科主任为卢竞如，俄文队队长常乾坤，副队长曹慕岳，政治协理员张培成。

军委俄文学校校长曾涌泉。曾涌泉（1902—1996），四川新都人。1925年加入中国共产党。曾就读于苏联列宁军政学院。曾任中央军委编译局局长兼军委俄文学校校长、延安外国语学校校长、石家庄警备司令等职。中华人民共和国成立后，历任驻苏联大使馆公使衔参赞、驻波兰大使、驻民主德国大使、中华人民共和国外交部副部长、驻罗马尼亚大使等职。是第十一届中共中央纪委常委、第六届全国政协常委。

军委俄文学校教务处处长卢竞如（摄于20世纪90年代）。卢竞如（1904—1993），湖南平江人。1925年8月加入中国共产党，早年先后在苏联国际列宁学校、东方大学学习。曾任中央妇女委员会秘书长、延安军事学院俄文科主任、军委俄文学校教务处处长、延安外国语学校俄文系主任等职务。中华人民共和国成立后，历任俄文《友好报》第一副总编辑、中央宣传部翻译组副组长、中央广播事业局苏联东欧部副主任等职务。

Zeng Yongquan (1902-1996), Principal of the Russian Language School of the Military Commission. Born in Xindu, Sichuan, Zeng joined the Communist Party of China in 1925; studied at the Lenin Military and Political Academy in the Soviet Union; served terms as Director of the Publication and Translation Bureau of the Central Military Commission and concurrently as Principal of Russian Department at Yan'an Military Academy and then as Principal of Yan'an School of Foreign Languages, Garrison Commander at Shijiazhuang. After the founding of the People's Republic, he took up such posts as Minister Counsellor at the Chinese Embassy to the Soviet Union, Ambassador to Poland, Ambassador to the German Democratic Republic, Vice Minister of Foreign Affairs, and Ambassador to Romania. He was on the Standing Committee of the 11th CPC Central Commission for Discipline Inspection and the Standing Committee of the 6th Chinese People's Political Consultative Conference.

Lu Jingru (1904-1993, picture taken in the 1990s.), registrar at the Russian Language School of the Military Commission. Born in Pingjiang, Hunan, Lu joined the CPC in August 1925 and studied at the International Lenin School and the Communist University of the Toilers of the East in the Soviet Union. She served as Secretary General of the Women's Work Division of the CPC Central Committee, Head of the Russian Department at Yan'an Military Academy, Director of Teaching Affairs at Yan'an Russian Language School, and Head of the Russian Department at Yan'an School of Foreign Languages. After the founding of the People's Republic, she took up posts such as the First-Deputy Chief Editor of the Russian language newspaper *Friendship Gazette*, Deputy Head of the Translation Division at the Propaganda Department of CPC Central Committee and Deputy Director of the Soviet Union and Eastern Europe Division at the Central Broadcasting Administration.

Russian Department at Yan'an Military Academy

At the direction of the CPC Central Committee in December 1941, Kangda's 3rd Campus was renamed Yan'an Military Academy. The military academy came under the direct governance of the Staff of the Central Military Commission and was under the stewardship of Zhu De (Academy President), Ye Jianying (Vice President) and Guo Huaruo (Registrar). The academy consisted of a Senior Cadre Department, Special Agents Department, Russian Department and Staff Officer Training Department.

The Russian Department had close to 200 people. The former Classes One and Two of the Russian Department of Kangda's Third Campus was organized into one Department, which split into five units. The former Class Three of the Russian Department of Kangda's Third Campus was assigned to the Engineering Department. The reconstituted Russian Department was led by Lu Jingru (Director), Chang Qiankun (Head), Cao Muyue (Deputy Head) and Zhang Peicheng (Political Assistant).

2

1. 延安大学校门。延安大学俄文系建立于 1941 年 9 月，当时在系学生 50 余人。延安军事学院成立后，延安大学俄文系被整合到延安军事学院中。
2. 军委俄文学校使用的教材，1941 年新文化出版社编印。

1. The entrance to Yan'an University. Its Russian Department was established in September 1941 with over 50 students. The department was later transferred into Yan'an Military Academy.
2. Russian Textbook used at the Russian Language School (compiled and printed by New Culture Press in 1941)

1942

军委俄文学校

1942 年 5 月，中央军委决定，延安军事学院俄文队单独建校，改名为军委俄文学校，归军委第四局（后改为中央军委编译局）领导。校长由局长曾涌泉兼任，王弼任秘书长，叶和玉任政治处主任，卢竞如任教务处处长，邹载道任校务处处长，曹慕岳任俄文队队长。

军委俄文学校在校学员 130 余人，编为一个队，分五个区队上课。为了便于对女生进行管理，另设一个女生区队，但学习仍分别编在五个区队内。学校师资力量有所增强，除原有的教师外，又先后调入刘群、钟毅、邵天任、王琏、刘风等人来校任教。

The Russian Language School of the Military Commission

In May 1942, the Central Military Commission decided that the Russian Department at Yan'an Military Academy was to become an independent school and be named the Russian Language School of the Military Commission. The school came under the governance of the Military Commission's Fourth Directorate (later named the Publication and Translation Directorate of the Central Military Commission), with the Head of the Directorate Zeng Yongquan serving concurrently as Principal of the school, Wang Bi as Chief Secretary, Ye Heyu as Political Director, Lu Jingru as Registrar, Zou Zaidao as Director of School Affairs, and Cao Muyue as Head of the Russian Department.

The Russian Language School of the Militaty Commission had just over 130 students on campus and was treated as a single department, but they were split into five units for lessons. To better manage the female students, a female unit was established, but all female students studied under the existing five units. The number of teaching staff at the school increased and in addition to the existing teachers, people like Liu Qun, Zhong Yi, Shao Tianren, Wang Lian and Liu Feng were recruited as teachers of the school.

俄 文 学 校

年 表　　　　罗俊才 1943·5·10

時　間	地　点	做什么？	證明人
1926（民国十五年）七岁—十一岁—1930	在太原市圆绢虎营街阳曲县立初级小学	上学	无
1930（民国十九年）十一岁—十三岁 1932	在太原市西绢虎营街阳曲县立高级小学	上学	无
1932年夏季（民国廿一年）十三岁—十四岁 1933	在太原市三桥街省立第一师范附属小学补习班	上学	王理（任某学院等習）
1933年夏季（民国廿二年）十四岁—十七岁 1936	在太原东绢虎营街私立友仁中学初中部	上学	邾涛（原名扈须明）现在中之二二○一班生产战斗改委
1936夏（廿五年）十七岁—十八岁（1937·4）	考入晋绥军军官教练所（有一时期在小北门外有一时期在新南门外尚上村离城十里）	当学兵	唐靖山（又名唐某斯）现在延大学習胡時敏现在由延厥行金库工作
1937·5（廿六年）十八岁—1937·9下旬	在山西祁县军士二团三营十二连（在距城五里名叫五里坑塔）	受训（当学员）	唐靖山 現在延大学習 蘇里国 现在军事学院工作
1937·9（廿六年）—12月 十八岁	在祁县军士二团自救抵者参加抗敌队（後开往临汾）	当队员	唐靖山 同上
1937年末 十八岁—1938·6月	由决死队调任政卫队（在临汾）	当队员（後任班长）	唐靖山
1938·6（廿七年）十九岁—1939（廿八年）·5月	在政卫队二大队四中队	任观察军士	唐靖山 鲁军（现在小石堡播子待委工作）
1939·7月（廿八年）二十岁至年底	在政卫队（又名二○九旅）八大队九中队	任政治工作员（後代指导）	王风 现在军事学院学習 唐靖山
1940·1（廿九年）—2月 廿一岁	在决死队干部学校（驻武乡县）二队	学習（任班长）	比爱田（原在姬兵队学習）現在武乡郡郡任深滨弹药的工作，現在秋政委晋调同志团队长
1940·2月（廿九年）—五月 廿一岁	在姬独一团政治部宣教科（武乡县）	任干事	王闰状（在决死二连隊，四团任事干事 由決死隊後不知往何处任职）
1940·5月（廿九年）—12月廿七日	在抗大总校二团一营二连（有一时期在武乡蟠龙镇有一时期在晋城入晋到冀西郡）	学習	张嘉英（在姬兵学習）現在此县一团及一工作多年 张爱田
1940年底—41年1月（廿二岁	在汾阳七区青年队（因敌扫荡不能回原部队 暂时为此工作）	任队长	柳珠（汾阳毕业現在和合化部队）
1940·2月（卅年）—三月 廿二岁	在决死二继队直属城队政治处	任教育干事	张一清（现在中甲学校学習（不知名字改仍叫张）
1941·3月（卅三年）—四月	仝上	调任青年干事	仝上
1941年·6月—一直特功在	在电器工程学校，抗大七分校，军事学校，俄文学校（延安）	学習	

1943 年军委俄文学校学员罗俊才填写的个人年表

A personal chronology table filled out by Luo Juncai, a student of the Russian Language School in 1943

■ 1943 年军委俄文学校旧址
（丁泉砭和尚塔）

Former site of the Yan'an Russian
Language School in 1943
(Heshangta at Dingquanbian)

■ 延安外国语学校英文系所在地车桥沟

Cheqiaogou, site of the English Department,
Yan'an School of Foreign Languages

1943

1943 年 10 月，军委俄文学校从延安东关黑龙沟搬迁到清凉山北麓丁泉砭原延安新文字干部学校的校址，并进行了小规模的校舍建设。

In October 1943, Russian Language School moved from Heilonggou in Dongguan, Yan'an, to Dingquanbian on the north side of Qingliang Mountain, former site of the Yan'an New Literature Cadre School. Some facilities were built at the site.

1　　　　　　　　　　　　　　　　　　　　　　2

1. 延安王家坪中央军委礼堂（当年延安外国语学校师生经常活动的场所）

2. 当时俄文系的教室延安和尚塔

1. The Central Military Commission's assembly hall at Wangjiaping, Yan'an, where staff and students from Yan'an School of Foreign Languages often gathered for activities

2. The Russian Department's classrooms at Heshangta in Yan'an

1944

延安外国语学校

1944 年 6 月，根据抗战形势的发展需要，军委俄文学校增设英文系，改名为延安外国语学校，归中央军委领导，仍由中央军委编译局局长曾涌泉兼任校长。中央军委副主席周恩来对学校的建设极为关切，指示一定要办好延安外国语学校，并亲自为英文系安排干部、聘请教师。在开学典礼上，周恩来发表了重要讲话，指出及早培养外交人才的必要性。同年 9 月，周恩来再次来校与师生见面，他强调，我们"不仅要培养军事翻译，而且要培养新中国的外交人才。这个问题，在办学思想上必须明确，组织领导上应早作准备"。

Yan'an School of Foreign Languages

In June 1944, to meet the needs arising from the new situation in the Chinese People's War of Resistance Against Japanese Aggression, the Russian Language School established an English Department and was renamed Yan'an School of Foreign Languages, which was placed under the governance of the Central Military Commission, with Zeng Yongquan, Director of the Publication and Translation Directorate still serving as Principal of the school. Zhou Enlai, Deputy Chairman of the Central Military Commission, was very attentive to the founding of the school and directed that it must be run well. He personally found senior staff and teachers for the English Department and gave a key speech at the school's opening ceremony, pointing out that the school must aim to train diplomatic personnel as quickly as possible. He returned to meet with staff and students at the school in September of the same year and reiterated that: "We must not only train translators for military affairs, but also diplomatic personnel for a new China. Senior school officials must bear this in mind when running the school and must prepare themselves for this challenge."

俄文系	英文系
Department of Russian	Department of English

◆ 系主任卢竞如

◆ 教员增调杨化飞、赵洵、韩斌、李荣华、唐国华等。

◆ 学员有 110 余人，分四个班上课。

◆ Lu Jingru (Department Head)

◆ New teachers: Yang Huafei, Zhao Xun, Han Bin, Li Ronghua, Tang Guohua, etc.

◆ More than 110 students, divided into four classes

◆ 系主任浦化人

◆ 专任教员有王大才、马牧鸣、唐海、温剑风、朱仲止等。

◆ 兼任教员有柯柏年、陈家康、黄华、马海德等。

◆ 学员有 70 余人，分编 A、B1、B2、C 四个班（不久改为 A、B、C 三个班）。

◆ Pu Huaren (Department Head)

◆ Full-time teachers included Wang Dacai, Ma Muming, Tang Hai, Wen Jianfeng and Zhu Zhongzhi, etc.

◆ Part-time teachers included Ke Bainian, Chen Jiakang, Huang Hua and George Hatem, etc.

◆ More than 70 students, divided into four classes A, B1, B2 and C (later condensed into three classes A, B and C)

▌延安外国语学校使用的部分教材

Some of the teaching materials used at Yan'an School of Foreign Languages

1945

1945 年 4 月至 6 月，中国共产党第七次代表大会在延安举行。会后曾涌泉调离延安外国语学校，校长由杨尚昆兼任。

1945 年 8 月，日本战败投降，学校除英文系部分师生留校继续学习外，大部分师生分批奔赴华北、东北解放区，承担外语翻译以及其他工作，一部分师生转移到张家口办学。

1946 年 4 月，卢竞如率领另一批师生到达吉林省长春市。其中一部分学生由东北局组织部分配了工作；一部分学生随卢竞如到哈尔滨办学，并于 1946 年 10 月成立了东北民主联军总司令部附设外国语学校。

After the Seventh Congress of the CPC, which was held in Yan'an from April to June 1945, Zeng Yong-quan was transferred elsewhere and Yang Shangkun took charge of the Yan'an School of Foreign Languages.

When the Japanese forces were defeated and Japan surrendered in August 1945, some of the English students continued to study at the School, but most of the students and staff left in batches and headed to the newly liberated North and Northeast regions to undertake translation and other work. Some of the students and staff moved to Zhangjiakou and started teaching there.

In April 1946, Lu Jingru led another group of students and staff to the city of Changchun in Jilin Province. Some of these students were assigned work by the Organization Department of the Northeastern Bureau. Other students followed Lu Jingru to Harbin where they established a School of Foreign Languages Affiliated to General Headquarters of Northeast Democratic Coalition.

第二章

辗转华北　坚持办学

（1946—1948年）

Chapter Two
With no fixed abode after relocation, yet remaining committed to teaching
(1946–1948)

　　1945 年 8 月抗日战争胜利，延安外国语学校师生大部分奔赴华北、东北解放区，承担翻译以及其他工作，一部分师生到张家口办学。1946 年至 1948 年，为适应革命形势发展的需要，中国共产党在晋察冀边区先后开办了四所外语教育机构，即华北联合大学外国语学院、晋察冀军政干部学校外语训练班、中央外事学校、华北大学二部外语系，进一步积累了办学经验，并培养出一批当时急需的外事工作干部。

After the Chinese people's War of Resistance Against Japanese Aggression came to a victorious end in August 1945, the majority of the teachers and students of Yan'an School of Foreign Languages went to the liberated areas in north and northeast China to work as translators or undertake other jobs, while the rest were relocated to Zhangjiakou where the school reopened. To adapt to the needs of the revolution, the Communist Party of China established four foreign language teaching institutions one after another in the Shanxi-Chahar-Hebei border region. They were the School of Foreign Languages at North China Union University, the Foreign Language Training Class at Shanxi-Chahar-Hebei Military and Political Cadre School, Central School of Foreign Affairs, and Foreign Languages Department at the Second Branch of North China University. This initiative provided the CPC with more experience in running foreign language schools and trained a much needed cohort of diplomatic personnel.

1

2

1. 1946 年 2 月延安外国语学校部分
   学员到达张家口时合影
2. 1946 年初张家口十三里营晋察冀
   军政干部学校外语训练班学员合影
3. 晋察冀军政干部学校外语训练班学
   员在校门外合影

1. A group photo of some of the students from Yan'an
   School of Foreign Languages when they arrived at
   Zhangjiakou in February 1946
2. A group photo of students from the Foreign Language
   Class at Shanxi-Chahar-Hebei Military and Political
   Cadre School taken in early 1946 at Shisanliying in
   Zhangjiakou
3. A group photo of students from the Foreign Language
   Class at Shanxi-Chahar-Hebei Military and Political
   Cadre School taken in front of the school gate

3

1946

华北联合大学文艺学院外语系、华北联合大学外国语学院

1945 年 9 月，中央军委决定，延安外国语学校师生分批离开延安，前往各解放区迎接新的任务。一部分师生到达晋察冀边区首府张家口，加入了由成仿吾任校长的华北联合大学（简称"华北联大"）。1946 年 1 月，华北联大文艺学院成立外语系，主要成员为来自延安外国语学校的师生，杨化飞任系主任。

1946 年 1 月，根据形势发展的需要，遵照周恩来"就地取材"的指示，重庆中共南方局外事组（组长王炳南）通过地下党组织和新民主主义青年社从重庆、成都等地大专学校的共产党员及有一定英语水平的进步学生中选拔了 79 人，由浦化人、罗清等带领，从重庆分三批飞往张家口，接着前往南郊十三里营晋察冀军政干部学校，成立外语训练班。军政干部学校校长张宗逊，政委朱良材，外文班主任浦化人，教务长罗清。

华北联大外国语学院院长浦化人（左）和英语系主任罗清

Head of the School of Foreign Languages Pu Huaren (L) with the Head of the English Department Luo Qing

Department of Foreign Languages in the School of Arts and Literature at North China Union University, and School of Foreign Languages at North China Union University

In September 1945, the Central Military Commission decided that students and teachers of Yan'an School of Foreign Languages should be sent to each of the liberated areas to undertake new assignments. A portion of those who left to Zhangjiakou, the regional capital of the Shanxi-Chahar-Hebei border region, was integrated into North China Union University, which was under the leadership of University President Cheng Fangwu. In January 1946, the Department of Foreign Languages was established within the School of Arts and Literature at North China Union University, and mainly consisted of those who had come from Yan'an School of Foreign Languages, with Yang Huafei as the department head.

Also in January 1946, to adapt to the changing situation and in accordance with Zhou Enlai's directive to "make use of local resources", the Foreign Affairs Division of the CPC Southern Bureau (headed by Wang Bingnan), with assistance from the CPC underground organisation and the New Democratic Youth Association, selected 79 bright students who had knowledge of English and who were Party members from vocational colleges around Chongqing and Chengdu. These students, led by teachers such as Pu Huaren and Luo Qing, went to Zhangjiakou in three groups and then went and setup the Foreign Language Training Course at the Shanxi-Chahar-Hebei Military and Political Cadre School, which was located at Shisanliying in the southern suburb of Zhangjiakou. The Cadre School was under the leadership of Principal Zhang Zongxun and Political Commissar Zhu Liangcai, with Pu Huaren as Course Director and Luo Qing as Director of Teaching Affairs.

1

2

　　1946 年 6 月，中共中央决定把晋察冀军政干部学校外语训练班全体师生转入华北联大，与华北联大外语系一起成立外国语学院，院长浦化人。学院有两个系：外语训练班和原华北联大外语系的 10 余名英语班学生组成的英语系，系主任罗清，政治助理员王季青；原华北联大外语系俄语班的 30 余名师生组成的俄语系，系主任杨化飞，政治助理员罗俊才。学院设在张家口东山坡原日本兵营家属宿舍内。

In June 1946, the CPC Central Committee decided to integrate all students and teachers from the Foreign Language Training Course at Shanxi-Chahar-Hebei Military and Political Cadre School into North China Union University, so that they could merge with the Department of Foreign Languages and form a new School of Foreign Languages within the University, with Pu Huaren as head of the school. The School had two departments: An English Department made up of those from the Foreign Language Training Course and a dozen or so students from the University's English Department, with Luo Qing as Department Head and Wang Jiqing as Political Assistant; A Russian Department was established, consisting of over 30 students and teachers from the University's Russian Language Class, with Yang Huafei as Department Head and Luo Juncai as Political Assistant. The School was established within the family quarters of the former Japanese army barracks at Dongshanpo in the city of Zhangjiakou.

1. 华北联大外国语学院旧址（张家口东山坡）

2. 1946 年 9 月，华北联大外国语学院迁至山西广灵县东加斗村，图为驻地院子大门（摄于 1985 年）。

3. 华北联大外国语学院在河北正定的学生宿舍

4. 华北联大外国语学院在河北正定的教师宿舍

3

4

1. Former site of the School of Foreign Languages at North China Union University (Dongshanpo, Zhangjiakou)

2. In September 1946, the NCUU School of Foreign Languages moved to East Jiadou Village in Guangling County, Shanxi. The photograph (taken in 1985) shows the main gate of the courtyard where the School was situated.

3. NCUU School of Foreign Languages' students' accommodation in Zhengding County, Hebei

4. NCUU School of Foreign Languages' teachers' accommodation in Zhengding County, Hebei

华北联大外国语学院成立不久，全体师生便于7月底停课赴宣化县农村参加土地改革运动。1946年9月，国民党军队进攻张家口前夕，华北联大撤离张家口，外国语学院英语系部分学生调入晋察冀中央分局组织部等待分配工作。其余师生随学校转移到山西广灵县东加斗村，两个月后，继续向冀中解放区进行大转移，12月到达冀中束鹿县路过村。罗清在转移到山西灵丘时离校，学校到束鹿县后英语系由施谷负责。

1948年5月，华北联大从冀中束鹿县迁至正定县，华北联大外国语学院驻在正定天主教堂内。

Shortly after the School of Foreign Languages was established at North China Union University, all lessons were suspended in July when its students and teachers joined the Land Reform initiative in rural areas of Xuanhua County, Hebei Province. In September of the same year, before the Kuomintang forces attacked Zhangjiakou, North China Union University evacuated from the city. Some of the students from the English Department were transferred to the Organisational Department of the Shanxi-Chahar-Hebei Branch of the Central Bureau to await further assignment, while the rest of the students and teachers moved with the University to East Jiadou Village in Guangling County, Shanxi Province. Two months later, the University moved again to the Central-Hebei Liberated Region and reached the Village of Luguo in Shulu County in December. Luo Qing had left the School when the University moved to Lingqiu County, Shanxi Province. His post was taken over by Shi Gu after the University reached Shulu.

In May 1948, North China Union University moved from Shulu County to Zhengding County and the School of Foreign Languages moved into the Zhengding Catholic Church.

浦化人（1887—1974），江苏无锡人。曾就读于上海圣约翰大学正馆。1927 年加入中国共产党，曾任中共临时上海局委员、宣传部部长。抗日战争爆发后奉调去延安，任中共中央英文翻译，新华通讯社翻译、社长，延安外国语学校英文系主任。1948 年任中央外事学校校长，1949 年 4 月至 1950 年 3 月任外国语学校校长。中国人民政治协商会议第三、四届全国委员会委员。

Pu Huaren (1887-1974) was born in Wuxi, Jiangsu. He studied at St John's University's Main Campus in Shanghai and joined the CPC in 1927. He was a member of the CPC Provisional Shanghai Bureau and served as Head of its Propaganda Department. After the War of Resistance Against Japanese Aggression began, he was assigned to Yan'an and served as the English Translator for the CPC Central Committee, Translator and Chief Editor of Xinhua News Agency, and Head of the English Department at Yan'an School of Foreign Languages. He became the Principal of the CPC Central School of Foreign Affairs in 1948 and was the Principal of Institute of Foreign Languages from April 1949 to March 1950. He was also a member of the National Committee at the 3rd and 4th Chinese People Political Consultative Conference.

时任中共中央工作委员会书记、中共中央华北局书记刘少奇关于外事学校教育方针的指示（抄件），提出不但要培养外事干部，还要培养翻译干部，并对课程设置等问题提出具体要求。

Hand-written copy of a directive by Liu Shaoqi, the then Secretary of the CPC Central Work Committee and Secretary of the CPC Central Bureau for North China, concerning the educational policy at the School of Foreign Affairs. He pointed out that the School should train translators as well as foreign affair officials. The directive also listed requirements for things such as the school curriculum.

中央外事学校

1948 年 6 月，为了迎接解放战争在全国的胜利，培养初级翻译和外事干部，中共中央决定成立中央外事学校（简称"外事学校"），由中央外事组领导，校址在河北省获鹿县南海山村，校长浦化人。学生主要是从重庆来到张家口、在华北联大外国语学院英语系学习的二十余人，加上英语系原有学生共三四十人。之后又陆续从解放区的北平、天津等地招收了一些进步大学生和优秀中学生，全校学生共七八十人。

CPC Central School of Foreign Affairs

In preparation for victory in China's War of Liberation and to train rudimentary translators and foreign affair officials, the Central Committee decided to establish a Central School of Foreign Affairs (abbreviated to School of Foreign Affairs). It came under the governance of the Foreign Affairs Division of the CPC Central Committee, and was established in Nanhaishan Village, Huolu County, Hebei, and was led by Principal Pu Huaren. Its 30 to 40 students consisted mainly of over 20 students who came from Chongqing to study at the English Department in the NCUU School of Foreign Languages in Zhangjiakou, and other students from the English Department. After the School was established, it continued to recruit capable university students and outstanding secondary students from areas such as Peking and Tianjin within the Hebei Liberated Region, and its student number reached 70 to 80 strong.

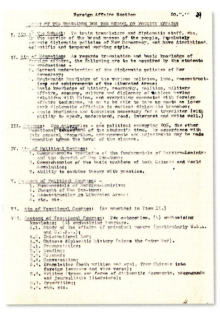

1

2

1. 2. 外事学校教育方针草案（英文）   1. 2. Draft educational policy of School of Foreign Affairs (in English)

3. 4. 5. 外事学校教育方针草案   3. 4. 5. Draft educational policy of School of Foreign Affairs

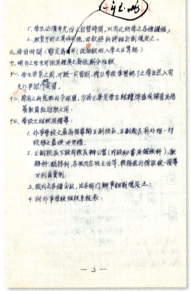

3

4

5

1

1948 年 10 月底，外事学校奉命向赞皇转移。1948 年 12 月，平津战役开始，北平军管会主任叶剑英命令外事学校迁往即将解放的北平，以应外事工作的需要。学校到达良乡时，北平尚未解放，学校暂驻良乡县城。1949 年 2 月，学校自良乡迁到北平城内御河桥原日本兵营内，和北平市军管会外事处相邻。

At the end of October 1948, the School of Foreign Affairs was ordered to relocate to Zan-huang County. In December of the same year, the military offensive to liberate Peking and Tianjin began and Ye Jianying, Director of the Peking Military Control Commission, ordered the School to move to Peking, which was about to be liberated, so as to be ready for the area's foreign affair needs. When the School arrived at Liangxiang, Peking had yet to be liberated so the School stayed in the county town of Liangxiang. In February 1949, the School was able to relocate to the former Japanese army barracks at Yuhe Bridge within Peking, which was next to the Foreign Affairs Department of the Peking Municipal Military Control Commission.

1. 1948 年，外事学校师生在行军途中休息。
2. 1949 年初，外事学校外籍教师在迁往北平的路上。

1. Students and teachers of the School of Foreign Affairs resting between military marches, taken in 1948
2. A foreign teacher from the School of Foreign Affairs enroute to Peking, taken at the start of 1949

2

1. 外事学校教育计划封面

2. 外事学校教育计划内页

3. 外事学校教学大纲

4. 外事学校教学大纲（英文版）

5. 外事学校教学计划（英文版）

1. Front page of the educational policy for the School of Foreign Affairs

2. A page from the educational policy for the School of Foreign Affairs

3. Curriculum for the School of Foreign Affairs

4. English version of the Curriculum

5. Educational Plan of the School of Foreign Affairs (in English)

华北大学二部外语系

Department of Foreign Languages at the Second Branch of North China University

　　原晋冀鲁豫边区的北方大学设有文教、文艺、财经、行政、工、农、医等学院。1947年7月，以张宗麟为院长的文教学院设立外文班，下分英文班和俄文班。1948年8月，华北联大与北方大学合并，改名华北大学。原华北联大外国语学院与北方大学的外文班合并为华北大学二部外语系，系主任杨化飞。

When the University of Northern China was still at the Shanxi-Hebei-Shandong-Henan border region, it had schools of Language Education, Arts and Literature, Finance and Economics, Government Administration, Engineering, Agriculture and Medicine. In July 1947, the School of Language Education headed by Zhang Zonglin set up two foreign language classes — English and Russian. In August 1948, North China University was formed from the merger of North China Union University and Northern University. The School of Foreign Languages at North China Union University merged with the Foreign Language Department at Northern University and became the Department of Foreign Languages at the Second Branch of North China University, with Yang Huafei as Head of the Department.

　　为了加强教学力量，中央外事组聘请国际友人马海德（George Hatem）、戴维·柯鲁克（David Crook）、伊莎白·柯鲁克（Isabel Crook）、韩丁（William Hinton）、葛兰恒（Betty Graham）等来校任教。他们到任时，中共中央后方委员会书记、华北军政大学校长兼政委叶剑英亲自主持召开欢迎大会。中国教员有曹汀、刘耕园、吴明、李正凌、周南、陈美娟等。

To strength the faculty's teaching ability, the Foreign Affairs Division of the CPC Central Committee invited such foreign nationals as George Hatem, David Crook, Isabel Crook, William Hinton and Betty Graham to teach at the School. When they arrived at the School, they were welcomed at a reception hosted by Ye Jianying, who was Secretary of the CPC Central Committee's Work Committee in the Rear, and President and Political Commissar of North China Military and Political University. Chinese faculty members of the School included Cao Ting, Liu Gengyuan, Wu Ming, Li Zhengling, Zhou Nan and Chen Meijuan.

　　戴维·柯鲁克（David Crook，1910—2000），英国人。1934年毕业于哥伦比亚大学，1935年加入英国共产党，1936年前往西班牙参加国际纵队，投身反法西斯斗争。1938年离开西班牙到上海圣约翰大学任教，后转移到成都金陵大学，结识了日后结为终身伴侣的加拿大人伊莎白。伊莎白·柯鲁克（Isabel Crook，1915—　　），加拿大人，出生于成都一个加拿大传教士家庭。成年后就读于加拿大多伦多大学，专攻心理学并获硕士学位。1938年回到成都，深入中国西部农村开展社会调查。1941年，柯鲁克返英加入英国皇家空军，抗击希特勒的侵略。战后就读于伦敦大学亚非学院。1947年11月，柯鲁克和伊莎白受英国共产党派遣，以国际观察员身份来到中国解放区河北省武安县十里店村，考察中国共产党领导下的土改复查和整党运动，见证了中国新民主主义革命的一个重要阶段，从此开始了他们始终不渝参与中国共产党和中国人民光辉事业的历程。

　　1959年，柯鲁克夫妇合作撰写的《十里店——一个中国村庄的革命》（*Revolution in A Chinese Village: Ten Mile Inn*）在英国伦敦出版，20年后，内容更为翔实的《十里店——一个中国村庄的群众运动》（*Mass Movement in A Chinese Village: Ten Mile Inn*）在美国纽约问世。这两部不可多得的历史文献，帮助西方人真实了解了中国的土地改革运动。1948年，中共中央外事组组长王炳南邀请他们留下来帮助新中国培养外语人才，他们欣然同意。同年加入由叶剑英、王炳南直接领导的南海山外事学校，成为新中国外语教育事业的拓荒者和奠基人。在其后半个多世纪的时间里，他们与中国人民同甘

伊莎白与柯鲁克（1948年
摄于南海山外事学校）

Isabel and David Crook (taken
in 1948 at the School of
Foreign Affairs at Nanhaishan)

共苦，把自己的命运与中华民族的命运紧密联结在一起。"文化大革命"（简称"文革"）期间，他们遭到监禁和迫害，后经周恩来总理亲自过问才得以出狱平反，但无怨无悔。他们为北京外国语大学的发展建设和我国的外语教育事业做出了杰出贡献，是中国人民永远的朋友。

David Crook (1910-2000) was born in Britain, graduated from Columbia University in 1934, joined the British Communist Party in 1935, fought in the Spanish Civil War as a member of the International Brigade against the fascists in 1936. He left Spain in 1938 to teach at St John's University in Shanghai and later moved to Jinling University in Chengdu (present-day Nanjing University), where he met his future wife and life-time soulmate. Isabel Crook (1915-), is a daughter of Canadian missionaries living in Chengdu. Isabel had studied Psychology at the University of Toronto and obtained a Master's degree in 1938. She then returned to Chengdu to conduct social and anthropological research in rural areas of Western China. In 1941 David returned to England and joined the Royal Air Force to fight the Nazi invasion. After the war, he studied at the School of Oriental and African Studies at the University of London. In November 1947, the British Communist Party sent the Crooks to China as International Observers. They were based at the village of Ten Mile Inn in Wu'an County, Hebei, a liberated region, and observed the Land Reform reviews undertaken by the Communist Party of China and the CPC's campaign to purify its own ranks. They were able to factually witness an important period in the history of China's new democratic revolution and this marked the start of their steadfast relationship with the CPC and the Chinese people.

In 1959, the book *Revolution in A Chinese Village: Ten Mile Inn* written by the Crooks was published in London, and 20 years later, the even more detailed *Mass Movement in A Chinese Village: Ten Mile Inn* was published in New York. These two extremely valuable works of historical literature have helped people of the West to accurately understand China's Land Reform. In 1948. Wang Bingnan, Head of the CPC Central Committee's Foreign Affairs Division, asked the Crooks to stay in China to help train foreign language professionals and the Crooks happily agreed. In the same year, they took up posts at the School of Foreign Affairs at Nanhaishan, which was under the leadership of Ye Jianying and Wang Bingnan, and became founders and pioneers of foreign language education in new China. In the next five decades, the Crooks shared hardship and happiness with the Chinese people and bonded their destiny closely with that of the Chinese nation. During the "Cultural Revolution", they were imprisoned and persecuted, and were only released and rehabilitated after Zhou Enlai intervened, but they never held a grudge or had any regrets. They have made outstanding contribution to the development and achievement of Beijing Foreign Studies University and to China's foreign language education, and are eternal friends of the Chinese people.

1

3

2

1. 外事学校时期的葛兰恒（摄于南海山）

2. 外事学校时期的韩丁（左）、柯鲁克（中）和伊莎白（右）

3. 1949年伊莎白在河北解放区行军途中。

4. 外事学校教师在读报。

5. 外事学校英语 C 班部分师生（1949 年）

4

1. Betty Graham at the School of Foreign Affairs (taken at Nanhaishan)

2. Isabel Crook (R), David Crook (M) and William Hinton (L) at the School of Foreign Affairs

3. Isabel Crook during a military march in the liberated region in Hebei in 1949

4. Teachers at the School of Foreign Affairs reading a newspaper

5. Some of the students and teachers of English Class C from the School of Foreign Affairs (1949)

5

第三章

继往开来　发展壮大

（1949—1958年）

Chapter Three
Building upon the past and growing stronger
(1949–1958)

　　1949年6月，华北大学二部外语系30余人并入外事学校，学校改名为外国语学校。1954年8月，外国语学校更名为北京外国语学院，成为新中国第一所多语种外语高等学府。自1949年中华人民共和国成立至1959年前，是学校的重要发展时期。其间虽然受到"反右"等政治运动的影响、干扰，但学校逐渐走向正规，规模不断扩大，在教学方面学习苏联，实践创新，逐步建立起具有鲜明特色的外语教育体系。

　　In June 1949, over 30 people from the Foreign Languages Department at the Second Branch of North China University were transferred to the School of Foreign Affairs, which was then renamed the Institute of Foreign Languages. In August 1954, the Institute of Foreign Languages was renamed Beijing Foreign Languages Institute, becoming the first institution of higher learning for multilingual studies in new China. The period from the founding of the People's Republic to 1959 was significant in the development of the university. During this period, although its teaching was distracted by political movements such as the "Anti-Rightist Campaign", the administration of the university gradually normalised, and the student population grew steadily. In terms of teaching methodology, by following the Soviet model and implementing innovative teaching practices, the University gradually built up a foreign language education system with distinct characteristics.

外国语学校校标（正、背面）

Insignia of the Institute of Foreign
Languages (Front & reverse)

初大告（1898—1987），山东莱阳人，九三学社中央委员、教授。曾就读于山东省立第一师范学校、北平高等师范学校、北平师范大学英语研究科。1924 年秋在北平创办志成中学，任董事兼第一任校长。1934 年秋赴英国剑桥大学学习英国文学、语音学。1938 年回国后至 1949 年，曾任河南大学英文教授、重庆复旦大学英文教授兼教务长、中央大学英文教授。1945 年 9 月 3 日与许德珩等民主人士一起发起成立九三学社。1949 年到外国语学校任教授。曾任英文部主任、英语系第一任系主任。

Chu Dagao (1898-1987), born in Laiyang, Shandong, was a member of the Central Committee for the Jiusan Society and a professor. He studied at Shandong No. 1 Normal School, Peking School of Advanced Teacher Training and the English Research Division at Peking Normal University. He established the Zhicheng Secondary School in Peking in the autumn of 1924 and was its Chairman and first Principal. He went to Cambridge University in England to study English Literature and Phonology in 1934 and returned to China in 1938. From then until 1949, he served successively as Professors of English at Henan University, Professor and Teaching Affairs Officer at Fudan University in Chongqing, and Central University. On September 3rd 1945, he and Xu Deheng and other democrats founded the Jiusan Society. In 1949, he became a professor at the Institute of Foreign Languages and was Head of the English Faculty and then the first Head of the English Department.

1949

外国语学校
（1949.6—1954.8）

1949 年 1 月北平和平解放，2 月外事学校奉命进城，全体师生 60 余人从良乡进驻北平御河桥 3 号原日本兵营旧址。三个英语班的学生，半年之内，陆续分配到北平、天津外事筹备处或留校工作。6 月，华北大学二部外语系 30 余人与外事学校合并，中央外事学校更名为外国语学校，仍隶属中央外事组领导。校长浦化人，副校长刘仲容。学校设英文、俄文两部，英文部主任初大告，俄文部主任杨化飞，教务处处长李遇安，党支部书记浦化人（兼）。

The Institute of Foreign Languages (June 1949 - August 1954)

In January 1949, Peking was liberated peacefully and the School of Foreign Affairs was ordered to enter the city in February. All of the students and staff from the School, over 60 people, moved from Liangxiang to the former Japanese army barracks at No. 3 Yuhe Bridge (present-day Zhengyi Road) in Peking. Within half a year, students from the three English classes were reassigned to the foreign affairs offices in Peking and Tianjin or became teachers at the School. In June, more than 30 people from the Foreign Languages Department at the Second Branch of North China University integrated with the School of Foreign Affairs, which was then renamed the Institute of Foreign Languages. The Institute still came under the governance of the Foreign Affairs Division of the CPC Central Committee and was led by Principal Pu Huaren (who was also the School Party Secretary) and Deputy President Liu Zhongrong. The Institute had an English Faculty headed by Chu Dagao and a Russian Faculty headed by Yang Huafei. The Director of Teaching Affairs was Li Yu'an.

杨 化 飞（1911—1989），辽宁辽阳人。曾就读于北平大学，1936年参加北平地下党工作。1939年9月至1944年9月在延安军委编译局工作，1944年至1945年在延安军委俄文学校担任教员。1945年任张家口华北联合大学外语系系主任。曾任外国语学校俄文部主任，北京俄文专修学校三部主任、教务长，北京俄语学院俄文部主任、副院长，北京外国语学院副院长。

Yang Huafei (1911-1989), born in Liaoyang, Liaoning, studied at Peking University and joined the CPC underground in Peking in 1936. From September 1939 to September 1944, he worked at the Bureau of Compilation and Translation under the Military Commission in Yan'an; then from 1944 to 1945, he worked as a teacher at the Military Commission Russian Language School in Yan'an. In 1945 he served as Head of the Foreign Language Department at North China Union University and then as Head of the Russian Department at the Institute of Foreign Languages, Head of the Third Division of Beijing Russian Language Training School and its Teaching Affairs Officer, Head of the Russian Faculty at Beijing Russian Language School, Vice President of Beijing Russian Language Institute and Vice President of Beijing Foreign Languages Institute.

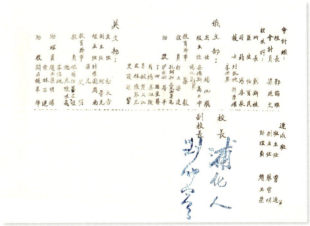

▌ 外国语学校组织机构干部配备表（1949年9月）

Organizational chart and staff list for the Institute of Foreign Languages (September 1949)

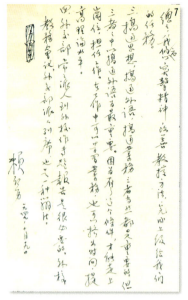

■ 外交部办公厅副主任、办公厅秘书处长赖亚力就外国语学校教务问题给外交部部长助理、办公厅主任王炳南的信

A letter to Wang Bingnan, Assistant to the Minister of Foreign Affairs and Director of the General Office at the Ministry of Foreign Affairs, from Lai Yali, Deputy Director of the General Office at the Ministry of Foreign Affairs and Chief Secretary of the General Office, regarding educational issues at the Institute of Foreign Languages

1

2

1. 1949 年，浦化人校长在外国语学校共青团代表大会上讲话。

2. 1949 年 10 月外国语学校在御河桥时的校门

1. President Pu Huaren speaking at a CPC Youth conference at the Institute of Foreign Languages in 1949

2. The main gate of the Institute of Foreign Languages at Yuhe Bridge in October 1949

1950 年外国语学校主要领导合影（右三为校长刘仲容，左二为党总支书记杨化飞）

A group photo of the top leaders of the Institute of Foreign Languages. President Liu Zhongrong (3rd right), Party Secretary Yang Huafei (2nd left)

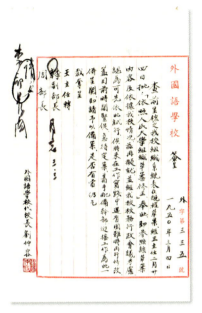

刘仲容校长就《外国语学校组织系统表及规程草案》签呈政务院总理、外交部部长周恩来，外交部副部长李克农、章汉夫的报告。左上角为周恩来总理亲笔批示。

President Liu Zhongrong drafted "A Proposal for the Organizational Structure and Draft Regulations" at the Institute of Foreign Languages and presented it to Zhou Enlai, Premier of the State Council and Minister of Foreign Affairs, and Deputy Ministers of Foreign Affairs Li Kenong and Zhang Hanfu. A hand-written remark by Zhou Enlai can be seen on the top left corner.

1950

1949 年 11 月，中央人民政府外交部正式成立，外国语学校隶属外交部领导。同月，学校迁到西苑华北革命大学校园内的一幢旧楼里。

1950 年 3 月，浦化人调任中国红十字会秘书长，刘仲容继任校长，总支书记由俄文部主任杨化飞兼任。12 月，教务长罗清兼任总支书记，杨化飞兼任总支副书记。同年，学校增设德文组和法文组，德文组主任由教务处处长李遇安兼任，法文组主任由韩惠莲担任。

In November 1949, the Ministry of Foreign Affairs was formally established under the central government and the Institute of Foreign Languages came under the governance of the Ministry. In the same month, the School moved to an old building within North China Revolutionary University's campus in the Xiyuan district of Beijing.

In March 1950, Pu Huaren became Chief Secretary of China Red Cross and Liu Zhongrong took over as President, while the Head of the Russian Faculty Yang Huafei served concurrently as Party Secretary for the Institute. In December, the then Director of Teaching Affairs Luo Qing took over as Institute Party Secretary, while Yang Huafei became Deputy Secretary. In the same year, the Institute added a German programme headed by Li Yu'an, who was also the Director of Teaching Affairs, and a French programme headed by Han Huilian.

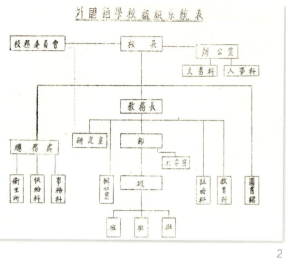

1

2

1. 外国语学校组织规程
2. 外国语学校组织系统表

1. Constitutive Regulations for the Institute of Foreign Languages
2. Organizational chart for the Institute of Foreign Languages

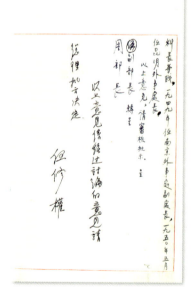

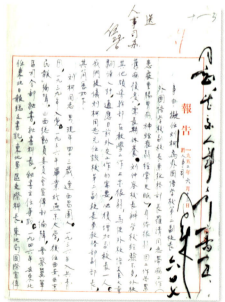

■ 拟任命刘柯为外国语学校第二
副校长的报告，周恩来总理批
示"同意"。

A report proposing to appoint Liu
Ke as the Number Two Deputy
Principal at the Institute of Foreign
Languages. It is marked "approved"
by Premier Zhou Enlai.

刘仲容（1903—1980），又名刘翠，湖南益阳（今桃江）人。1923年加入国民党，1925年任黄埔军校国民党特别党部执行委员，同年赴莫斯科中山大学学习。1955年11月加入民革，历任民革第三、四届中央常委，第五届中央副主席。曾任外国语学校校长、北京外国语学院院长。1959年北京俄语学院与北京外国语学院合并后任副院长。1978年后任北京外国语学院顾问。

Liu Zhongrong (1903-1980), otherwise known as Liu Hui, was born in Yiyang (present-day Taojiang), Hunan. He joined the Kuomintang in 1923 and served as a member of the Kuomintang Special Executive Committee at Huangpu Military Academy in 1925 and in the same year, he went to study at Moscow Sun Yat-sen University. In November of 1955, he joined the Revolutionary Committee of the Chinese Kuomintang and served on its Central Committee's Standing Committee during its 3rd and 4th congresses and was the Deputy Chairman at its 5th congress. He served as the Principal of Institute of Foreign Languages and the President of Beijing Foreign Languages Institute. After Beijing Russian Language Institute merged with Beijing School of Foreign Languages in 1959, he served as its Vice President. After 1978, he became a consultant for the Beijing Foreign Languages Institute.

刘柯（1911—2006），辽宁昌图人。1936年毕业于燕京大学，同年加入中国共产党。曾任八路军晋冀军区司令部秘书处副处长、中共中央东北局宣传部国际宣传科科长。1949年后任云南省外事处处长，外国语学校副校长、党总支书记（1952—1957），北京外国语学院党委书记（1957—1959）兼副院长。1959年北京外国语学院与北京俄语学院合并后，先后任党委第二书记兼副院长、院长。

Liu Ke (1911-2006), born in Changtu, Liaoning Province, graduated from Yenching University in 1936 and joined the CPC in the same year. He served as Deputy Head of the Secretariat for the Headquarters of the Eighth Route Army's Shanxi-Hebei Military Command and then as Chief of the International Propaganda Section within the Propaganda Department of the CPC Central Committee's Northeast Bureau. After 1949, he served first as Head of the Foreign Affairs Division of the Yunnan Provincial Government, then as Deputy Principal of Institute of Foreign Languages, and Secretary of the School Branch of the CPC (1952-1957), then Secretary of the Party Committee and Vice President of Beijing Foreign Languages Institute. After the Institute merged with Beijing Russian Institute in 1959, he became Number Two Secretary of the Party Committee and Vice President, then President of the Institute.

1952年，经周恩来总理批准，刘柯调入外国语学校任第二副校长。1953年，经周恩来总理批准，李棣华调入外国语学校任第三副校长。

In 1952, after approval from Premier Zhou Enlai, Liu Ke was transferred to the Institute of Foreign Languages and became its Number Two Deputy Principal. The same happened in 1953 when Li Dihua became its Number Three Deputy Principal.

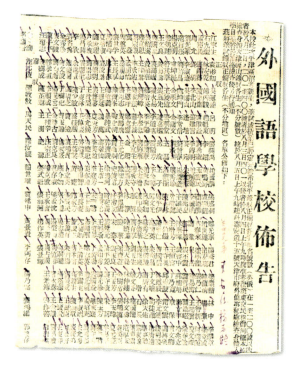

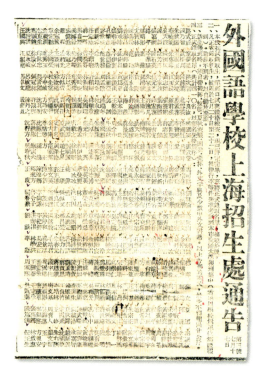

■ 外国语学校布告及招生通告

Student recruitment notices for the
Institute of Foreign Languages

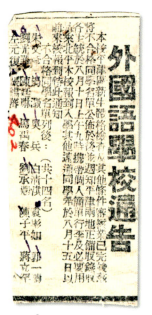

1949年6月成立外国语学校之后，根据形势发展和外事工作需要，中央指示扩大招生。

After the Institute of Foreign Languages was established in June 1949, the Central authorities, in anticipation for an increase in the need for foreign affairs personnel as a result of the changing situation at the time, directed the Institute to increase student admissions.

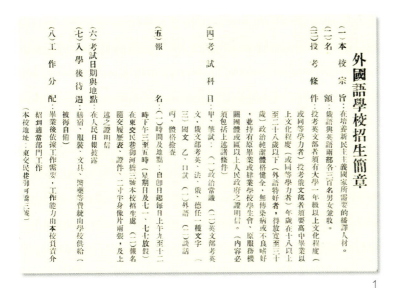

1

2

1. 外国语学校招生简章

2. 外国语学校入学证

3. 1949 年，新生在上海北站等车。

4. 1949 年 7 月，新生搭轮渡到达南京浦口乘火车北上。

1. Students' admission guide for the Institute of Foreign Languages

2. Certificate of Admission for the Institute of Foreign Languages

3. New students waiting for their train at Shanghai North Station in 1949

4. New students arriving at Nanjing Pukou Station by ferry to take the train up north in July 1949

3

4

1949 年 8 月，南京区同学在天津站换乘到北京的火车。

Students from the Nanjing region changing trains for Beijing at Tianjin Station in August 1949

中譯英試題

將下列各句譯成英文：　　　　　　　　　　　第一種

1）昨天當我正在車站等候時，我碰見一位多年不見的朋友。

2）根據官方消息，四外長會談已在巴黎召開并開始討論德國問題。

3）昨天，當他開始工作之後，他發現這項工作比他所預期的要困難一些。

4）中國青年工人，農民和學生，在中國新民主主義過程中，有着已很光榮的歷史。自五四運動以來，他們都曾站在英勇斗爭的最前綫，對人民革命運動，作了很大的貢獻，三十年來的革命史澄明中國青年運動是中國革命運動中的一個重要部份。

將下列各短語譯成英文：

1）為人民服務　　　　2）實質上　　　　　　3）將革命進行到底

4）盡量的早　　　　　5）您多您好　　　　　6）減輕人民負担。

READING EXAMINATION　　　　　　　　NAME
　　　　　　　　　　　　　　　　　　　NUMBER

Section 1.

Under the new Five-Year Plan railways should nearly double their traf-
River and sea transport should increase three times. Motor transport
e multiplied by sixteen. The canal between the White Sea and the
is to be completed, and also those between Moscow and the Volga Ri-
d between the Volga River and the Don River.

As far as the factories are concerned, workers' dwellings with a floor-space
out 54 million square yards are to be constructed.

The actual wages of the workers will, in 1937, be two and a half times
they were in 1932.

Illiteracy is to be completely wiped out—as completely as unemploy-
was under the preceding Plan; every citizen in the Soviet Union wil
le to read and to write. The total number of pupils in schools and
tes will be 197 per 1,000 of the population, instead of 147 per 1,000
present.

The funds of national insurance will be doubled.

"It is an impossible Plan," some people will say. For answer they have
to look at the results of the previous Five-Year Plan.

NAME
NUMBER　　　　MARK

AM 1　　　　GRAMMAR

Section 1

(1) In the afternoon I went for a walk. (2) Because it was
ly late, I did not plan to go far. I met a
good friend of mine, little Jane Smith, whom I had not seen
three years. (4) I was persuaded to go to her house and as a
it, it was already dark when I returned home. (5) If it had
been so late, I would have telephoned you then.

1. List all the common nouns in sentences 1 and 2.

2. List the first 4 pronouns you come to, starting at the beginning of 3rd
sentence, omitting possessive and relative pronouns.

3. List all the possessive pronouns.

4. List the first 4 adjectives in the selection.

5. List all the prepositions in sentences 2, 3, and 4.

6. List all the verbs in sentences 1 and 4, omitting the infinitive.

7. List all the phrases in sentence 1.

8. How many clauses are there in sentences 2 and 3. Give the number　( )

9. How many of the sentences are compound-complex? Give number　　( )

10. What is the voice and mood of the first verb in sentence 4?

Section II

1. Change the following sentence into a question:
She will be here in an hour.

2. Fill in the prepositions in the following sentences:
The house＿＿＿＿ the end＿＿＿＿the street was empty.
＿＿＿＿ the evening I went＿＿＿＿a play.

3. Fill in the articles in the following sentences:
＿＿＿＿ China has＿＿＿＿largest population of any country in＿＿＿＿world;
it is＿＿＿＿country with＿＿＿＿large resources as well as＿＿＿＿moderate
climate.

4. Punctuate and supply capital letters:
Its time to go I think he said or I will be late john my brother is waiting
for me at my brown house

English-Chinese Translation

Mr. Wang left home that morning in a very cheerful state of mind. Even
the weather seemed delightful, although it is true the sun might have felt a bit
too hot but for a slight wind that cooled the air. As it was still early, the streetcar
(tram) was not yet as crowded as it would be in another hour, and so he was able
to find an empty seat by an open window where he settled down comfortably to read
his newspaper.

No sooner had he glanced at the front page than his spirits rose still
higher. According to front-line reports from the New China News Agency, the People's
Liberation Army was continuing its steady, resolute and astoundingly rapid drive
to the south, not permitting the shattered Kuomintang forces time to regroup themselves along any new line of defense.

Meanwhile, he noted with pleasure, the workers and peasants in the
rear were demonstrating as much tireless energy and initiative as their armies. The
newspaper carried many descriptions of their outstanding accomplishments in not only
restoring industrial and agricultural production, but even in raising output beyond
pre-war levels. It was, one might say, as if the workers had changed into an entirely
new race of men after their liberation. Now they thought nothing of increasing their
efforts day by day and week by week, achieving successes that formerly would have
been considered completely out of the question.

He read in an editorial commenting on the liberation of Shanghai how
the progressive democratic peoples throughout the world were rejoicing over the
recent revolutionary victories in China. Shanghai, a key commercial and industrial
center, had served the imperialists as their principal base for systematically exten-
ding their economic domination over semi-feudal China. Now, to the contrary, Shanghai would in the future become one of the major bases of the world democratic
camp from which to resist capitalist aggression.

Translate the following expressions and phrases:

1) in order to arrive on time　　　　4) even up to the present

2) impossible though the problem may seem　　5) by no means too early

3) without the least hesitation whatsoever　　6) regardless of whether you go or not

---

外国语学校入学考试试题

Admissions test for the Institute of Foreign Languages

1

2

3

4

1949 年 8 月，外国语学校在北京、天津、上海、南京、杭州等地区招收的新生 800 余人来校报到。新生入学后，先到华北人民革命大学学习政治半年，改造思想，树立革命人生观。

In August 1949, the Institute of Foreign Languages recruited over 800 students from around Beijing, Tianjin, Shanghai, Nanjing and Hangzhou. After the students were enrolled, they spent the first six months studying politics at North China People's Revolutionary University so that they could adopt the revolutionary philosophies and change their way of thinking.

1. 1949 年 8 月，外国语学校的新生都转入华北人民革命大学学习。

2. 3. 4. 1949 年在华北人民革命大学学习的部分外国语学校学生

1. In August 1949, all new students from the Institute of Foreign Languages went to study at North China People's Revolutionary University.

2. 3. 4. Some of the students from the Institute of Foreign Languages studying at North China People's Revolutionary University in 1949

1

2

3

4

5

■ 1949 年外国语学校全体在校师生合影

A group photo of all students and teachers for the Institute of Foreign Languages taken in 1949

6

1. 2. 北上前和在华北人民革命大学学习时的学生李伊丽

3. 1949 年秋，外国语学校学生在华北人民革命大学上大课。

4. 5. 华北人民革命大学毕业证书

6. 华北人民革命大学证章

1. 2. Li Yili, a student before going to Beijing (left) and when studying at North China People's Revolutionary University (right)

3. Students from the Institute of Foreign Languages studying at North China People's Revolutionary University in the autumn of 1949

4. 5. Graduation certificate from North China People's Revolutionary University

6. North China People's Revolutionary University's badge

　　1950 年 3 月，在华北人民革命大学学习的 800 余名新生政治学习结业返校，多数分在英文、俄文两部学习英语、俄语。学过德语、法语者参加德法文组建组考试，德文组录取学生 14 名，法文组录取学生 30 名。

　　1950 年 4 月 1 日，学校正式开学，新生开始专业外语学习。

In March 1950, the 800 odd students who had studied at North China People's Revolutionary University returned to the Institute of Foreign Languages. Many of them were split into the English and Russian Departments to learn English and Russian. Those who had learnt German or French were tested for the newly established German and French programmes, which admitted 14 students of German and 30 students of French.

The Institute officially commenced lessons on 1st April 1950 and the new students started learning foreign languages as their professional subjects.

1

1. 1950 年，学生参加抗美援朝妇女大游行。

2. 1950 年，参加中国人民志愿军的部分师生合影。

1. Students participated in a women's march expressing their support for "resisting US aggression and aiding Korea" in 1950.

2. A group photo of some of the teachers and students who joined the Chinese People's Volunteer Army in 1950

2

1950 年 6 月，朝鲜战争爆发。10 月，中国人民志愿军入朝参战，全国开展抗美援朝运动。外国语学校师生、干部踊跃报名参军，志愿赴朝。英文部三年级男生几乎全部获准入伍，赴朝参加美军俘虏的教育管理工作。11 月，赴朝人员由周南、李正凌带队出发，全校举行欢送大会。

The Korean War started in June 1950 and in October of that year, the Chinese People's Volunteer Army entered the Korean peninsula and began to assist the Korean people in resisting the advance of the US-led UN forces. In a nationwide movement to "resist US aggression and aid Korea", students, faculty and staff from the Institute of Foreign Languages leapt at the chance to join the war and almost all male third-year students from the English Department were given permission to join the expeditionary force in order to supervise and re-educate American prisoners of war. Those heading to Korea were led by Zhou Nan and Li Zhengling and the whole Institute gave them a big send-off in November.

3

4

3. 学生踊跃报名参加中国人民志愿军。

4. 1951 年，参加志愿军的陈文伯，摄于战场。

3. Students queuing to volunteer for the Chinese People's Volunteer Army

4. A photo of Chen Wenbo in 1951 when he was in the battlefield after he joined the Volunteer Army

1951

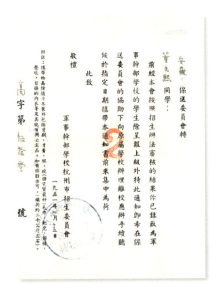

董光熙的军事干部学校录取通知书

Letter of admissions to the Military Cadre School for Dong Guangxi

1951 年 1 月，上海、江苏、山东、安徽、福建参加抗美援朝军事干部学校的学员 500 余人被分配到外国语学校学习，分别学习英语、德语、法语，学制定为三年，给予干部学习待遇，享受供给制。

In January 1951, more than 500 students originating from the provinces of Shanghai, Jiangsu, Shandong, Anhui and Fujian who attended the Military Cadre School were assigned to the Institute of Foreign Languages to learn English, German or French. The length of learning was three years and they enjoyed the privileges of cadres, as everything was provided for them.

1

3

2

1. 军事干部学校校标（胡文仲提供）

2. 1951 年，军事干部学校的学员转来
   外国语学校，到达北京火车站。

3. 1951 年开学典礼现场

4. 1951 年，外交部副部长伍修权在开
   学典礼上讲话。

1. Insignia of Military Cadre School (supplied
   by Hu Wenzhong)

2. Students from the Military Cadre School
   arriving at a Beijing train station on their way
   to the Institute of Foreign Languages in 1951

3. Matriculation ceremony in 1951

4. Vice Foreign Minister Wu Xiuquan speaking
   at the matriculation ceremony in 1951

4

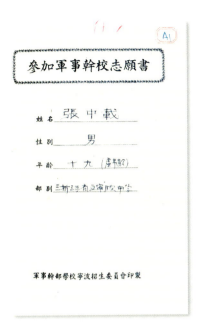
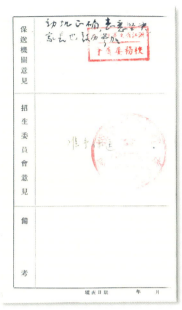
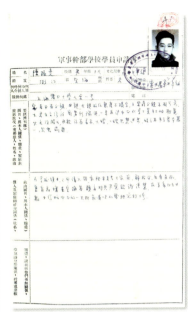

张中载、陈振尧、庄元泳参加军事干部学校的志愿书、申请书

Military Cadre School's application forms and letter of intent from Zhang Zhongzai, Chen Zhenyao and Zhuang Yuanyong

　　1950 年 12 月，外国语学校俄文部并入北京俄文专修学校，成立俄专三部。1951 年 9 月，北京俄文专修学校新校舍落成，俄专三部迁出外国语学校，并入鲍家街北京俄文专修学校本部。

　　1951 年，学校机构逐步健全，校长刘仲容，副校长罗清（兼党总支书记、教务长）。学校成立"学习委员会"，由罗清提名，王佐良为主任，王毓桂为副主任，石春来、吴道生等为委员。

In December 1950, the Russian Faculty at the Institute of Foreign Languages was merged into Beijing Russian Language School, and became its Third Faculty. In September 1951, the new campus for the Beijing Russian Language School was completed and its newly formed Third Faculty was able to move out of the Institute of Foreign Languages and into the newly built campus of Beijing Russian Language Institute on Baojia Street.

In 1951, the administrative structure of the Institute of Foreign Languages took shape, with Liu Zhongrong as President and Luo Qing (the School's Party Branch Secretary and Teaching Affairs Officer at the same time) as Deputy Principal. A Learning Committee was set up and nominated by Luo Qing. Wang Zuoliang was elected as Committee Chairman, Wang Yugui as Deputy Chairman, and Shi Chunlai, Wu Daosheng and others as committee members.

1

2

1952

1952 年 4 月，遵照周恩来总理指示，外国语学校增设西班牙语专业。1953 年初，正式建立西班牙文组，并入德法文系，合称德西法文系。西班牙文组组长王飖，秘书柳小培，教员李体乾、孟复，助教肖振吉、岑楚兰，并由国际友人、亚洲及太平洋地区和平委员会秘书长、智利画家万徒勒里夫人帮助授课。西班牙文组成立之初，从英文系二年级抽调学生 24 名，改学西班牙语，于 2 月正式上课。

1. 为给 1952 年 10 月在北京召开的亚洲及太平洋地区和平会议提供西班牙语翻译和工作人员，外交部从学校法文组抽调学生 15 名突击学习西班牙语，为大会服务。

2. 1952 年，西班牙语教师和出席亚洲及太平洋地区和平会议的智利代表在中山公园。

3. 1953 年德西法文系教师合影

In April 1952, at the direction of Premier Zhou Enlai, the Institute of Foreign Languages added Spanish to its range of languages. The Ministry of Foreign Affairs assigned Wang Xie to the School to establish the Spanish programme with the help of Liu Xiaopei from the French programme. At the beginning of 1953, the Spanish programme was formally established and became a part of the German-French Department, which was renamed the German-Spanish-French Department. The Director of the Spanish programme was Wang Xie, with Liu Xiaopei serving as secretary, Li Tiqian and Meng Fu as teachers, and Xiao Zhenji and Cen Chulan as teaching assistants. The teaching of Spanish was assisted by Madam Venturelli, a Chilean artist and Secretary General of the Asia Pacific Region Peace Commission. To begin with, 24 second-year students from the English Department was transferred to the Spanish programme and they formally started lessons in February.

3

1953 年全国高等学校统一招生
考试登记表

Registration form for the 1953
National Higher Education Entrance
Examination

1. In order to provide Spanish translation and related services at the Asia Pacific Region Peace Conference that was going to take place in Beijing in October 1952, the Ministry of Foreign Affairs selected 15 students from the French programme to intensively learn Spanish.

2. Teachers from the Spanish programme and a Chilean delegate to the Asia Pacific Region Peace Conference at Zhongshan Park in 1952

3. A group photo of teachers from the German-Spanish-French Department in 1953

1953

1953 年夏季，学校第一次参加全国统一招生，学制由三年改为四年。第一届四年制新生主要是从京、津、沪、宁等大城市招收的高中毕业生。外事专业属绝密专业，学校招生按国防军工院校政治标准，提前到中学选拔推荐。这一届共招新生 94 人。学生从该学年起全部实行助学金制。

In the summer of 1953, the Institute, for the very first time, joined the National Higher Education Admissions process and changed the length of its courses from three years to four years. The first intake of students taking the four-year course mainly consisted of high school graduates from large cities such as Beijing, Tianjin, Shanghai and Ningbo. As the foreign affairs course was deemed to be top secret, the Institute followed the same protocols as institutions under the Ministry of Defence and went to high schools to select the students. A total of 94 students were selected in 1953, all receiving student grants from that year.

1. 1950 年西苑校区伊莎白与学生合影
2. 外籍教师陈梅洁与学员在一起。
3. 陈梅洁与学生游览长城。

1. Isabel Crook photographed with students in the Xiyuan campus of the School in 1950
2. Margaret Turner photographed with a student
3. Margaret Turner visiting the Great Wall with students

　　自 1949 年至 1951 年，一大批来自国内外、学有所成的中青年学者、教师加入外国语学校，投身新中国的外语教育事业。在这期间先后进入外国语学校任教的有吴景荣、程镇球、王佐良、许国璋、周珏良、许孟雄、许渊冲等人。外籍教师有陈梅洁、史克、安德斯、米申、李欧丽嘉等人。

　　From 1949 to 1951, a large number of young and middle-aged accomplished scholars and teachers from China and abroad joined the Institute of Foreign Languages and began to help new China in its foreign language education endeavour. Chinese nationals who joined the Institute include Wu Jingrong, Cheng Zhenqiu, Wang Zuoliang, Xu Guozhang, Zhou Jueliang, Xu Mengxiong and Xu Yuanchong. Foreign teachers included Margaret Turner, Bertha Sneck, Anders, Mishin, Olga Lee, etc.

▌ 王佐良进入华北人民革命大学学习时所填写的履历表

Wang Zuoliang's resume when he was admitted to
North China People's Revolutionary University

4. 1950 年外国语学校聘任姚可崑担任教授的聘书

5. 6. 吴景荣介绍刘世沐来外国语学校工作的材料

4. Employment contract for the appointment
   of Yao Kekun as professor at the Institute of
   Foreign Languages

5. 6. Wu Jingrong's letter of recommendation for
   Liu Shimu to work at the Institute

王佐良的自传

Wang Zuoliang's autobiography

王佐良（1916—1995），浙江上虞人，英语教育家、作家、翻译家、英国文学专家。1929年至1934年，在武昌文华中学读书。1935年考入清华大学外文系，抗战爆发后，随校迁往云南昆明。1939年毕业于西南联合大学外文系（原清华大学外文系），并留校任教。1947年赴英国牛津大学，师从著名学者威尔逊教授，专攻英国文学。1949年回国入外国语学校任教授。曾任北京外国语学院英文系主任、副院长，国务院学位委员会第一、二届学科评议组外国文学组组长，国家教委高等学校专业外语教材编审委员会主任，第六届全国政协委员。著有《英国诗史》《英国散文的流变》《论契合——比较文学研究集》等重要著作。

Wang Zuoliang (1916-1995), educator of English, writer, translator and expert of English literature, was born in Shangyu, Zhejiang. He studied at Bishop Boone Memorial School from 1929 to 1934 and was admitted to the Foreign Languages Department at Tsinghua University in 1935. After the start of the War of Resistance Against Japan, he moved with the University to Kunming, Yunnan, where Tsinghua and two other universities formed National Southwestern Associated University. He remained at the University as a teacher after graduating in 1939, then went to study at Oxford University under the tutelage of Professor Frank Percy Wilson. He returned to China in 1949 and became a professor at the Institute of Foreign Languages. He later served as Head of the English Department at Beijing Foreign Languages Institute and Vice President of the Institute, Head of the Appraisal Panel for Foreign Literature under the Academic Degrees Committee of the State Council for the first two terms (1981-1991), Chairman of the State Education Commission Review Committee for Higher Education Foreign Language Teaching Materials, and a member of the National Committee of the 6th CPPCC. Among the important literary works he authored are *A History of English Poetry*, *Development and Change of British Prose*, *Degrees of Affinity—Studies on Comparative Literature and Translation*.

许国璋（1915—1994），浙江海宁人，英语教育家、语言学家。1934年毕业于苏州东吴中学，曾先后就读于上海交通大学及清华大学外文系。1939年毕业于西南联合大学外文系。毕业后曾任教于上海交通大学、复旦大学。1947年赴英国留学，相继在伦敦大学、牛津大学攻读英国文学。1949年入外国语学校任教授。曾任北京外国语学院英文系主任、外国语言研究所所长、中国英语教学研究会会长、中国语言学会常务理事、全国高等教育自学考试英语专业指导委员会主任。著有《语言的定义、功能、起源》《语言符号的任意性》《论语法》《〈马氏文通〉及其语言哲学》《论语言》等重要论著。

Xu Guozhang (1915-1994), linguist and educator of English, was born in Haining, Zhejiang. He graduated from Soochow University Middle School in 1934 before studying at National Chiao Tung University in Shanghai and the Department of Foreign Languages at Tsinghua University. He graduated from National Southwestern Associated University in 1939 and taught at Chiao Tung University and Fudan University. He went to England in 1947 to study English literature at the University of London and Oxford University. Upon returning to China in 1949, he became a professor at the Institute of Foreign Languages and served as Head of the English Department at Beijing Foreign languages Institute, Director of the Institute of Linguistics and Foreign Languages, President of China English Language Education Association, member of the Executive Council of the Chinese Language Society, and Chairman of the English Steering Committee of National Higher Education Self-Learning Examinations. Among his important publications are *The Meaning, Function and Origin of Language*, *The Arbitrariness of the Linguistic Sign*, *On Grammar*, *Ma's Grammar and Its Philosophy of Language*, and *On Language*.

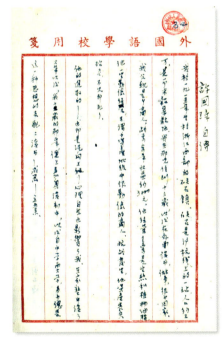

许国璋的干部登记表及自传

Xu Guozhang's cadre registration form and autobiography

周珏良（1916—1992），安徽至德人，翻译家、中西比较文学专家。毕业于天津南开中学，后考入清华大学外文系，先后在昆明西南联合大学、昆明清华大学研究院外文部学习。曾任天津工商学院女子学院、清华大学外文系讲师。1947年赴美国入芝加哥大学深造。1949年回国入外国语学校任教。1953年赴朝鲜，任朝鲜军事停战委员会中国人民志愿军秘书处翻译。1975年调外交部任翻译室副主任。1980年调回北京外国语学院任教授。曾任中国比较文学研究会常务理事、美国文学研究会常务理事等职。参加过《毛泽东选集》第五卷、《周恩来选集》上卷、毛泽东诗词等英译本的定稿工作。

Zhou Jueliang (1916-1992), translator and expert in China-Western comparative literature, was born in Zhide, Anhui. He graduated from Nankai High School in Tianjin and was admitted by the Department of Foreign Languages at Tsinghua University. He studied at National Southwestern Associated University and the Foreign Languages Faculty of the School of Graduate Studies at Tsinghua University in Kunming. He worked as a lecturer at the Women's College of Tianjin Institute of Higher Education and Commerce (Institut des Hautes Études et Commerciales) and the Department of Foreign Languages at Tsinghua University. He went to the United States to study at the University of Chicago in 1947 and returned to China in 1949 to teach at the Institute of Foreign Languages. He went to North Korea in 1953 and worked as a translator for the Secretariat of Chinese People's Volunteer Army at the Korea Military Armistice Commission. In 1975, he was transferred to the Ministry of Foreign Affairs where he became Deputy Head of its Department of Translation and Interpreting. In 1980, he was transferred back to Beijing Foreign Languages Institute to become a professor. He also served as a member of the Executive Council of Chinese Comparative Literature Association and of China Association for the Study of American Literature. He took part in revising the English translations of the *Selected Works of Mao Zedong: Volume V*, *Selected Works of Zhou Enlai*: Volume I, and *Mao Zedong Poems*.

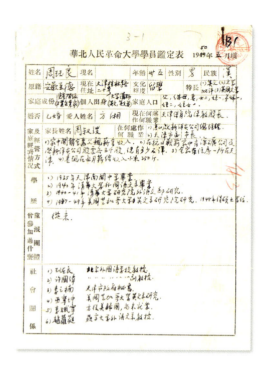

周珏良在华北人民革命大学学习结业时的鉴定表

Zhou Jueliang's Identification Form from North China People's Revolutionary University

陈梅洁的干部登记表及英文自传

Margaret Turner's cadre registration form and English autobiography

2

1. 1953年马列教研室教师合影

2. 第一届德语专业学生与教师合影，
二排左起：李康、姚可崑、李遇安。

1. A group photo of teachers from the Marxism-Leninism Teaching and Research Section

2. Photograph of the first intake of students of German with their teachers. Second row from the left: Li Kang, Yao Kekun, Li Yu'an.

外国语学校早期教师（部分）

Some of the faculty members of the Institute of Foreign Languages

薄冰

1921年生，山西应县人。毕业于浙江大学外文系，1950年来外国语学校任教。

Bo Bing, born in 1921 in Yingxian, Shanxi, graduated from the Foreign Languages Department at Chekiang University (present-day Zhejiang University) and became a teacher at the Institute in 1950.

郭迪诚

1907年生，北京人。毕业于法国巴黎电机高等专科学校，曾任北京中法大学副教授，1950年来外国语学校任教。

Guo Dicheng, born in 1907 in Beijing, graduated from the College of Electrical Engineering (École supérieure d'électricité) in Paris and was an Associate Professor at the French-Chinese University (l'Université Franco-Chinoise) before becoming a teacher at the Institute in 1950.

外国语学校早期教师（部分）　Some of the faculty members of the Institute of Foreign Languages

岑楚兰

1933 年生，广东南海人。毕业于堤岸中法学堂，1951 年入外国语学校学习，1953 年留校任教。

Cen Chulan, born in 1933 in Nanhai, Guangdong, graduated from French-Chinese School (Lycée Franco-Chinois) at Cholon in Saigon, Vietnam, was enrolled in the Institute of Foreign Languages in 1951 and, upon graduation, became a teacher at the Institute in 1953.

陈　琳

1922 年生，北京人。南京金陵大学毕业，1950 年来外国语学校任教。

Chen Lin, born in 1922 in Beijing, graduated from the former University of Nanking and became a teacher at the Institute in 1950.

丁往道

1924 年生，安徽无为县人。毕业于四川大学外文系，1950 年来外国语学校任教。

Ding Wangdao, born in 1924 in Wuwei, Anhui, graduated from the Department of Foreign Languages at Sichuan University and became a teacher at the Institute in 1950.

房仲民

1906 年生，安徽桐城人。先后就读于北京女子师范大学、德国耶拿大学。曾任北京大学兼任讲师、同济大学副教授、兼任复旦大学副教授，1952 来外国语学校任教。

Fang Zhongmin, born in 1906 in Tongcheng, Anhui, studied at Beijing Women's Normal University and the University of Jena in Germany. She was a part-time lecturer at Peking University, Associate Professor at Tongji University and part-time Associate Professor at Fudan University before becoming a teacher at the Institute in 1952.

李欧丽嘉

1901 年生于瑞士圣加仑城。曾就读于美国哥伦比亚大学，1951 年来外国语学校任教。

Olga Lee, born in 1901 in St Gallen, Switzerland, studied at Columbia University in the US before becoming a teacher at the Institute in 1951.

李廷揆

1916 年生，北京人。毕业于北京大学，并先后就读于瑞士洛桑大学、法国巴黎大学，曾在北京大学任教，1951 年来外国语学校任教。

Li Tingkui, born in 1916 in Beijing, graduated from Peking University and studied at the University of Lausanne in Switzerland and University of Paris in France. He taught at Peking University before becoming a teacher at the Institute in 1951.

刘承沛

1922 年生，江西信丰人。毕业于昆明西南联合大学外文系，1949 年 8 月考入外国语学校，于 1950 年留校任教。

Liu Chengpei, born in 1922 in Xinfeng, Jiangxi, graduated from the Department of Foreign Languages at National Southwestern Associated University in Kunming. He was admitted into Beijing School of Foreign Languages in August 1949 and, upon graduation, became a teacher at the Institute in 1950.

刘世沐

1913 年生，江苏南京人。先后就读于清华大学、英国爱丁堡大学，1951 年来外国语学校任教。

Liu Shimu, born in 1913 in Nanjing, Jiangsu, studied at Tsinghua University and the University of Edinburgh in the UK, and became a teacher at the Institute in 1951.

柳小培

1928年生，江苏武进县人。曾就读于上海私立东吴大学、外国语学校，1950年留外国语学校任教。

Liu Xiaopei, born in 1928 in Wujin, Jiangsu, studied first at Soochow University at Shanghai and then at Beijing School of Foreign Languages; and upon graduation, became a teacher at the Institute in 1950.

孟 复

1916年生，江苏常州人。曾就读于上海沪江大学、清华大学及英国伦敦政治经济学院，1952来外国语学校任教。

Meng Fu, born in 1916 in Changzhou, Jiangsu, studied at the University of Shanghai(predecessor of the University of Shanghai for Science and Technology), Tsinghua University, and London School of Economics and Political Sciences. He became a teacher at the Institute of Foreign Languages in 1952.

唐进伦

1924年生，山东牟平县人。毕业于燕京大学政治系，曾就读于日本东京帝国大学法学院，1949年来外国语学校学习，1951年留校任教。

Tang Jinlun, born in 1924 in Mouping, Shandong, graduated from the Department of Political Science at Yenching University and studied in the School of Law at Tokyo Imperial University; enrolled at the Institute of Foreign Languages in 1949 and, upon graduation, became a teacher at the Institute in 1951.

唐祖培

1906年生，四川成都人。毕业于巴黎大学政治学院，法学博士，1951年来外国语学校任教。

Tang Zupei, born in 1906 in Chengdu, Sichuan, was awarded a Doctorate in Law from the School of Political Science at the University of Paris (Institut d'Études Politiques de Paris) and became a teacher at the Institute of Foreign Languages in 1951.

王锡钧

1911年生，辽宁沈阳人。哈佛大学研究院政治系毕业，曾就读于天津南开大学、伦敦大学，1951年来外国语学校任教。

Wang Xijun, born in 1911 in Shenyang, Liaoning, graduated from the Department of Government at Harvard Graduate School of Arts and Science and had studied at Nankai University in Tianjin and University of London before becoming a teacher at the Institute of Foreign Languages in 1951.

危东亚

1920年生，四川綦江县人。毕业于南京金陵大学，曾任南京美国大使馆翻译，1949年来外国语学校任教。

Wei Dongya, born in 1920 in Qijiang, Sichuan, graduated from the University of Nanking and worked as a translator at the American Embassy in Nanjing. He became a teacher at the Institute in 1949.

熊德锐

1927年生，江西南昌人。先后就读于牛津大学、巴黎大学，并获硕士学位，1951年来外国语学校任教。

Xiong Deni, born in 1927 in Nanchang, Jiangxi, studied at the University of Oxford and then the University of Paris, where he received a Master's Degree. He became a teacher at the Institute in 1951.

熊 健

1920年生，湖北礼山县人。曾就读于日本第一高等专科学校及广西大学经济系，1949年7月来外国语学校任教。

Xiong Jian, born in 1920 in Lishan, Hubei, studied at Number One Special Training School in Japan and the Economic Department at Guangxi University. He became a teacher at the Institute in July 1949.

杨树勋

1918年生，湖北应城县人。曾就读于南京金陵大学外文系、美国纽约州汉密尔顿学院，并于哥伦比亚大学师范学院研究院毕业，1951年来外国语学校任教。

Yang Shuxun, born in 1918 in Yingcheng, Hubei, graduated from the Foreign Languages Department at the University of Nanking, and studied at Hamilton College in New York and the Teachers College at Columbia University. He became a teacher at the Institute in 1951.

姚可崑

1904年生，河北临榆人。曾就读于德国柏林大学及海德堡大学，曾任北京师范大学国文系教授，1950年来外国语学校任教。

Yao Kekun, born in 1904 in Linyu, Hebei, studied at Berlin University and Heidelberg University in Germany, and was a professor in the Chinese Department at Beijing Normal University before becoming a teacher at the Institute in 1950.

应曼蓉

1928年生，浙江鄞县人。毕业于上海圣约翰大学英文系，1950年来外国语学校任教。

Ying Manrong, born in 1928 in Yin County, Zhejiang, graduated from the English Department at St John's University in Shanghai before becoming a teacher at the Institute in 1950.

张道真

1926年生，湖北沙市人。毕业于南京中央大学外文系，曾就读于美国华盛顿大学、哈佛大学和法国巴黎大学，1950年来外国语学校任教。

Zhang Daozhen, born in 1926 in Shashi, Hubei, graduated from the Department of Foreign Languages at National Central University (present-day Nanjing University) in Nanjing and studied at the University of Washington, Harvard University and University of Paris. He became a teacher at the Institute in 1950.

张汉熙

1921年生，广东梅县人。毕业于印度加尔各答大学，曾任沈阳中正大学副教授、兼任北京师范大学副教授、天津市政府秘书，1949年来外国语学校任教。

Zhang Hanxi, born in 1921 in Mei County, Guangdong, graduated from Calcutta University in India and was an Assistant Professor at Chong Cheng University in Shenyang, part-time Associate Professor at Beijing Normal University and Secretary to the Tianjin Municipal Government. He became a teacher at the Institute in 1949.

周谟智

1927年生，湖北黄陂人。毕业于外国语学校，1951年留校任教。

Zhou Mozhi, born in 1927 in Huangbei, Hubei, graduated from the School of Foreign Languages and, upon graduation, became a teacher at the Institute in 1951.

祝彦

1926年生，江苏江阴人。曾就读于南京中央大学外文系，1951年于外国语学校德语专业毕业后留校任教。

Zhu Yan, born in 1926 in Jiangyin, Jiangsu, studied in the Department of Foreign Languages at National Central University in Nanjing, graduated from the German Department at the School of Foreign Languages in 1951 and, upon graduation, became a teacher at the Institute.

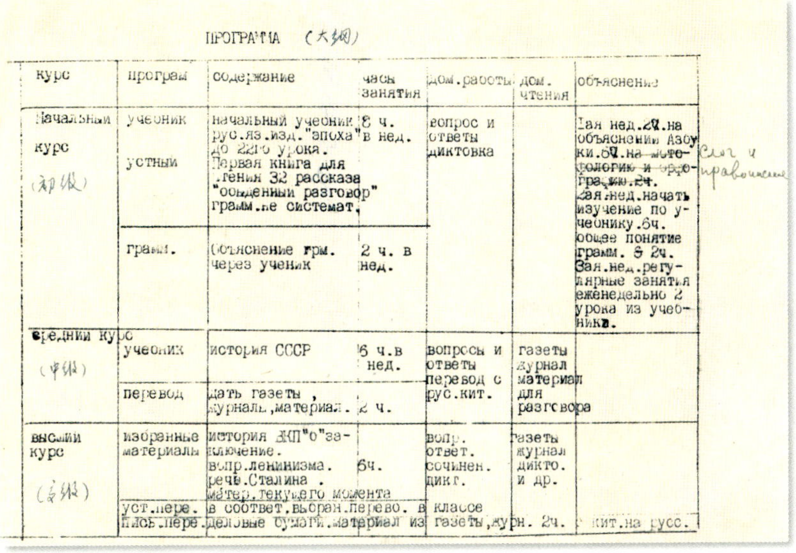

1. 1950 年外国语学校俄文部教学大纲

2. 3. 外国语学校俄文部一、二年级语法教学大纲

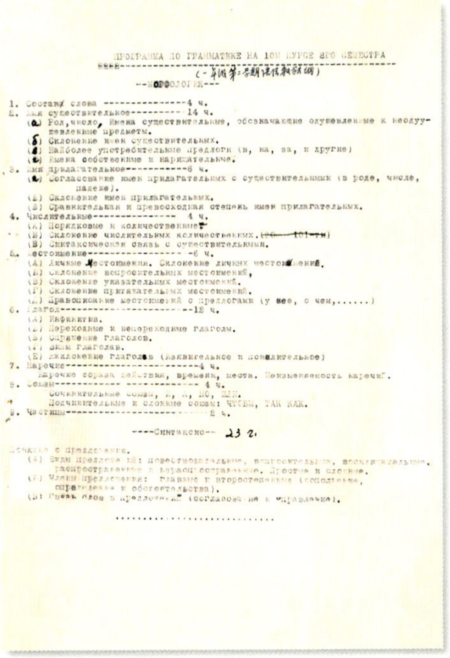

1. Syllabus of the Russian Faculty at the Institute of Foreign Languages in 1950

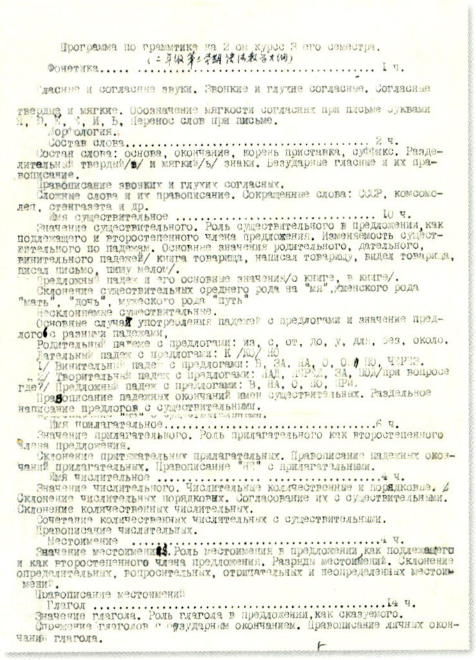

2. 3. Grammar syllabus for first- and second-year students of Russian at the Institute

1

2

3

4.5. 外国语学校俄文部一、二年级
阅读课教学大纲

4.5. Reading Syllabus for first- and
second-year students of Russian
at the Institute

4

5

外国语学校建校初期，目标为培养德才兼备的外
事翻译干部。学制暂定两年，如工作需要可以随时调
出工作。课程设政治和外语两门。外语分读本、语法、
翻译等课型，选材主要是政论文章。政治学习主要是
结合运动，采取听报告、讨论、辅导等方式进行。在
课时分配上，政治课占 20%，外语课占 80%。

When the Institute of Foreign Languages was first
established, its aim was to educate translators with both professional ability and political integrity to undertake foreign
affairs work. The length of the courses were two years, but
the students could be assigned to work duties when there was
need. The school curriculum only had two subjects, Politics
and Foreign Languages. Foreign Language classes were split
into categories such as reading, grammar and translation, and
the teaching materials were mainly selected from political
treatises. Political studies were constantly combined with
political movements and took mainly the form of group
activities where students listened to reports, debated and
received tuition. Political classes took up 20% of the teaching
time, with foreign languages 80%.

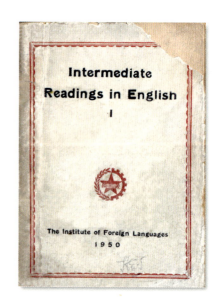

■ 1950 年外国语学校
使用的英语教材

English textbooks used at
the Institute in 1950

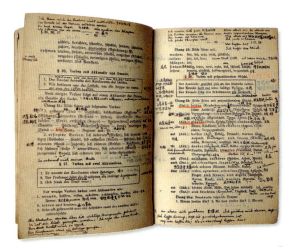

1、2、3. 外国语学校时期伊莎白使用的英语教材（伊莎白提供）

4、5. 外国语学校德语教材

6. 外国语学校政治课使用的 1949 年版的《共产党宣言》

1. 2. 3. English textbooks used by Isabel Crook
when she taught at the Institute (provided by
Isabel)

4. 5. German textbooks used at the Institute

6. The 1949 edition of the *Communist Manifesto* used
in political studies classes at the Institute

■ 外国语学校 1952 年教学大纲

The Institute syllabus for 1952

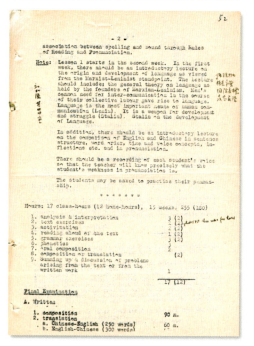

1951 年外国语学校开始大力贯彻"学习苏联"的方针。首先是采用苏联的大学课本，英文部以莫斯科外语师范学院的《高级英语》为教材，德法文组以苏联外贸学院的课本为教材。学校还请中国人民大学和北京俄文专修学校的苏联专家来校介绍苏联的教学经验，开始采用苏联的教学大纲、教学方案、教学制度和五分制，建立专业教研室。1952 年 6 月，英文部改称英文系，德法文组改称德法文系，各系制订三年教学计划。根据外交部的决定，学校规模缩小为 600 人，成立校务委员会和系务委员会。

In 1951, the Institute sought to comply with directives to "learn from the Soviet Union", and began to use university textbooks from the Soviet Union. The English Faculty started using *Advanced English* brought back from Moscow Foreign Language Teacher Training College as textbooks, and the German and French programmes began to use textbooks brought back from Moscow Foreign Trade College. The Institute also invited Soviet experts from Renmin University of China and Beijing Russian Language School to share their experience of Soviet teaching methods. The Institute started to use Soviet syllabuses, teaching plans, teaching systems and their five grades marking system, and a teaching and research section was set up for each language or subject area. In June 1952, the English Faculty was renamed the English Department, the German and French programmes were renamed the German and French Departments, and each department made its own three-year teaching plan. At the behest of the Ministry of Foreign Affairs, the Institute shrank its size to 600 people and established a Institute Affairs Committee and Departmental Affairs Committee.

1

1. 1954年初外国语学校就招收研究生事宜请示高教部的文件（草稿）

2. 3. 外国语学校《对学校培养研究生的初步意见》

1. A proposal to recruit research students (draft) submitted to the Ministry of Higher Education for approval in 1954

2. 3. "A preliminary proposal concerning setting up a programme of research students at the Institute" drafted by the Institute of Foreign Languages

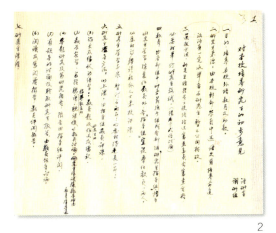

2

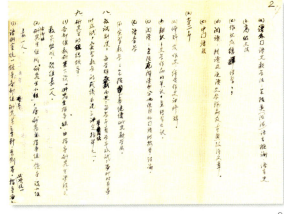

3

　　1953年外国语学校开始学习过渡时期总路线，贯彻高等教育部杨秀峰部长提出的"一切以教学为中心""全面学习和运用苏联先进经验"的思想，学校召开了翻译教学、口语教学、课外阅读、课外活动等专业会议，总结并交流编写教材和课堂教学的经验，明确提出了要听、说、写、读、译全面发展，重视口语和翻译训练，重视实际运用的锻炼。

　　1954年，由军事干部学校分配来校学习的三年制学生，全部毕业分配工作。为培养师资，学校从英语、法语、德语三个专业的应届毕业生中选拔10人，作为第一批研究生。

In 1953, the Institute started its transitional period and sought to follow the directives of Yang Xiufeng, Minister of Higher Education, who asked colleges and universities to "place teaching at the core" and "comprehensively learn and use advanced Soviet teaching methods". To this end, the Institute organized special meetings on translation teaching, oral lessons, extracurricular reading, after-class foreign language activities and so on to sum up and exchange experience in teaching material development and classroom teaching. The Institute made it clear that students' abilities in listening, speaking, writing, reading, translation and interpreting should be developed comprehensively, with emphasis placed on speaking, translation and interpreting training and on exercises based on real life situations.

In 1954, the students who had been transferred from the Military Cadre School completed their three years of study and were all assigned work upon their graduation. To cultivate its own source of teaching staff, the Institute selected ten graduating students from the English, French and German Departments to become the Institute's first intake of research students.

外国语学校第一批研究生（缺瞿则诚）

The first intake of research students at the Institute of Foreign Languages (missing Qu Zecheng)

陈振尧（Chen Zhenyao）

董光熙（Dong Guangxi）

金国芬（Jin Guofen）

姜文霞（Jiang Wenxia）

吴千之（Wu Qianzhi）

张载梁（Zhang Zailiang）

郑荣成（Zheng Rongcheng）

庄绎传（Zhuang Yichuan）

庄元泳（Zhuang Yuanyong）

1

2

外国语学校建校初期，办学条件十分艰苦。但全校师生同心协力，教师创造条件努力教学，学生满怀热情勤奋学习。与此同时，师生积极参与或组织各种社会活动和文体活动，校园生活丰富多彩。

When the Institute of Foreign Languages was first established, its teaching conditions were severely lacking, but everyone worked together with teachers doing the best they could to teach and the students learning diligently. At the same time, the students and the teachers organized or participated in all kinds of social and cultural activities to make their life on campus more varied and colourful.

3

5

4

6

1. 学生在露天就餐。

2. 1949 年 10 月 1 日，全校师生 1,000 余人到天安门参加开国大典。毛泽东主席在天安门城楼上见到外国语学校师生队伍后，高喊："外国语学校的同志万岁！"图为 1949 年 10 月 1 日从学校出发参加开国大典的游行队伍。

3. 参加 1950 年"五一"游行的外国语学校女同学队伍

4. 1950 年"五一"游行队伍

5. 1950 年"七一"，党员代表向党组织献旗（右一为杨化飞）。

6. 为庆祝中华人民共和国成立，外国语学校学生上街演出。

1. Students eating outside

2. On 1st October 1949, more than 1,000 teachers and students from the Institute attended the founding ceremony for the People's Republic. When Chairman Mao Zedong saw the Institute in the parade, he shouted "Long live the comrades from the Institute of Foreign Languages!" The photograph shows members of the Institute setting off from the Institute to join the founding ceremony parade on 1st October 1949.

3. Female students from the Institute marching to join the May 1st parade to celebrate International Labour Day in 1950

4. The May 1st parade in 1950

5. Party member representatives presenting a banner to the CPC organization in the Institute in celebration of the anniversary of the founding of the CPC on July 1st 1950 (First right: Yang Huafei)

6. Students from the Institute performing on the street in celebration of the founding of the People's Republic

7

8

9

10

---

7. 学校腰鼓队表演

8. 朝鲜留学生和中国学生进行拔河比赛。

9. 欢送俄专三部迁入宣武校区及庆祝 1951 年开学的文艺演出会

10. 欢送俄专三部迁入宣武校区及庆祝 1951 年开学的文艺演出会，
   学生表演京剧《打渔杀家》。

7. Performance by the Institute's drum team

8. Students from DPRK studying in China competing with Chinese students in
   a tug of war

9. A group photo of the performers at the gala marking the start of the Institute
   year in 1951 and the relocation of the BRLS's Third Faculty to its new
   campus

10. Students performing the Peking opera *A Fisherman's Fury* in a gala marking
    the start of the school year in 1951 and the relocation of the BRLS's Third
    Faculty to its new campus

1

2

1. 1954 年迁入苏州街新校区，师生在校园内植树
   （左起第四人为陈梅洁）。

2. 苏州街新校舍一角

1. Teachers and students planting trees after the Institute
   relocated to its new campus on Suzhou Street (4th
   from the left: Margaret Turner)

2. A corner of the new campus on Suzhou Street

1954

1954 年成立 北京外国语学院

The establishment of Beijing Foreign Languages Institute in 1954

1954 年 8 月，外国语学校由西苑迁至西郊苏州街新校区；同时经高教部呈请国务院批准，学校改名为北京外国语学院。1955 年 8 月，学校行政关系由外交部改隶高等教育部领导。

In August 1954, the Institute of Foreign Languages relocated from Xiyuan to its new campus on Suzhou Street in the west suburb of Beijing. At the same time, with the approval of the State Council after an application from the Ministry of Higher Education, the School renamed itself Beijing Foreign Languages Institute. In August 1955, governance of the Institute was transferred from the Ministry of Foreign Affairs to the Ministry of Higher Education.

■ 1957 年庆祝俄国十月革命 40 周年时的校门

The Institute's main gate decorated to mark the 40th anniversary of the Russian October Revolution

■ 高等教育部就批准外国语学校改名
为北京外国语学院致外交部的文件

The approval document from the Ministry of Higher Education to the Ministry of Foreign Affairs for the renaming of the Institute to Beijing Foreign Languages Institute

1955

　　根据高教部《1954—1955 学年工作计划指导要点》中"今后我部对各校的指导重点是进一步全面地学习苏联，进一步使学校纳入正常轨道"的要求，学校制订《1954—1955 学年工作计划纲要》，提出以"积极认真全面地学习苏联先进经验"作为全校各项工作的指导思想。12 月，参照莫斯科外语师范学院的教学方案，制订了四年制的《北京外国语学院教学计划（草案）》，其中规定："外语学院的任务是培养德才兼备、口笔译兼能的所学外国语文的翻译人才。毕业生应该掌握马列主义理论知识，具有较广博的中外语言文学及外国历史地理的基础知识与初步国际事务知识……"计划中规定开设的课程共计 18 门。

Responding to the "Main Points of Guidance on the Work Plan for the 1954-1955 Academic Year" issued by the Ministry of Higher Education, which stated that "from now on, this Ministry's main points of guidance for higher education institutions will be to make further efforts to learn from the Soviet Union on all levels and further their efforts to set themselves onto a normal track", the Institute drew up "Outlines of the Work Plan for the 1954-1955 Academic Year", in which it proposed that all members of staff at the Institute should "enthusiastically, earnestly and comprehensively draw on the advanced methods of the Soviet Union and regard this as the guideline for all the work of the Institute". In December 1954, the Institute, with reference to the teaching plan at Moscow Foreign Languages Teacher Training College, drew up a four-year "Beijing Foreign Languages Institute Teaching Plan (draft)", which stipulates that "the aim of the Institute is to train translators who are not only proficient in both oral and written translation but also possess moral integrity. Graduates from the Institute should have a solid understanding of Marxist ideology and possess a fairly wide array of basic knowledge about Chinese and foreign language and literature, history and geography of foreign countries, and preliminary knowledge of international affairs…" The plan also specified for the creation of 18 courses.

1. 1954 年开学典礼，刘仲容院长讲话。

2. 1954 年开学典礼，外交部办公厅主任王炳南讲话。

1. Institute President Liu Zhongrong speaking at the 1954 matriculation ceremony

2. Wang Bingnan, Director of the General Office at the Ministry of Foreign Affairs, speaking at the 1954 matriculation ceremony

1955 年，苏联专家、顾问陆续到校任职，指导教学工作。苏联英语专家杜鲁妮娜任院长顾问，参加院长联合办公会议，参与重大教学问题的讨论，并以英文系为重点，指导教师进行科研，开设语言理论课和文学史课。

苏联专家指导中国教师上课。

A Soviet expert instructing a Chinese teacher as she taught her class

In 1955, Soviet experts and consultants started to arrive and took up posts at the Institute to help the Institute's teachers in their work. The Soviet English expert Drunina became a consultant to the Institute's President, attended the administrative meeting of Institute's President and Vice Presidents, engaged in discussions about important issues in teaching, advised teachers, especially those in the English Department, on how to do research, and offered classes in linguistic theories and histories of literature.

■ 李棣华副院长和院长顾问杜鲁妮娜的合影

Vice President Li Dihua photographed with the
President's consultant Drunina

1

1956年9月，学制延长为五年，第一届五年制新生七十二人入学。同年根据中罗文化协定，增设罗马尼亚语专业，属法文系领导。罗马尼亚专家迪亚康奈斯库来校任教。

In September 1956, the length of study at the Institute was lengthened to five years and the first intake under this new system numbered 72 students. In the same year, under a cultural agreement between China and Romania, the Institute added Romanian to its range of subjects. The new subject came under the French Department and Romanian expert Ion Diaconescu arrived at the Institute to teach the language.

2

3 4

5

1. 1954 年德文系教师讨论教学改革。

2. 1955 年 8 月，从民主德国聘请的第一位德语专家汉斯·艾彻来校任教。图为艾彻与董光熙合影。

3. 罗马尼亚专家迪亚康奈斯库指导罗马尼亚语学生学习。

4. 罗马尼亚专家史德方带领学生进行口语实习。

5. 1956 年部分西班牙语教师和西班牙专家梅廉多（后排左二）在颐和园。

1. Teachers from the German Department discussing teaching reform in 1954

2. In August 1955, Hans Eicher, the first German expert from the German Democratic Republic, arrived at the Institute. He is pictured in the photograph with Dong Guangxi.

3. Romanian expert Ion Diaconescu supervising students in the study of Romanian

4. Romanian expert Stefan Giosu taking students out of the classroom to practise speaking Romanian

5. Some of the teachers of Spanish photographed with Spanish expert Abaúlfo Melendo (second from the left, second row) at the Summer Palace in Beijing

2

1

3

1. 迁入苏州街新校舍时的西班牙语教师

2. 20 世纪 50 年代法文系教师合影

3. 20 世纪 50 年代末法文系教师与第一位法国专家
   安德烈（后排左三）合影

1. Teachers of Spanish photographed after the Institute relocated to
   Suzhou Street

2. A group photo of teachers from the French Department taken in
   the 1950s

3. Teachers from the French Department photographed with the
   Institute's first French expert Andre (3rd from the left, back row)

4

5

6

4. 英文系应曼蓉夫妇与杜鲁妮娜

5. 1956 年英文系陈琳与杜鲁妮娜

6. 1956 年外国专家研究录音配合授课问题。

4. Ying Manrong and her husband from the English Department photographed with Drunina

5. Chen Lin from the English Department photographed with Drunina in 1956

6. Foreign experts working on the issue of combining recordings with classroom teaching in 1956

1956

　　高教部要求我校顾问和专家对其他院校外语系和中学外语教学发挥指导作用。英文系在《1955—1956 学年工作计划草案》中把"在专家指导下开展科学研究、稳定教材以提高教学质量"作为中心任务，并把专家工作规定为"科研工作、培养师资和教学组织领导工作"。应高教部要求，在专家指导下，由刘世沐、应曼蓉负责为全国高中、初中开设的英语课制订教学大纲，1956 年起在全国执行；陈琳、姚可崑等分别负责编写全国通用的大学英语、德语专业学生用课本；中学使用的英语教科书由英文系教师负责编写。

The Ministry of Higher Education required that foreign consultants and experts at the Institute provide guidance for teachers of foreign language departments at other higher education institutions and secondary schools. The Institute's English Department, in its "Work Plan for the 1955-1956 Academic Year", identified it as the central core priority "to carry out scientific research under the guidance of experts so as to fix teaching materials and elevate the quality of teaching ", and specified that the work of the experts were "undertaking academic research, training teachers and playing a leadership role in teaching". At the request of the Ministry of High Education and under the guidance of foreign experts, Liu Shimu and Ying Manrong led an initiative to write a syllabus for English language teaching in middle and high schools nationwide. The syllabus was implemented in 1956. Chen Lin, Yao Kekun and others were responsible for writing standard English and German textbooks for university English and German majors, which were used nationwide. Secondary school English textbooks were written by teachers from the English Department.

▌1956 年我校受教育部委托，编写并正式
出版了中华人民共和国成立后的第一套
全国通用大学英语、德语课本。

Commissioned by the Ministry of Education,
the Institute compiled and published new
China's first set of College English and German
textbooks for nationwide use.

1

2

1.《西方语文》创刊号，1959 年改
　名为《外语教学与研究》。

2.《西方语文》创刊号目录及创刊词

1. The front page of the first edition of *Western Languages
and Literature*. Its title was changed to *Foreign Language
Teaching and Research* in 1959.

2. The contents page and words from the publisher in the
first issue of *Western Languages and Literature*

■ 外语科学讨论会日程

The schedule for the conference

1956年5月，学校召开第一次外语科学讨论会，全院教师和兄弟院校代表300余人参加了会议。会后将论文汇成专集，铅印出版，每篇论文发给奖金100元。1957年6月，我国第一本专门研究西方语言文学的学术刊物《西方语文》创刊。

In May 1956, the Institute convened its first foreign language academic conference, which was attended by the entire faculty at the Institute and other partner institutions, over 300 attendees. After the conference, the submitted papers were compiled into the conference proceedings and published in lead print, each contributor receiving 100 *yuan* as a bonus. In June 1957, *Western Languages and Literature*, China's first academic journal on the study of Western languages and literature was born.

1

1. 英国共产党名誉主席加拉赫与英文系学生合影

2. 1956 年，罗马尼亚语学生与罗马尼亚政府代表团联欢。

3. 1956 年，法文系学生与挪威青年联欢。

4. 1957 年，法国著名演员菲利普来访时和法文系学生在一起。

2

3

4

20 世纪 50 年代中期，学校除了和苏联大力发展友好关系外，和其他一些国家也开始了民间友好交往，在配合国家外交政策的同时，扩展学生视野，活跃校园生活。

In the mid-1950s, the Institute not only forged friendly relations with the Soviet Union, but also started to befriend its counterparts in other nations. This endeavour not only served the country's diplomatic policies, it also expanded the academic horizon of its students and enriched campus life.

1. Willie Gallacher, Honorary President of the Communist Party of Great Britain photographed with students from the English Department

2. Students of Romanian gathered together with a Romanian government delegation in 1956

3. Students from the French Department gathering together with a Norwegian youth in 1956

4. The famous French actor Gérard Philippe photographed with students from the French Department when he visited the Institute in 1957

6

7

5

5. 1957 年，西班牙语系学生接待来访的墨
西哥歌舞团演员。

6. 1960 年，阿尔巴尼亚来宾参观电化教室。

7. 1960 年，剑桥大学代表来校访问。

5. Students from the Spanish Department receiving
visiting performers from a Mexican dance troupe in
1957

6. Guests from Albania visiting an audio-visual classroom
in 1960

7. A representative from the University of Cambridge
visiting the Institute in 1960

1957

1957 年 2 月，学院党总支改为党委，刘柯任党委书记，郝金禄任副书记。英文系和德西法文系分别成立党支部。

1957 年 6 月，人民日报发表题为《这是为什么》的社论，全国开展"反右"运动，学校 200 多名教师及学生被打成"右派分子"，受到不同程度的错误处理，这对学校工作造成严重破坏。

In February 1957, the CPC General Branch at the Institute became a CPC Committee, which was responsible for overseeing the running of the Institute. Liu Ke became Secretary and Hao Jinlu became Deputy Secretary of the committee. The Departments of English, German, Spanish and French each set up their own CPC branches.

In June 1957, the People's Daily published an editorial with the title "Why Is This" and people all over China were involved in an "Anti-Rightist" campaign. Over 200 teachers and students at the Institute were branded as "Rightists" and endured a variety of wrongful treatment, which did serious damage to the Institute.

1

▌《北京外国语学院跃进计划纲要》提出"大干特干，苦战五年，把我院建成为一个先进的共产主义的外国语学院""彻底批判一切资产阶级教育思想和学术思想"等口号。

"An Outline Plan for Beijing Foreign Languages Institute to Leap Forward" contained slogans such as "Get stuck in, work hard for the next five years, and turn our Institute into an advanced communist foreign languages institute" and "Thoroughly repudiate all bourgeois educational thinking and academic theories."

2

1958

　　1958 年 6 月，院党委向全院传达中共八大二次会议精神和毛泽东主席在会议上的讲话，全院开展学习建设社会主义的总路线。在"左"的思想指导下，全国出现"大跃进"，高等学校掀起了"教育革命"高潮：进行教学整改，大搞群众性的科学研究，集体编教材、写论文、编词典，师生辩论教学方案，制订跃进规划，开办校办工厂，校内大炼钢铁，师生上山下乡参加劳动。

　　In June 1958, after the Institute's Party Committee relayed the message of the 2nd Plenum of the 8th CPC National Congress and Mao Zedong's speech at the plenum to the whole Institute, everyone started learning about the Party's general guideline for China's socialist reconstruction. Under the guidance of "Leftist" ideology, the whole nation started a "Great Leap Forward" and higher education institutions started a wave of "Educational Revolution" featuring rectifying current educational practices, conducting mass scientific research, and authoring teaching materials, dictionaries and essays collectively, holding teacher-student debates on teaching plans, formulating plans for "leaping forward", setting up factories affiliated to the Institute, building small furnaces on the Institute premises for smelting iron, and participating in manual labour in rural areas.

3

4

5

6

1. 庆祝建党 37 周年及学院"跃进规划"诞生

2. 1958 年"国庆献礼"

3. 4. 召开全校"跃进大会"，各单位献决心书。

5. 学生在焦油厂参加生产劳动。

6. "大跃进"期间的文艺演出

1. A performance to celebrate the 37th anniversary of the founding of the CPC and the formation of the Institute's plan for "Leaping Forward"

2. A "gift" prepared for China's National Day celebrations in 1958

3. 4. Each department delivering their letter of determination during the Institute's "Leaping Forward" meeting

5. Students engaging in productive labour at a tar factory

6. A dance performance during the "Great Leap Forward"

1

2

3

1. 师生一起扭秧歌。

2. 师生在京郊密云县参加大炼钢铁。

3. 学生参加京密运河劳动，休息时组织娱乐活动。

1. Teachers and students doing the Yanko dance

2. Teachers and students engaging in mass smelting of iron in Miyun County, on the outskirts of Beijing

3. Students organizing recreational activities during work on the Beijing-Miyun Canal

4

5

6

7

4. 迁入苏州街校区后柯鲁克和英文系部分学生合影

5. 1954—1955 学年暑期毕业留念

6. 第一届西班牙语专业学生与教师合影

7. 1955—1956 学年西班牙语专业毕业生合影纪念

4. David Crook photographed with some of the students from the English Department after the Institute relocated to its Suzhou Street campus

5. A group photo of students graduating in the summer during the 1954-1955 academic year

6. The first intake of students of Spanish photographed with their teachers

7. A group photo of students of Spanish graduating in the 1955-1956 academic year

北京外国语学院是我国第一所多语种外国语学院。从 1954 年到 1958 年，学校规模不断扩大，师资力量进一步增强，人才培养规格逐步提高，学校为国家培养了一批英、法、德、西等语种的外语专门人才。

Beijing Foreign Languages Institute was China's first multilingual foreign language institute. From 1954 to 1958, the Institute grew continuously and its faculty was strengthened. It was able to gradually upgrade its teaching programmes, providing the nation with a significant number of foreign language professionals proficient in languages such as English, French, German and Spanish.

1

2

3

1. 1955—1956 学年西班牙语专业毕业生与英文系进修学生结业合影

2. 1957 年刘仲容院长向学生颁发毕业证书。

3. 1957 年许国璋在毕业典礼上讲话。

1. Graduating students of Spanish photographed with students from the English Department who had completed their Spanish training course in the 1955-1956 academic year

2. Institute President Liu Zhongrong presenting a student with his graduation certificate in 1957

3. Xu Guozhang speaking at the graduation ceremony in 1957

4. 1958 年英文系 3 班学生

5. 1958 年德文系师生

6. 1957—1958 学年全体毕业生合影

4. Class Three students from the English Department in 1958

5. Teachers and students from the German Department in 1958

6. A group photo of all graduating students of the 1957-1958 academic year

4

5

6

第四章

俄语教育　独树一帜

（1949—1958年）

——从北京俄文专修学校到北京俄语学院

Chapter Four
Russian language teaching,
unique and outstanding

From Beijing Russian Language School to Beijing

Russian Institute

(1949-1958)

　　1949 年成立的北京俄文专修学校，以及在此基础上成立于 1955 年的北京俄语学院，是新中国外语教育的一支重要力量。自 1949 年建校至 1959 年与北京外国语学院合并，学校培养了一大批俄语教学、翻译以及外事人才，在社会主义建设事业中发挥了重要作用。1952 年 3 月增设的留苏预备部向苏联派出了数以千计的优秀学员，这些留苏学生回国后大都成为国家各个领域的骨干力量。

　　Set up in 1949, Beijing Russian Language School, the predecessor of Beijing Russian Institute founded in 1955, was an important institution for foreign language education in new China. From its establishment in 1949 to 1959 when it was merged into Beijing Foreign Languages Institute, it trained a large number of Russian language teachers, translators and foreign affairs personnel, all of whom played important roles in building China into a socialist country. The Training Division for Studying in the Soviet Union created in March 1952 gave Russian proficiency to thousands of trainees, most of whom after studying in the Soviet Union became leading figures in various fields in China.

师哲（1905—1998），陕西韩城人，俄语翻译家。曾先后随毛泽东、周恩来、朱德等人访问苏联及东欧。曾在中共中央俄文编译局、北京俄文专修学校和外文出版社任首任局长、校长、社长，同时还兼任毛泽东、周恩来、刘少奇、朱德等中央领导的俄语翻译。

Shi Zhe (1905-1998), born in Hancheng, Shaanxi, was a Russian translator. He accompanied Mao Zedong, Zhou Enlai, Zhu De and others on state visits to the Soviet Union and countries in Eastern Europe. He served as Director of the CPC Central Committee Russian Compilation and Translation Bureau, Principal of the Russian Language School, and the first President of Foreign Languages Press. He also served as the Russian translator for the top leaders of CPC such as Mao Zedong, Zhou Enlai, Liu Shaoqi and Zhu De.

北京俄文专修学校（1949—1954）

Beijing Russian Language School (1949-1954)

1949 年，为了配合新中国成立后在国际政治关系上实行"一边倒"（即倒向以苏联为首的社会主义阵营）的方针，满足国家对俄语人才的需要，中共中央决定成立一所专门教授俄语的学校，责成当时的中共中央俄文编译局负责筹建。学校从组建伊始就受到党中央的关怀，毛泽东主席亲自为学校确定并题写了校名。1949 年 10 月，北京俄文专修学校（简称"北京俄专"）正式成立，附属于中共中央俄文编译局，由编译局的正、副局长师哲、张锡俦兼任正、副校长，党的关系隶属于中共中央直属机关党委（当时由党中央办公厅主任杨尚昆任书记）。1953 年 3 月，北京俄专举行第一次党代表大会，党总支改为校党委，实行党委制，选举产生新的党委会。由于学校改隶高教部领导，学校党的关系从 1953 年 9 月起，也由中直党委转到北京市委。

In 1949, to implement the policy of "falling on one side" (the camp of socialist countries led by the Soviet Union) adopted by the People's Republic in dealing with international relations and to satisfy the country's need for people with Russian language skills, the CPC Central Committee decided to establish a school to solely teach Russian and the task was given to its Russian Compilation and Translation Bureau. The school had received a lot of attention from the Party leadership even before it was established and Chairman Mao Zedong personally decided on the name for the school and wrote it in calligraphy. The Beijing Russian Language School (BRLS) was formally established in October 1949 and was affiliated with the Russian Compilation and Translation Bureau and as such, the Bureau Director Shi Zhe and Deputy Director Zhang Xichou became the School's Principal and Vice Principal. The School's Party affiliation was with the Party Committee for Departments immediately under the CPC Central Committee, whose Secretary was Yang Shangkun, Director of the General Office of the CPC Central Committee.

1. 位于宣武区鲍家街的北京俄专校门，校名为毛泽东主席亲笔题写。

2. 1951年北京俄专学生在宣武区鲍家街校舍。

3. 1951年北京俄专鲍家街新校舍

1. The gate of Beijing Russian Language School on Baojia Street in Xuanwu District, Beijing. The calligraphy on the school plaque was written by Mao Zedong.

2. Students of BRLS at its campus on Baojia Street in Xuanwu District in 1951

3. BRLS new school buildings at its new campus on Baojia Street in 1951

北京俄专校址初为北京西城南宽街13号，与设在西斜街的俄文编译局邻近。后迁至鲍家街21号醇亲王府旧址。1950年下半年开始在鲍家街21号院内兴建新校舍，1951年暑假落成。

The School was initially situated at No.13 Nankuan Street in the Xicheng District of Beijing, close to the Russian Compilation and Translation Bureau, which was on Xixie Street. It later relocated to No.21 Baojia Street, the former site of Prince Chun Mansion. In the second half of 1950, the School began to build new school buildings on the site and the work was completed in the summer of 1951.

1951 年欢迎俄专三部（原外国语学校俄文部）师生迁入鲍家街新校舍。

The School welcoming the arrival of the its Third Faculty (formerly the Russian Faculty of the Institutel of Foreign Languages) at the new campus at Baojia Street in 1951

1950 年初，中央人民政府副主席刘少奇接见北京俄专科级以上干部，指出俄文编译局和北京俄专工作的重要意义：中苏两国友好合作的前景和大批苏联专家即将来华帮助我国进行建设，国家急需大批俄语翻译干部。他的讲话指明了学校的办学方向。

1951 年 8 月，鲍家街新校舍落成，俄专三部从西苑迁来，部的建制撤销。杨化飞担任北京俄专教务长。

At the start of 1950 when meeting with officers from the School above the rank of office chief, Liu Shaoqi, Vice President of the Central People's Government, pointed out the importance of the Russian Compilation and Translation Bureau and the Russian Language School, saying that the prospect of friendly relations and cooperation between China and the Soviet Union meant that large numbers of Soviet experts were about to arrive in China to help with the country's economic reconstruction, so the nation needed large numbers of Russian translators. His remarks cast light on the direction the School was to take.

In August 1951, after the construction of its new campus on Baojia Street was completed, the Third Faculty of the School moved in from Xiyuan and the system of faculties was abolished. Yang Huafei became the Teaching Affairs Officer of BRLS.

北京俄专建校初期的学生构成（1950 年）

The makeup of the student body in the early days of the School (1950)

一班：原哈尔滨外国语专门学校 17 班全体学生 50 名
三班：从原哈尔滨外国语专门学校其他班抽调的学生

Class One: All 50 students of Class 17 from Harbin School of Foreign Languages
Class Three: Students transferred from the other classes of Harbin School of Foreign Languages

二班：从大连解放军俄专调来的 20 余名学生

Class Two: 20-odd students transferred from Dalian People's Liberation Army Russian Language School

四班、五班：西苑外国语学校俄文部调来的学生
六班：其他大学在校生

Classes Four and Five: Students transferred from the Russian Faculty at the Institute of Foreign Languages in Xiyuan
Class Six: Current students from other universities

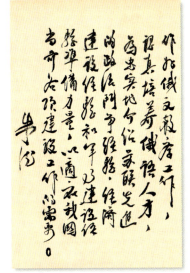

中央人民政府副主席刘少奇、朱德，政务院总理周恩来，副总理兼文教委员会副主任郭沫若为《俄文教学》题词。

Russian Language Teaching magazine received inscriptions by Vice Presidents Liu Shaoqi and Zhu De, Premier Zhou Enlai, and Vice Premier and Deputy Chairman of the Cultural and Education Committee Guo Moruo

1950 年 10 月 1 日，由毛泽东主席题写刊名的《俄文教学》创刊号出版。1951 年 9 月，中共中央宣传部、中央人民政府教育部、中共中央俄文编译局联合召开了第一次全国俄文教学工作会议。会议决定成立全国俄文教学指导委员会，隶属教育部，并建议将北京俄专筹备创办的《俄文教学》杂志作为该会的机关刊物。

On 1st October 1950, the first issue of *Russian Language Teaching* was published and its title was written by Chairman Mao. In September 1951, the first National Russian Language Teaching Conference was convened by the CPC Propaganda Department, the Ministry of Education and CPC Russian Compilation and Translation Bureau. Discussion at the conference revolved around important topics such as the guidelines and aims of Russian language education. The conference delegates decided to establish a National Russian Language Education Steering Committee affiliated to the Ministry of Education, and suggested that the *Russian Language Teaching* magazine that Beijing Russian Language School was due to publish should become the official publication for the committee.

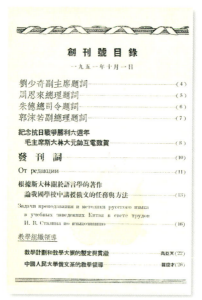

《俄文教学》创刊号

First issue of *Russian Language Teaching*

《俄文教学》创刊号目录

Contents page of *Russian Language Teaching*

1953 年《俄文教学》编辑部成员与苏联顾问合影

A group photo of editorial staff from *Russian Language Teaching* with Soviet advisers

在 1953 年 8 月召开的全国俄文教学工作会议上，北京俄专制订的讲读、翻译、语音及语法等课程的教学大纲被中央高等教育全国俄文教学指导委员会推荐给全国各俄语教学机构。

At the National Russian Language Teaching Conference held in August 1953, the syllabuses designed by Beijing Russian Language School for Speaking and Reading, Translation, Phonology and Grammar Courses were recommended by the Central Higher Education National Russian Language Teaching Steering Committee for its use in institutions of Russian language teaching nationwide.

全国俄文教学指导委员会成立后，加强了对俄文教学工作的组织领导。此后苏联专家来华任教的人数逐年增加，当时在文教部门中，北京俄专是拥有苏联专家人数最多的高等学校之一。在苏联专家的指导和帮助下，学校开展制订教学计划、教学大纲、教学制度，研究教学方法，培养师资，编写教材等基本建设，开始了学习苏联、逐步实现正规化的新阶段。

The establishment of the National Russian Language Teaching Steering Committee strengthened the organizational leadership of Russian language education in China. Afterwards, the number of Soviet experts arriving in China increased every year. In China's cultural and educational sectors, Beijing Russian Language School had one of the largest numbers of Soviet experts among higher educational establishments. Under the guidance and help of Soviet experts, the School started to learn from the Soviet Union in drawing up teaching plans, syllabuses and regulations, researching teaching methods, training teachers, compiling teaching materials and so on. By laying such groundwork for a proper educational establishment, the School moved to a new phase of its development.

留苏预备部

1952 年 3 月，为了适应国家建设需要派遣大量人员赴苏联学习苏联建设经验的情况，上级决定，北京俄专设立留苏预备部，派往苏联学习人员先在此集中学习一年俄语。当时为留苏预备部确定的教学方针是："在一年之内，教会学生基础俄语，使之具有初步用俄语听讲、阅读、记录、会话的能力，并提高其政治理论水平，锻炼健全的体魄，为留苏准备条件。"留苏预备生的来源为：国内大学在校生或毕业生、高中生和工农速成中学的部分学生，以及部分机关干部。

留苏预备部初期借用定阜大街原辅仁大学部分校舍，后在西郊魏公村苏州街兴建新址，1955 年底新校舍落成并投入使用。1956 年暑假后，校本部本科学生激增，鲍家街校舍不能容纳，决定与留苏预备部易位，校本部迁来西郊。

Training Division for Studying in the Soviet Union

In March 1952, to prepare for the large numbers of people who were about to go to the Soviet Union to learn from the Soviet experience in economic development, the superior of BRLS decided to create at the School a Training Division for Studying in the Soviet Union, so that those going to the Soviet Union can learn Russian for a year before leaving the country. At the time, the guiding principle set for the Training Division was: "Enable trainees to master basic Russian and have rudimentary skills in listening comprehension, reading, note-taking and conversation within a year; enhance their understanding of political theory, strengthen their physique, and prepare them for living and studying in the Soviet Union." Trainees for the Training Division came from several sources: undergraduates and graduates from Chinese universities, high school students, students from crash courses for workers and peasants, and cadres from various departments.

The Training Division initially utilised some of the teaching facilities of the former Fu Jen Catholic University on Dingfu Street. Later it started to build a new campus at a site on Suzhou Street in the Weigongcun area in the western suburb of Beijing. The new facilities were completed and ready for use at the end of 1955. After the summer of 1956, as BRLS's student population had grown significantly and could no longer be facilitated at its main campus on Baojia Street, the School decided to swap campuses with the Training Division and moved to the western suburb of Beijing.

北京俄语学院成立

1955 年 6 月，经高教部呈请国务院批准，北京俄专改名为北京俄语学院。

1955 年 7 月，经高教部决定，中国人民大学俄文系与北京俄语学院合并，系主任罗俊才等干部 10 人、教师 13 人、学生 367 人从北京西郊人民大学迁入市内鲍家街北京俄语学院，成立俄语师范翻译系，学制四年。北京俄语学院领导班子进行了相应调整。

The Establishment of Beijing Russian Institute

In June 1955, with the approval of the Ministry of Higher Education and the State Council, Beijing Russian Language School was renamed Beijing Russian Institute.

In July 1955, the Ministry of Higher Education decided to merge the Russian Department of Renmin University of China with Beijing Russian Institute. As a result, the Department Head Luo Juncai, its 10 staff members, 13 teachers and 367 students moved from the Renmin University campus in the western suburb of Beijing to Beijing Russian Institute's city centre campus on Baojia Street, where they formed a new Russian Teacher Training and Translation Department offering 4-year programmes. The governing body of the Institute was adjusted following the merger.

张锡俦（1905—1989），重庆涪陵人，1926年加入中国共产党。曾任共青团重庆地委学委书记、中共重庆地委组织部部长等职。1927年冬被派往苏联莫斯科东方大学学习，后转入中国劳动者孙中山共产主义大学，毕业后被派到海参崴（今"符拉迪沃斯托克"）工作，任国际师范大学副校长兼中国部主任、中国高级列宁学校校长等职。1939年9月调至共产国际直属外文出版局任编辑、翻译，将《卓娅和舒拉的故事》《青年近卫军》等译成中文。1946年，被苏联最高苏维埃主席团授予卫国战争时期的劳动奖章。1948年8月回国。历任哈尔滨外国语专门学校第一副校长、中共中央俄文编译局副局长、北京俄专副校长、北京俄语学院院长、北京外国语学院院长兼党委书记等职务。

Zhang Xichou (1905-1989), born in Fuling, Chongqing, joined the CPC in 1926 and served as Secretary of the Students Work Committee of Communist Youth League Chongqing Committee, and Head of the CPC Chongqing Committee's Organization Department. In 1927 he was sent to the Soviet Union to study at Communist University of the Toilers of the East in Moscow. Later he was transferred to Sun Yat-sen Communist University of the Toilers of China. After his graduation, he was assigned to Vladivostok, where he served first as Vice President of the International Teacher Training University and Director of its Chinese Faculty, then as Principal of Higher Lenin School of China. In September 1939, he was transferred to Foreign Languages Publishing House under Communist International and worked there as an editor and translator. Among the Russian books he translated were *The Story of Zoya and Shura* and *The Young Guard*. In 1946, he was awarded the Medal for Labour for his work during the Great Patriotic War by the Presidium of the Supreme Soviet of the USSR. He returned to China in August 1948 and served as Pro-Deputy Principal of Harbin School of Foreign Languages, Deputy Director of the CPC Central Russian Compilation and Translation Bureau, Deputy Principal of Beijing Russian Language School, President of Beijing Russian Institute, President and Party Secretary of Beijing Foreign Languages Institute.

1955年北京俄语学院领导班子结构图

The organizational structure of Beijing Russian Institute in 1955

院长兼党委书记：张锡俦
副院长：杨化飞
党委副书记：杨岗、高秀山

President and Party Committee Secretary: Zhang Xichou
Vice President: Yang Huafei
Deputy Party Secretaries: Yang Gang, Gao Xiushan

教务处处长：罗俊才
科学研究处处长：高亚天
行政处处长：熊正阳

Teaching Affairs Officer: Luo Juncai
Research Officer: Gao Yatian
Administrative Officer: Xiong Zhengyang

师范翻译系主任：赵辉
系党总支书记：齐平
翻译专修科主任：李琛
科党总支书记：李培林

Head of Teacher Training & Translation Department: Zhao Hui
Department Party Branch Secretary: Qi Ping
Head of Translation Section: Li Chen
Section Party Branch Secretary: Li Peilin

留苏预备部主任：朱允一
分党委书记：霍毓贵

Director of Training Division for Studying in the Soviet Union: Zhu Yunyi
Division Party Committee Secretary: Huo Yugui

1

2

1. 中国人民大学副校长聂真在人民大学俄文系并
入北京俄语学院大会上讲话。

2. 北京俄语学院学生在校门前合影

1. Vice President of Renmin University Nie Zhen speaking
at the merger ceremony

2. A photograph of students Beijing Russian Institute at
the main gate

1. 1954 年冬捷克语班学生与中外教师
   在北京大学俄语楼前合影
2. 1956 年张锡俦院长与波兰语专业学
   生在波兰大使馆合影

1

2

1. Students photographed with Czech and Chinese
   teachers in front of the Russian Language Building at
   Peking University during the winter of 1954
2. Institute President Zhang Xichou photographed with
   students of Polish at the Polish Embassy in 1956

　　1956 年暑假，北京大学波兰语、捷克语班调整到北京俄语学院。当时两个语种各有学生 35 人（一年级 15 人，二年级 20 人），波兰、捷克专家各 2 人，波兰、捷克语中国教员各 1 人，行政干部 2 人，并入北京俄语学院后组建波捷语系，由史迁任系主任。同年又各招一个班新生，每班 20 人。波兰、捷克方面再增派两位专家来华任教。北京大学波兰语、捷克语班并入，打破了北京俄语学院只有俄语专业的格局，学校向多语种迈出了重要的一步。

　　In the summer of 1956, the Polish and Czech programmes at Peking University were moved to Beijing Russian Institute. At the time, each programme had 35 students (15 first-years and 20 second-years), two Polish and two Czech teachers, two Chinese instructors teaching Polish and Czech respectively, and two administrative staff. After merging into Beijing Russian Institute, they formed the Department of Polish and Czech, with Shi Qian appointed as Head of the department. In the same year, a class of new students was enrolled for each language, and Poland and Czech each sent two additional teachers to the Institute. The addition of the Polish and Czech programmes at the Institute broke new ground and marked the start of a multilingual institute.

3

4

5

3. 1957 年张锡俦看望即将回国的波兰语专家尤拉舍克（右三）。

4. 1958 年高教部部长杨秀峰（前左一）来校看望北京俄语学院师生。

5. 1958 年波兰语、捷克语师生与专家及院领导合影

3. Zhang Xichou visiting Polish expert Juraschek (3rd from the right) before she was due to return to Poland in 1957

4. Minister of Higher Education Yang Xiufeng(front left) visiting the Institute in 1958

5. Students, teachers and foreign experts from the Department of Polish and Czech photographed with Institute leaders in 1958

李莎（1914—2015），原名叶丽萨维塔·基什金娜，北京外国语大学教授、著名俄语教育家，第六、七、八、九届全国政协委员。出生于俄罗斯萨拉托夫州，1936年与李立三（1889—1967，无产阶级革命家，中国共产党早期领导人之一，曾任中共中央政治局常委兼秘书长、中华全国总工会副主席等职务）结为夫妻。1941年毕业于莫斯科外语师范学院法语系，1946年随李立三来华，改名李莎（1964年加入中国国籍）。1947年曾在中国人民解放军哈尔滨俄语专科学校任教，1951年入北京俄文专修学校任教，其后从事俄语教学及研究工作40余年，是北京外国语大学俄语教育事业发展过程的亲历者，参与培养了一大批杰出的俄语教师和学科带头人。李莎在"文革"中蒙冤入狱8年，但1979年出狱后不久，就以昔日的专注和热情投入刚刚恢复的研究生教学中，共参与培养了13届研究生。她热爱中国，珍视中俄两国人民的友好关系，为我国的俄语教育事业和中俄友好关系的发展做出了杰出贡献，并为此得到俄罗斯政府和民间组织的多次奖励表彰。2013年7月，法国驻华大使林白向李莎颁发了法国政府授予的荣誉军团勋章。

Li Sha (1914-2015), Russian maiden name Elizaveta Kishkina, professor at Beijing Foreign Studies University, famous Russian language educator, and member of the National Committee of the 6th, 7th, 8th, and 9th CPPCC. She was born in the Russian state of Saratov and in 1936 married Li Lisan (1889-1967; a proletarian revolutionist and one of the earliest CPC leaders; served as Secretary General and a member of the CPC Politburo Standing Committee, and Deputy Chairman of All-China Federation of Trade Unions). She graduated from the French Department at Moscow State Pedagogical Institute of Foreign Languages in 1941, came to China with Li Lisan in 1946, and changed her name to Li Sha (became a Chinese national in 1964). She taught at Chinese People's Liberation Army Harbin Russian Language School in 1947 and then became a teacher at Beijing Russian Language School in 1951. For the next 40 years, as a faculty member of the Russian Department at Beijing Foreign Languages Institute and its successor Beijing Foreign Studies University, she dedicated herself to Russian language teaching and research in China, helping to train a large number of outstanding Russian language teachers and leaders of this field. During the "Cultural Revolution", she was falsely accused and imprisoned for eight years, but shortly after she was released in 1979 she took up teaching research students with the same concentration and enthusiasm as before and was involved in teaching 13 intakes of research students. She loved China and treasured the friendly relationship between China and Russia. For her immense contributions to China's Russian language education and friendly relations between China and Russian, she was honoured by the Russian government and non-government organizations many times with commendations and prizes. In July 2013, Sylvie Bermann, French Ambassador to China, presented Li Sha with the Order of Legion of Honour on behalf of the French government.

北京俄专初期课程设置只有俄语（包括翻译和俄语实践）和政治两门，没有固定教材及固定教员。教员一部分是由编译局俄文翻译干部兼任，另一部分由莫斯科东方语言学院中文系派到苏联驻中国大使馆实习的学生兼任。1950年2月中苏签订《中苏友好同盟互助条约》，开始从苏联聘请专家来校担任专职教师，他们中间多数是苏联的中学语文教师。1951年，李莎进入北京俄专任教。

When Beijing Russian Language School was initially established, it only offered two subjects, Russian (including translation and practical Russian) and Political Science, and it did not have any set teaching materials or dedicated teachers. Teaching was done partly by the translators from the Compilation and Translation Bureau, partly by interns from the Chinese Department at Moscow Institute of Oriental Studies working at the Soviet Embassy in China. In February 1950, China and the Soviet Union signed the Sino-Soviet Alliance Treaty of Friendship and Mutual Assistance, after which China began to recruit experts from the Soviet Union to work in China as teachers. Those who came to China were mostly secondary school teachers of Russian. In 1951, Li Sha became a teacher at Beijing Russian Language School.

1

2

3

1．2．1950 年北京俄专欢迎第一批苏联专家。

3．1952 年张锡俦与苏联专家合影

1．2．Beijing Russian Language School welcoming the
arrival of the first group of Soviet teachers in 1950

3．Zhang Xichou photographed with Soviet teachers in 1952

4

5

6

4. 1953年张锡俦和苏联专家合影（前排左一教务处处长高亚天，左二苏联专家组组长马蒙诺夫，左三张锡俦）

5. 1954年副院长杨化飞与苏联专家研究工作。

6. 苏联专家萨哈罗夫向院领导汇报工作。

4. Zhang Xichou photographed with Soviet teachers in 1953 (Front row from the left: Gao Yatian-Teaching Affairs Officer, Mamonov-Head of the Soviet team of experts, and Zhang Xichou.)

5. Deputy Principal Yang Huafei discussing work with a Soviet expert in 1954

6. Soviet expert Sakharov reporting to the School leadership

20 世纪 50 年代中期

部分俄语教师

Some of the Russian language
teachers from the mid-1950

蔡 毅 (Cai Yi)

曹书勋 (Cao Shuxun)

丁树杞 (Ding Shuqi)

段世骥 (Duan Shiji)

干肇敏 (Gan Zhaomin)

顾亚玲 (Gu Yaling)

金世杰 (Jin Shijie)

李传明 (Li Chuanming)

李新春 (Li Xinchun)

刘环宇 (Liu Huanyu)

刘 若 (Liu Ruo)

吕 凡 (Lü Fan)

吕慕樵 (Lü Muqiao)

任蔓莉 (Ren Manli)

谭自强 (Tan Ziqiang)

王天成 (Wang Tiancheng)

肖 敏 (Xiao Min)

赵 辉 (Zhao Hui)

赵陵生 (Zhao Lingsheng)

赵作英 (Zhao Zuoying)

周 圣 (Zhou Sheng)

周 允 (Zhou Yun)

20 世纪 50 年代初期，北京俄专的师资以苏联专家、教师为主。1954 年后，学校自己培养的青年教师开始成长起来，陆续走上讲台。他们在苏联专家的指导和帮助下，教学方法不断改进，教学水平不断提高。

In the early 1950s, the Russian Language School depended on Soviet experts and teachers for teaching. From 1954 young teachers trained by the School started teaching. With the help and guidance from the Soviet experts, these young teachers continually improved their teaching methods and raised their teaching ability.

1

3

---

1. 1954 年苏联教师在上课。

2. 1954 年苏联专家在专家休息室答疑。

3. 1954 年苏联专家进行课文录音。

    1. A Soviet teacher giving a lesson in 1954

    2. A junior teacher from the Training Division for Studying in the Soviet Union preparing lessons under the supervision of a Soviet expert

    3. A Soviet expert making a recording of a text in 1954

2

    苏联专家带来了苏联高等学校和中学语文教学的经验、教材和教法，帮助学校建立教研室、资料室等，制订教学计划、大纲、制度，提出教学要求，传授教学方法。在他们的倡导下，课程逐渐增多，除俄语实践课外，先后开设了语言学引论、语音学、语法学、词汇学、修辞学、教学法等一系列语言理论课程。

    1955 年 9 月，北京俄语学院开始全面执行高教部颁发的俄语专业全国通用四年制教学计划。1956 年招收副博士研究生 10 名。在青年教师中择优评选出一批讲师共 37 人。

    The Soviet teachers brought over their experience of Russian language teaching in colleges and secondary schools, together with their teaching materials and teaching methods, helping the Institute set up teaching and research sections, reference rooms, etc., draw up teaching plans, syllabuses and regulations, set out teaching requirements, and imparted their teaching methods to the Chinese teachers. Following their advice, the number of courses gradually increased. Apart from Russian language skill courses, a series of linguistic courses were instituted, including Introduction to Linguistics, Phonetics, Grammar, Lexicology, Rhetoric, and Pedagogy.

    In September 1955, the Russian Language School started implementing the National Russian Language Four-year Teaching Plan promulgated by the Ministry of Education in a comprehensive manner. In 1956 ten Master students were enrolled, and a total of 37 outstanding young teachers were appointed lecturers.

1

2

3

1. 1954 年苏联专家与青年教师研究教学工作。

2. 1954 年苏联专家指导留苏预备部青年教师备课。

3. 1956 年俄语系主任赵辉与苏联专家研究教学工作。

1. A Soviet expert discussing work with junior teachers in 1954

2. A Soviet expert answering questions in the Experts' Lounge in 1954

3. Head of the Russian Department Zhao Hui discussing work with a Soviet expert in 1956

4

5

6

---

4. 中国教师在听苏联专家讲课。

5. 1953 年北京俄专青年教师在上课。

6. 1954 年北京俄专教师在资料室备课。

4. Chinese teachers listening to Soviet experts giving a lecture

5. A BRLS junior teacher giving a lesson in 1953

6. BRLS teachers preparing lessons in the reference room in 1954

从 1953 年秋季开学后，学校开办讲读课教师进修班，为期一年，系统地开设各种俄语理论课程，积极培养师资，提高教师的语言实践能力和理论水平。经过一年的培训，到 1954 年秋季开学时，一批青年教员开始登上俄语实践课讲坛，承担一年级俄语讲读课的教学工作。1955 年 3 月，北京俄专开设研究生班（学习期限两年半），招收教师脱产进修，同时开办夜大。

After the School started in the autumn of 1953, it had run a one-year refresher course in reading for teachers and systematically offered various courses on theories about the Russian language, so that those who took those courses could both improve their language proficiency and have a better understanding of theory. By the autumn of 1954, after one year of training, a cohort of junior teachers started filling vacancies in Russian language skill courses, undertaking the teaching of first-year Russian reading. In March 1955, BRLS started a two-year postgraduate programme for the full-time development of teachers; at the same time it opened a night school.

1

2

3

4

1. 1954 年苏联专家给北京俄专青年教师上课。

2. 1954 年北京俄专教师正式开课前试讲。

3. 1954 年北京俄专学生利用课外时间听外语唱片。

4. 1955 年苏联专家指导青年教师上课。

    1. A Soviet expert giving a lesson to junior teachers at BRLS in 1954

    2. A BRLS trainee teacher giving a test lecture in 1954

    3. Students listening to foreign language records after class in 1954

    4. A Soviet expert tutoring junior teachers in 1955

5

7

6

8

9

---

5. 1954 年副院长杨化飞（右二）参加学生口试。

6. 师生一起练习俄语对话。

7. 1956 年俄语系师生在资料室听录音。

8. 1956 年苏联专家和语音教研组教师讨论教学工作。

9. 1958 年词汇教研组教师讨论教学工作。

5. Deputy Principal Yang Huafei (2nd right) taking part in a student oral exam in 1954

6. Teachers and students practising Russian conversation

7. Teachers and students listening to a recording in the reference room in 1956

8. Soviet experts and teachers from the Phonetics Teaching and Research section discussing work in 1956

9. Teachers of the Lexicology group discussing work in 1958

■ 1955 年北京俄专毕业证书存根

Beijing Russian Language School's graduation certificate (school's copy) issued in 1955

■ 1950 年北京俄专第 4 班毕业生和校领导合影

Graduates from Class 4 of Beijing Russian Language School photographed with School leaders in 1950

1959

　　从北京俄专创建、北京俄语学院成立到 1959 年与北京外国语学院合并期间，政治运动不断，有些运动在"左"的思想指导下，对学校工作形成严重干扰，造成不良后果。但就整体而言，学校在正规化道路上不断发展，人才培养数量、质量与规格明显提高，培养出了一大批俄语专门人才和留苏预备生。

　　From the establishment of the Beijing Russian Language School and the formation of Beijing Russian Institute to its merger with Beijing Foreign Languages Institute in 1959, the School experienced a series of political campaigns. Some of the campaigns driven by "Leftist" ideology caused severe disruptions to the running of the School and left unwanted result. Overall, however, the school continued to institutionalise itself, enhanced its teaching capacity, and raised its standard of teaching, producing a large number of Russian language professionals and students qualified for studying in the Soviet Union.

1

2

3

1. 1952年留苏预备部第一批（部分）
   学员毕业留影，前排左起第8人为
   班主任杨化飞。

2. 1953年北京俄专24班毕业生合影

3. 1955年北京俄专部分师生合影

1. A graduation photograph showing some of
   the first cohort of graduates from the Training
   Division in 1952. Form Tutor Yang Huafei is
   8th from the left in the front row

2. Students from Class 24 graduating from
   Beijing Russian Language School in 1953

3. A group photo of some of the students and
   teachers from Beijing Russian Language
   School in 1955

1. 1955 年留苏预备部派出的留学生
   在苏联实习。

2. 1957 年北京俄语学院毕业生合影

   1. A graduate of the Training Division on
      a work experience programme in the
      Soviet Union in 1955

   2. A group photo of students from Beijing
      Russian Institute graduating in 1957

1

2

1950 年北京俄专第一届运动大会

The first Sports Meet at Beijing Russian Language
School in 1950

3

5

3. 1950 年北京俄专第一届运动大会

4. 1953 年新民主主义青年团北京俄专第一次代表大会

5. 1954 年北京俄专学生上体育课。

6. 1955 年学生演出俄语短剧。

3. The first Sports Meet at Beijing Russian Language School in 1950

4. The first New Democratic Youth Corps of Beijing Russian Language School's Congress in 1953

5. Students taking a physical education class in 1954

6. Students performing a short Russian play in 1955

6

1

3

1. 1955 年在俄语朗诵会上朗诵的学生

2. 1955 年学生联欢会

3. 1957 年暑假北京俄语学院四年级学生与西伯利亚大学生旅行团在一起。

1. Students on stage at a Russian poetry reading in 1955

2. Student Gala in 1955

3. Fourth-year students from the Beijing Russian Institute pictured with Siberian visiting students in the summer of 1957

4

5

6

7

4. 北京俄语学院师生在十三陵水库工地劳动，党委副书记杨岗在讲话。

5. 北京俄语学院的学生去四季青公社参加抗旱劳动。

6. 1958 年在十三陵水库建设工地上，师生和解放军战士一起劳动并表演节目。

7. 1958 年"大跃进"运动时期，校园内在大炼钢铁。

4. Teachers and students working at the Shisanling (Ming Tombs) Reservoir. The photograph shows Deputy Party Secretary Yang Gang making a speech

5. Students from the Bejijing Russian Institute on their way to the Sijiqing Commune to help with alleviating draught

6. Teachers and students with soldiers from the Liberation Army working and performing entertainment at the Shisanling Reservoir in 1958

7. Smelting iron on campus as a part of the "Great Leap Forward" in 1958

第五章

两院合并　曲折前进

（1959年2月—1966年5月）

——从北京俄语学院与北京外国语学院合并成立
新的北京外国语学院至"文革"前

Chapter Five
After the merger, following a rocky path

From the merger of Beijing Russian Institute and Beijing Foreign
Languages Institute to the eve of "the Cultural Revolution"

(February 1959–May 1966)

　　1959 年 2 月，北京外国语学院、北京俄语学院合并成立新的北京外国语学院。从两院合并到 1966 年 5 月"文革"开始前，虽然受到 1959 年的"反右"运动干扰，以及 1962 年中共八届十中全会提出的阶级斗争"要年年讲、月月讲、天天讲"等指导思想的影响，但在总理周恩来、副总理兼外交部部长陈毅的关怀和直接指导下，全校师生员工共同努力，学校事业取得了长足的进步，师资队伍不断发展壮大，教授语种从并校时的 8 个增加到 27 个，其中多个语种在我国高校首次开设，同时进一步明确了以培养外事翻译为主的人才培养目标。

　　In February 1959, Beijing Foreign Languages Institute and Beijing Russian Institute merged to form a new Beijing Foreign Languages Institute. From the merger to the eve of "the Cultural Revolution" in May 1966, the Institute was distracted by the "Anti-rightist" campaign in 1959 and suffered negative impact from the campaign to constantly instil the idea of class struggles "year after year, month after month, day after day", which was advocated at the 10th Plenary Session of the CPC's 8th Central Committee. Yet under the care and direct guidance of Premier Zhou Enlai and Vice Premier and Foreign Minister Chen Yi and through the concerted efforts of all its staff and students, the Institute made significant progress, with the number of staff steadily growing and the number of foreign languages taught increasing from the initial eight at the time of the merger to 27, many of which were being offered for the first time at an institution of higher learning in China. At the same time it was clearly specified that the aim of the Institute was to train translators for departments of foreign affairs.

1959 年 2 月 21 日，教育部部长杨秀峰
在两校合并大会上讲话。

Minister of Education Yang Xiufeng speaking
at the meeting marking the merger of the two
institutes on 21st February 1959

1958

　　1958 年 10 月，经教育部报请国务院批准，北京俄语学院与北京外国语学院合并，成立新的北京外国语学院，张锡俦任党委书记、院长，刘仲容任副院长。1959 年 2 月 21 日举行并校大会，教育部部长杨秀峰出席讲话，强调要"认真读书""尊师爱生""建立稳定的教学秩序"。合校后，对 1958 年"大跃进"运动和"教育革命"进行了总结。

　　从 1949 年到 1959 年北京外国语学院、北京俄语学院合并前，两校共为国家培养外语人才 11,000 余人，其中本科各语种毕业生 4,739 人，留苏预备生 6,648 人。本科毕业生中，俄语毕业生 3,246 人，英语毕业生 1,145 人，德语毕业生 111 人，法语毕业生 146 人，西班牙语毕业生 91 人。

　　In October 1958, following the approval of a MOE request by the State Council, Beijing Russian Institute and Beijing Foreign Languages Institute merged to become a new Beijing Foreign Languages Institute, with Zhang Xichou appointed as its CPC Committee Secretary and President, and Liu Zhongrong as its Vice President. On 21st February 1959, a general meeting was held to mark the merger. Minister of Education Yang Xiufeng attended the meeting and spoke, emphasizing the need for "earnest reading", "respect for teachers and care for students", and "establishing a stable order for teaching". After the merger, the Institute wound up the "Great Leap Forward" and the "educational revolution" in 1958.

　　From 1949 to before their merger in 1959, more than 11,000 foreign language students graduated from the two institutes, of whom 4,739 were regular undergraduate students, 6,648 were students preparing to study in the Soviet Union. Of the regular undergraduates, 3,246 were students of Russian, 1,145 students of English, 111 students of German, 146 students of French, and 91 students of Spanish.

教育部关于成立北京俄语学院与北京外国语
学院并院筹备委员会的通知

The MOE's notification on setting up a preparatory
committee for the merger of Beijing Russian Institute
and Beijing Foreign Languages Institute

1. 1959 年 2 月 21 日，张锡俦院长在两校合
   并大会上讲话。
2. 1959 年 2 月 21 日，院党委第二书记刘柯
   在两校合并大会上讲话。

1. Institute President Zhang Xichou
   speaking at the merger meeting
2. Liu Ke, Second Secretary of the
   Institute's Party Committee, speaking at
   the merger meeting

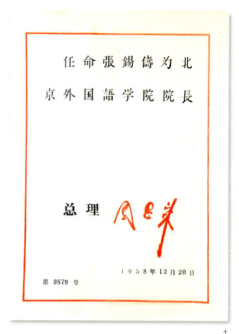

1

2

1. 周恩来总理签发的张锡俦任命书
2. 教育部就国务院任免张锡俦职务等事宜转告北京外国语学院的文件

1. The letter appointing Zhang Xichou signed by Premier Zhou Enlai
2. The MOE document notifying Beijing Foreign Languages Institute about the appointment of Zhang Xichou by the State Council

1959 年合校后的教学单位和语种
Teaching units and languages after the merger

教学单位 Teaching unit	语种 Language
英语系 English Department	英语 English
俄语系 Russian Department	俄语 Russian
德语系 German Department	德语 German
法语系 French Department	法语 French
西班牙语系 Spanish Department	西班牙语 Spanish
波捷罗语系 Polish, Czech and Romanian Department	波兰语、捷克语、罗马尼亚语 Polish, Czech, Romanian
留苏预备部 Training Division for Studying in the Soviet Union	俄语 Russian

1959 年两院合并后院系主要领导干部

Major leaders of the Institute and departments after the merger in 1959

院长、党委第一书记张锡俦

President & Number One Secretary of the CPC Committee: Zhang Xichou

副院长刘仲容
Vice President: Liu Zhongrong

副院长、党委第Ⅰ书记刘柯
Vice President & Number Two Secretary of the CPC Committee: Liu Ke

副院长李棣华
Vice President: Li Dihua

副院长杨化广
Vice President: Yang Huafei

党委副书记杨岗
Vice Secretary of the CPC Committee: Yang Gang

党委副书记高秀山
Vice Secretary of the CPC Committee: Gao Xiushan

党委副书记郝金禄
Vice Secretary of the CPC Committee: Hao Jinlu

教务处处长罗俊才
Director of Teaching Affairs Office: Luo Juncai

人事处处长张仪容
Director of Personnel Office: Zhang Yirong

总务处处长熊正阳
Director of General Logistics Office: Xiong Zhengyang

俄语系主任、总支书记赵辉
Head of the Russian Department & Secretary of the CPC's Russian Department Branch: Zhao Hui

英语系代主任王佐良
Acting Head of the English Department: Wang Zuoliang

英语系总支书记石春来
Secretary of the CPC's English Department Branch: Shi Chunlai

德语系主任熊健
Head of German Department: Xiong Jian

法语系主任沈毅
Head of French Department: Shen Yi

西班牙语系副主任孟复
Deputy Head of the Spanish Department: Meng Fu

德西法总支书记杨淦春
Secretary of the CPC's German, Spanish and French Departments: Yang Ganchun

波捷罗语系主任、支部书记史迁
Head of the Polish, Czech and Romanian Department & the CPC Branch Secretary: Shi Qian

留苏预备部主任朱允一
Head of the Training Division for Studying in the Soviet Union: Zhu Yunyi

图书馆馆长初大告
Director of the Library: Chu Dagao

▌ 1959 年 6 月成立的院务委员会名单

List of members of the Council set up in June 1959

王佐良、史迁、司徒锦才、朱允一、孙鸿祥、刘世沐、刘克良、刘芷、刘柯、初大告、沈毅、李茂祥、李隶华、孟复、罗俊才、林丰年、郝金禄、姚可崑、赵申、赵辉、高秀山、郭迪诚、张仪容、张锡俦、杨化飞、杨岗、熊正阳、熊健、魏兆平

Chu Dagao, Gao Xiushan, Guo Dicheng, Hao Jinlu, Li Dihua, Li Maoxiang, Lin Fengnian, Liu Ke, Liu Keliang, Liu Shimu, Liu Zhi, Luo Juncai, Meng Fu, Shen Yi, Shi Qian, Situ Jincai, Sun Hongxiang, Wang Zuoliang, Wei Zhaoping, Xiong Jian, Xiong Zhengyang, Yang Gang, Yang Huafei, Yao Kekun, Zhang Xichou, Zhang Yirong, Zhao Hui, Zhao Shen, Zhu Yunyi

▌ 1959 年 8 月两院合并后第一届党代会产生的党委会成员名单（25 人）

List of members of the Party Committee elected at the 1st Party Congress in August 1959 after the merger

常 委 **Standing committee members**	张锡俦、刘柯、杨岗、高秀山、郝金禄、李隶华、罗俊才、熊正阳、张仪容、赵辉、石春来 Gao Xiushan, Hao Jinlu, Li Dihua, Liu Ke, Luo Juncai, Shi Chunlai, Xiong Zhengyang, Yang Gang, Zhang Xichou, Zhang Yirong, Zhao Hui
委 员 **Committee members**	彭典卿、彭伯勋、于一夫、梁克、齐平、孙鸿祥、程镇球、朱允一、文棋、杨淦春、凌志、张柏新、刘克良、杨化飞 Cheng Zhenqiu, Liang Ke, Ling Zhi, Liu Keliang, Peng Boxun, Peng Dianqing, Qi Ping, Sun Hongxiang, Wen Qi, Yang Ganchun, Yang Huafei, Yu Yifu, Zhang Baixin, Zhu Yunyi

1959

　　1959 年 6 月，学校成立院务委员会，作为最高行政领导机关，由 29 名委员组成。

　　1959 年 8 月 9 日，两院合并后第一届党员代表大会召开。刘柯代表中共北京外国语学院临时委员会向大会作工作报告。报告提出："群众运动已经告一段落，学校工作转入正常教学。形势的变化，要求党把主要领导力量转向教学，要进一步领导好教学，使教师教好，学生学好，提高教学质量。"党代会选出党委会委员 25 人，其中常委 11 人。

　　In June 1959, the Institute established its Council, the highest administrative governing body of the Institute made up of 29 members.

　　On 9th August 1959, the 1st Party Congress was held after the merger. On behalf of the CPC Beijing Foreign Languages Institute Provisional Committee, Liu Ke delivered a work report to the Congress, which pointed out: "The mass movement has come to an end and the Institute's work has shifted to its normal teaching. The changing situation requires that the Party turn its focus to teaching, give better guidance to teaching, ensure that teachers teach well and students learn well and that the standards of teaching is raised." The Congress elected a committee of 25 members, including a standing committee of 11 members within.

▌这一时期，学校增设、调整了一些教学单位：

During this period, the Institute set up some more teaching units and restructure some existing ones:

1959 年

- ◆ 1959 年 9 月，学院增设附属中学，除开设普通高中课程外，还开设了英、俄、德、法、西五种外语，当年按机密专业参加北京市高级中学联合招生，录取高中一年级学生 253 名。
- ◆ 到 1963 年又扩展成为包括中学部和小学部的附属外国语学校。

- ◆ In September, the Institute established an affiliated middle school, which, apart from offering the courses of an ordinary upper middle school, set up five foreign languages as subjects, i.e. English, Russian, German, French, Spanish. In the same year, it participated as a confidential academic discipline in the unified students admission administered by Beijing upper middle schools, accepting 253 upper middle school year-one students.
- ◆ In 1963 the affiliated school was expanded into the Affiliated Foreign Language School which included both a middle school division and a primary school division.

1960 年

- ◆ 留苏预备部停办。留苏预备部机构改组为外国留学生办公室和出国留学生部，开始接纳一批非洲国家留学生入校学习汉语。
- ◆ 1962 年教育部在原外国留学生办公室和出国留学生部基础上成立"外国留学生高等预备学校"，是北京语言学院前身。

- ◆ The Training Division for Studying in the Soviet Union was discontinued. The Division was transformed into the Office for Overseas Students and the Division for Studying abroad, which started to accept the first intake of students from African countries to study Chinese at the Institute.
- ◆ In 1962, on the basis of the Office for Overseas Students and the Division for Overseas Studies, the MOE founded the "Advanced Preparatory School for Overseas Students", which was the predecessor of Beijing Language Institute.

1961 年

- ◆ 波捷罗语系更名为东欧语系，增设匈牙利语、保加利亚语、阿尔巴尼亚语三个专业。
- ◆ 筹建亚非语系，陈振宜为系主任。筹备增设亚非国家使用的一些语种。

- ◆ The Department of Polish, Czech and Romanian was renamed the Department of Eastern European Languages, adding Hungarian, Bulgarian and Albanian.
- ◆ A Department of Asian and African Languages was established, with Chen Zhenyi as head of the department, making preparation for offering languages used in Asian and African countries.

1962 年

- ◆ 外交学院的阿拉伯语教研室、日语教研组、印尼语教研组、德语教研组分别并入我院亚非语系和德语系，西班牙语和俄语本科生也转入我院西语系、俄语系学习。
- ◆ 纳忠任亚非语系主任，陈振宜任第二主任，康崇儒任系党总支书记。

- ◆ The Arabic Teaching and Research Section, and Japanese, Indonesian and German teaching units of China Foreign Affairs Univercity were merged respectively into the Department of Asian and African Languages and the German Department of this Institute, the College's undergraduates of Spanish and Russian were also transferred to the Spanish and Russian Departments of this Institute.
- ◆ Na Zhong was appointed as Head of the Asian and African Languages, Chen Zhenyi as Number Two Head, and Kang Chongru as Secretary of the CPC Department Branch.

1963 年

- ◆ 德语系与东欧语系合并，成立新的东欧语系，齐平任代主任，史迁为副主任，张高铎任系党总支书记。

- ◆ The German and Eastern European departments merged into a new Department of Eastern European Languages, with Qi Ping appointed as its acting Head, Shi Qian as Deputy Head, and Zhang Gaoduo as Secretary of the CPC Department Branch.

1

1. 1959 年国庆节时的北京外国语学院东院校门

2. 1965 年西院大门。1961 年 11 月，北京外国语学院由教育部转归外交部领导，但学院外国留学生办公室、出国留学生部的全体师资与干部仍归教育部领导，在此基础上于 1962 年成立"外国留学生高等预备学校"，1965 年 1 月更名为北京语言学院。1971 年北京语言学院与北京第二外国语学院合并，迁出北京外国语学院西校区。

2

1. The gate of the east campus of Beijing Foreign Languages Institute during the National Day period of 1959

2. The gate of the west campus of the Institute in 1965.
   In November 1961, the governance of Beijing Foreign Languages Institute was transferred from the Ministry of Education to the Ministry of Foreign Affairs, however, all the teachers and staff of the Institute's Office for Overseas Students and the Division for Studying Abroad still remained under the governance of the MOE, which founded the "Advanced Preparatory School for Overseas Students" on the basis of these two units in 1962, and renamed it as Beijing Language Institute in January 1965. In 1971 Beijing language Institute merged with Beijing Second Foreign Languages Institute and moved out of the west campus of Beijing Foreign Languages Institute.

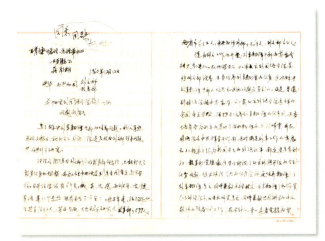

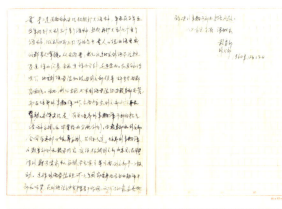

外交部、教育部《关于北京外国语学院领导关系问题的报告》

"Report Concerning the Jurisdiction over Beijing Foreign Languages Institute" made by the Ministry of Foreign Affairs and the Ministry of Education

1960

　　1960 年，学校经中央批准列为全国重点高等学校。1960 年 12 月 12 日，外交部、教育部在《关于北京外国语学院领导关系问题的报告》中提出，虽然将北京外国语学院划归外交部领导在培养外事翻译方面较为有利，"但是外语院校中需要有一所北京外国语学院这样的全国重点学校，除担负培养外事翻译的任务外，还要培养高水平的其他方面的翻译和外语师资，并在外语院系中发挥骨干作用，这对满足外事工作的需要和从根本上提高我国学生的外语水平，都是有利的"。报告还指出了北京外国语学院今后的工作方针："一是靠提高质量，二是用各种办法积极扩大语种，争取在三年到五年内扩大到三十多个语种，然后再扩大到七十余个语种，做到世界上凡有相当数量人口说的语言我们都有人掌握。从全面看，我们认为北京外国语学院担负这样的任务，采取这样的方针是适当的。"周恩来总理在报告上批示"同意"。

　　In 1960, with the approval of the Central authorities, the Institute entered the list of national key institutions of higher education. On 12th December 1960, in the "Report Concerning the Jurisdiction over Beijing Foreign Languages Institute", which was submitted jointly by the Ministry of Foreign Affairs and Ministry of Education to the Central authorities, it was pointed out that although it was more advantageous in terms of training foreign affairs translators to place Beijing Foreign Languages Institute under the jurisdiction of Ministry of Foreign Affairs, "yet considering the need among foreign languages institutes for a national key higher education institution like Beijing Foreign Languages Institute, which apart from undertaking the task of training foreign affairs translators, it also has the obligation to train highly qualified translators in other fields and educate foreign language teachers and play a central role among foreign languages institutes, which would be advantageous in terms of both meeting the needs of foreign affairs work and raising the foreign language standards of Chinese students." The report also laid out the following guidelines for the future development of Beijing Foreign Languages Institute: "First, by raising the quality of teaching; second, by increasing the number of foreign languages taught at the Institute in whatever way possible, so that in three to five years there will be more than 30 languages, and then expanding to over 79. In this way, we will have people speaking all the languages that are spoken by a sizable number of people in the world. From all points of view, we think it is appropriate for Beijing Foreign Languages Institute to undertake this task and follow such guidelines." The directive Premier Zhou gave on top of the report was "Agree".

教育部《关于北京外国语学院今后方针任务的请示报告》
（60 教党蒋字第 179 号）

The MOE's "Report Concerning the Future Guidelines and Tasks
of Beijing Foreign Languages Institute" (No. 179, 1960)

1960 年 12 月，教育部在《关于北京外国语学院今后方针任务的请示报告》（60 教党蒋字第 179 号）中提出："根据我国社会主义建设的需要和国际形势的发展，迫切需要加强外语教育，培养世界各国语言的外语干部，特别是质量较高的翻译干部和外语师资。""国内培养的任务，应该主要由北京外国语学院来承担，首先要做到所有亚洲各国的语言，我们都有人掌握。北京外国语学院在高等外语院校中又是历史较久、基础较好的学校，因而应该进一步努力发展成为高质量、多语种的外语学院。""作为全国重点高等学校，北京外国语学院应该在全国外语院系中发挥骨干作用。"

In December 1960, in a MOE's "Report Concerning the Future Guidelines and Tasks of Beijing Foreign Languages Institute" (No. 179, 1960), it was pointed out: "In view of the needs of China's socialist development and the changing international situation, there is a crying need for strengthening foreign language education in order to educate cadres of various languages of the world, especially high-quality translators and foreign language teachers." "The task of educating such people at home should be undertaken mainly by Foreign Languages Institute and the first step is to ensure that we have the ability to teach all the languages of Asian countries. Beijing Foreign Languages Institute is one with a longer history and better foundation than other foreign languages institutes, therefore it should be further developed into a high-quality and multilingual foreign languages institute." "As a national key institution of higher education, it should play a central role among foreign languages institutes in the whole country."

周恩来总理批示的《北京外国语学院准备陆续增设的新专业或课程的初步规划》

"A preliminary planning for Beijing Foreign Languages Institute to add more languages or courses", with Premier Zhou's handwritten directive on it

周恩来总理对学校的发展极为重视，并给予具体指导。1960年12月，外交部在呈报周恩来总理的《北京外国语学院准备陆续增设的新专业或课程的初步规划》中，建议尽快开办葡萄牙语等二十一个新专业。周恩来总理批示："这二十一种语言要加以调整，如朝鲜、越南、蒙古、缅、印、巴基斯坦、印尼、阿拉伯、日本、尼泊尔、刚果、阿尔巴尼亚、柬埔寨、老挝、阿富汗、伊朗、马来亚等国语言均应加入，数目稍多，也可扩大。"周恩来总理的批示为北京外国语学院的专业建设指出了明确的方向。

根据周恩来总理的批示，从1961年至1966年"文革"前，学校增开语种十九个，开办语种达到二十七个。

Premier Zhou placed immense importance on the development of the Institute. In "A preliminary planning for Beijing Foreign Languages Institute to add more languages or courses", which the Ministry of Foreign Affairs submitted to Premier Zhou, it was proposed that 21 languages including Portuguese should be available as soon as possible. The directive Premier Zhou gave was: Adjustments should be made to the 21 languages; other languages, such as Korean, Vietnamese, Mongolian, Burmese, Hindi, Pakistani, Indonesian, Arabic, Japanese, Nepali, Congo, Albanian, Cambodian, Laotian, Afghan, Persian, Malay, etc. should also be added. The number of languages to be offered can be increased. This directive by Premier Zhou pointed out a clear direction for the academic development of Beijing Foreign Languages Institute.

Following Premier Zhou's directive, from 1961 to the eve of "Cultural Revolution" in 1966, the Institute added 19 foreign languages, the total number of foreign languages reaching 27.

1941—1949 年（开设 2 个语种）

◇ 俄语　◇ 英语

1941-1949 Starting with 2 languages
Russian, English

1950—1960 年（增设 6 个语种）

◇ 德语　◇ 法语　◇ 西班牙语
◇ 波兰语　◇ 捷克语
◇ 罗马尼亚语

1950-1960 Adding 6 languages
French, German, Spanish, Polish,
Czech, Romanian

1961—1965 年（增设 19 个语种）

◇ 葡萄牙语　◇ 瑞典语　◇ 匈牙利语
◇ 阿尔巴尼亚语　◇ 保加利亚语
◇ 意大利语　◇ 塞尔维亚语
◇ 斯瓦希里语　◇ 阿拉伯语　◇ 老挝语
◇ 柬埔寨语　◇ 僧伽罗语　◇ 马来语
◇ 缅甸语　◇ 印尼语　◇ 日语
◇ 豪萨语　◇ 泰语　◇ 越南语

1961-1965 Adding 19 languages
Portuguese, Swedish, Hungarian, Albanian, Bulgarian,
Italian, Serbian, Swahili, Arabic, Laotian, Cambodian,
Sinhala, Malay, Burmese, Indonesian, Japanese,
Hausa, Thai, Vietnamese

1966 年前开设的语种

Languages offered before 1966

1961

1961 年 3 月，院务委员会讨论贯彻全国重点高等学校工作会议精神，提出：我院贯彻"八字方针"，要求实现"一高二全"，"一高"要求高质量，"二全"要求多语种；从现在起，要筹备开设瑞典语、葡萄牙语、意大利语，以及僧伽罗语、柬埔寨语、豪萨语、斯瓦希里语等亚非语言。学校规模定为本科生 3,500 人，研究生 400 人。

In March 1961, the Institute Council discussed how to carry out the spirit of the meeting on the work of national key institutions of higher education and proposed to take the following measures: the Institute will strive to be high in quality and comprehensive in language cover; from now on, preparation should start on introducing Swedish, Portuguese, Italian, and Asian and African languages such as Sinhala, Cambodian, Hausa and Swahili. The student population is set to be 3,500 undergraduates and 400 research students.

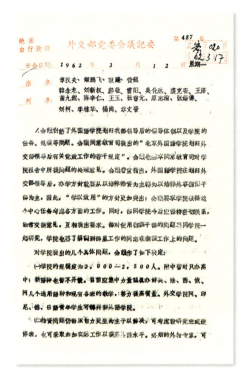

外交部党委会纪要（1962 年）

Minutes of Ministry of Foreign Affairs
Party Committee meeting (1962)

罗士高（1905—1995），广东大埔人。1927 年加入中国共产党。曾任重庆市副市长、重庆市委副书记。1957 年调入外交部任驻阿尔巴尼亚大使。1964 年至 1966 年，任外交部党委委员、北京外国语学院党委书记。1978 年后，任中国人民对外友好协会副会长、中非友好协会副会长。

Luo Shigao (1905-1995), born in Dapu, Guangdong, joined the CPC in 1927, served as Deputy Mayor of Chongqing, Vice Secretary of the CPC Chongqing Municipal Committee before he was transferred into the Ministry of Foreign Affairs and appointed as ambassador to Albania in 1957. From 1964 to 1966, he was a member of the CPC Ministry of Foreign Affairs Committee and Secretary of the CPC Beijing Foreign Languages Institute Committee. After 1978, he served as Vice Chairman of Chinese People's Association for Friendship with Foreign Countries and Vice Chairman of the Chinese-African People's Friendship Association.

1962

　　1962 年，经外交部报中央书记处批准，北京外国语学院重新划归外交部领导。1964 年 9 月，中央决定学校党的关系由北京市委改隶外交部党委领导，并派罗士高任党委书记。

　　1961 年 9 月和 1962 年 3 月，国务院副总理、外交部部长陈毅先后两次来校视察并向全体师生作报告。1962 年 1 月 17 日，陈毅副总理在中南海紫光阁接见北京外国语学院和外交学院的干部教师代表，大家就办学方针、发展方向等问题进行了深入讨论。

In 1962, the Secretariat of the CPC Central Committee approved the request made by the Ministry of Foreign Affairs that Beijing Foreign Languages Institute revert back to be under the governance of the Ministry of Foreign Affairs. In September 1964, the Central authorities decided to transfer the affiliation of the Institute's Party organisation from the CPC Beijing Municipal Committee to the CPC Ministry of Foreign Affairs Committee and appointed Luo Shigao as Secretary of the Institute's Party Committee.

In September 1961 and March 1962, Vice Premier and Foreign Minister Chen Yi came to the Institute twice for inspection and gave talks to the whole institute. On 17th January 1962, Chen Yi received representatives of staff and faculty of Beijing Foreign Languages Institute and the Foreign Affairs College in the Hall of Purple Light (Ziguangge) at Zhongnanhai and held in-depth discussions with them about educational guidelines and the directions of future development of the two institutions.

1

2

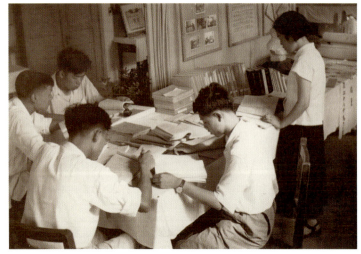

3

1. 1959 年朝鲜留学生在上课。

2. 1960 年学生在听录音。

3. 1960 年学生在一起自习。

1. Students from DPRK having a class in 1959

2. Students listening to a recorder in 1960

3. Students self-studying together in 1960

4

5

7

6

4. 1960 年的课堂教学

5. 1960 年资料室工作人员给学生介绍资料查询方法。

6. 1960 年初的听力课

7. 1966 年的德语系课堂

4. A classroom teaching in 1960

5. A reference room staff member explaining to the students how to use the catalogue

6. A listening class in early 1960

7. A class of the German Department in 1966

1

2

1960

这一时期，由于受到各种运动的冲击以及"以阶级斗争为中心"的错误思想的指导，学校的发展受到严重制约和影响。"批判修正主义文艺思想""反修教材大检查""教育改革"等活动对学校的教学工作和教材建设造成严重干扰。尽管如此，学校努力贯彻《教育部直属高等学校暂行工作条例（草案）》（即《高校六十条》），坚持把提高教学质量作为工作中心，在全校开展教学方案修订、教材与教学大纲的编写与审定，以及教学经验研讨、交流等工作。

3

During this period, due to the distractions of various political movements and the misguidance of the erroneous concept of "taking class struggle as the central task", the development of the Institute was severely constrained and affected. "Criticising the revisionist ideology in arts", "an anti-revisionist general re-examination of teaching materials" and "educational reforms" caused serious damage to the development of the teaching and teaching materials of the Institute. Despite all this, the Institute tried its best to implement the "Interim Work Regulations of Institutions of Higher Education Directly under the Ministry of Education (draft)", which was commonly known as the "Sixty Articles of Institutions of Higher Education", unswervingly treated raising teaching standards as the focus of the Institute's work, and carried out Institute-wide teaching plan revisions, compiled and reviewed new textbooks and syllabuses, and organised teaching experience discussions and exchanges.

1. 1960 年教师讨论制订新的教学方案。

2. 1960 年德语系师生共同讨论教学方案。

3. 1960 年英语系扩大系务员会听取教师对教学改革的意见。

1. A group of teachers discussing a new teaching plan in 1960

2. Teachers and students of the German Department discussing a teaching plan together in 1960

3. An enlarged departmental affairs committee of the English Department listening to teachers voicing their opinions on teaching reforms in 1960

■ 1960 年俄语系教师听取学生对教学改革的意见。

Teachers of the Russian Department listening to students' opinions about the teaching reforms in 1960

1

2

3

1. 创刊于 1958 年的《英语学习》是中国第一本英语辅导刊物，图为 1959 年第一期《英语学习》。

2. 1959 年第一期《俄语学习》

3. 4. 1960 年第一期《外语教学与研究》及目录

1. *English Monthly*, launched in 1958, is the first English language tutorial magazine in China. The photo shows the front cover of its No 1 issue in 1959.

2. The 1st issue of *Russian Language Learning* in 1959

3. 4. The 1st issue of *Foreign Language Teaching and Research* in 1960 and its table of contents

4

1962 年制订的《北京外国语学院教学方案》

"Teaching Plan of Beijing Foreign Languages Institute" drawn up in 1962

1960

学校重视教学经验交流，不仅提倡老教师带新教师，还努力加强全校乃至全国性的交流活动。1960 年 7 月，学校举行第一届外语教学经验交流会，校外 100 多个单位派代表前来参加。

Paying great attention to the exchange of teaching experience, the Institute not only encouraged senior teachers to act as mentors for junior teachers, but also organised a number of Institute-wide and nation-wide workshops for exchanging teaching experience. In July 1960, the 1st Foreign Language Teaching Experience Exchange Conference was held at the Institute, which was attended by representatives from over 100 colleges and universities.

1960 年《外语教学经验交流会快报》

Bulletins of the Foreign Language Teaching Experience Exchange Conference in 1960

■ 1960 年外语教学经验交流会，院领导和部分与会兄弟院校代表合影，
前排左一至左五：党委书记刘柯、俄语系主任赵辉、副院长刘仲容、外
交部副部长刘新权、院长张锡俦；前排右一：副院长李棣华。

Institute leaders photographed with some of the representatives from other colleges
and universities at the 1960 Teaching Experience Exchange Conference (1st left
to 5th left:Institute Party Secretary Liu Ke, Head of the Russian Department Zhao
Hui, Vice President Liu Zhongrong, Vice Foreign Minister Liu Xinquan, Institute
President Zhang Xichou; 1st right: Institute Vice President Li Dihua)

■ 1960 年外语教学经验交流会文件

Papers presented at Foreign Language
Teaching Experience Exchange
Conference in 1960

1. 1960 年，教师与学生研究如何编写教材。

2. 1960 年，教师与学生举行座谈会，共同研究如何编写教材。

1. Teachers and students studying how to write teaching materials in 1960

2. Teachers and students holding a discussion in 1960 on how to join forces to compile teaching materials

1960

　　1960 年下半年开始，中宣部和教育部出面抓高等学校教材工作。后成立文科教材办公室，由周扬负责。1961 年，中宣部、教育部决定，由我院副院长李棣华任外语教材组组长。我院承担的全国通用外语教材的编写任务有：英语、俄语、德语、法语、西班牙语教材；分别由许国璋、赵辉、姚可崑、李廷撰、孟复任主编。

　　Starting from the second half of 1960, the Propaganda Department of the CPC Central Committee and the Ministry of Education took the initiative to take care of the development of higher education teaching materials. An office for arts and humanities teaching material was set up with Zhou Yang, the Minister of Education, personally in charge. In 1961 the Propaganda Department and the Ministry of Education appointed the Institute Vice President Li Dihua as Chairman of the Committee for the Development of Foreign Language Teaching Materials. The Foreign language teaching materials that the Institute was commissioned to compile were: English, Russian, German, French, and Spanish, with Xu Guozhang, Zhao Hui, Yao Kekun, Li Tingzhuan, and Meng Fu as respective chief editors.

1

2

3

4

5

6

1. 1960 年出版的由朱德委员长题写书名的《汉德词典》

2. 1962 年出版的由周恩来总理题写书名的《西汉辞典》

3. 4. 20 世纪 60 年代初编写的西班牙语教材

5. 1963 年出版的英语教材

6. 1962 年和 1963 年英语系编印的精读课本

7. 1963 年出版的德语教材

7

1. *A Chinese-German Dictionary* published in 1960 bearing the title written by Mr Zhu De

2. *A Spanish-Chinese Dictionary* published in 1962 bearing the title written by Premier Zhou Enlai

3. 4. A set of Spanish textbooks compiled in the early 1960s

5. A set of English textbooks published in 1963

6. Intensive reading textbooks compiled and printed by teachers of the English Department in 1962 and 1963

7. A set of German textbooks published in 1963

纳 忠（1909—2008），云南通海人，阿拉伯史专家、阿拉伯语教育家。1931—1940 年在埃及爱兹哈尔大学学习。1936 年获爱兹哈尔大学最高委员会授予的该校最高学位"学者证书"。1942 年底被聘为中央大学历史系教授。1947 年到云南大学历史系任教。1958 年，调外交学院筹建阿拉伯语系并出任系主任。1962 年，外交学院阿拉伯语系并入北京外国语学院亚非语系，纳忠任亚非语系主任。曾任亚非洲史学会第一、二、三届会长，巴基斯坦"希吉来国际学术奖金"提名委员，第六届全国政协委员。长期从事阿拉伯历史、伊斯兰文化的研究。著有《回教诸国文化史》《埃及近现代史》《阿拉伯通史》等学术著作。2001 年 10 月 25 日，被联合国教科文组织授予首届"阿拉伯文化沙迦国际奖"。

Na Zhong (1909-2008), born in Haitong, Yunnan, is an expert in the history of Arabia and an Arabic language educator. He studied at Al-Azhar University in Egypt from 1931 to 1940 and was awarded a "Scholar's Certificate", the highest degree of the University, by the highest committee of the University in 1936. He was appointed as a professor at the History Department of National Central University at the end of 1942, moved to the History Department of Yunnan University in 1947, and was transferred to Foreign Affairs College in 1958 to establish an Arabic department and serve as its Head. In 1962, the Arabic Department of the Foreign Affairs College was merged into the Department of Asian and African Languages at Beijing Foreign Languages Institute, and Na Zhong was appointed as Head of the department. He served successively as the first, second and third President of Historical Society for Asian and African Histories, and a member of the National Committee of the 6th CPPCC. A long-time scholar on Arabic history and Islamic culture, he authored a significant number of academic works, such as *A Cultural History of Islamic Countries*, *A Modern History of Egypt*, and *A General History of Arab Countries*. On 25th October 2001 he was awarded the 1st "Sharjah Prize for Arab Culture" by UNESCO.

从 1959 年至 1966 年，学校师资队伍不断发展壮大，学校自己培养的优秀青年教师逐步走上教学一线，非通用语种的教师队伍初步形成。1962 年外交学院阿拉伯语、日语、印尼语、德语教师并入我校，进一步加强了学校的师资力量。

From 1959 to 1966, the faculty of the Institute grew steadily, with the excellent young teachers gradually taking up frontline teaching posts and the faculty of minor languages taking shape. After the teachers of Arabic, Japanese, Indonesian and German from China Foreign Affairs University transferred to the Institute in 1962, the strength of its faculty was further boosted.

1

2

3

1. 英语系青年教师讨论教学工作。

2. 20 世纪 50 年代末英语系中外教师游览北海公园。

3. 1961 年在莫斯科召开的社会主义国家高校第四届
   俄语教师会议期间，苏联教师在指导中国教师备课。

1. Junior teachers from the English Department discussing
   their teaching

2. Chinese and foreign teachers from the English Department visiting Beihai Park in the late 1950s

3. A Soviet teacher tutoring a group of Chinese teachers
   on how to prepare lessons during the 4th Conference
   of Teachers of Russian in Socialist Countries held in
   Moscow in 1961

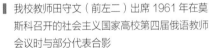

我校教师田守文（前左二）出席1961年在莫斯科召开的社会主义国家高校第四届俄语教师会议时与部分代表合影

Tian Shouwen (Second left in the front) from the Institute photographed with some of the delegates when attending the Fourth Conference of Teachers of Russian in Socialist Countries held in Moscow in 1961

4

5

4. 20世纪60年代初亚非语系部分教师合影

5. 1961年5月，德语系一年级教学组教师与民主德国专家诺伊米勒女士合影，从左至右：颜承翰、殷桐生、李逵六、诺伊米勒、梁敏、董光熙。

4. A group photo of some of the teachers from the Department of Asian and African Languages taken in the early 1960s

5. Teachers of Year One teaching group of the German Department photographed with Ms Neumueller, an expert from German Democratic Republic in May 1961. From left to right: Yan Chenghan, Yin Tongsheng, Li Kuiliu, Neumueller, Liang Min and Dong Guangxi.

1

2

3

4

1. 波兰专家尤拉舒克给青年教师程继忠、吴英增上小课。

2. 波捷罗语系主任史迁（中）与罗马尼亚专家乔苏商讨工作。

3. 20 世纪 60 年代的波兰语教研室教师

4. 20 世纪 60 年代东欧语系字典组教师在工作。

1. A Polish expert tutoring Cheng Jizhong and Wu Yingzeng, two junior teachers

2. Shi Qian (in the middle), Head of the Department of Polish, Czech and Romanian Languages , discussing departmental affairs with a Romanian expert

3. Teachers of the Polish programme in the 1960s

4. Teachers of the Lexicography Unit of Eastern European Languages Department at work in the 1960s

5

6

5. 捷克语专业第一届毕业生（部分）合影

6. 罗马尼亚语专业第一届毕业生与院领导及教师合影（前排左起：赵申、杨顺禧、张高铎、李棣华 、刘柯、张锡俦、杨淦春）

5. A group photo of the first cohort of graduates (incomplete) of Czech

6. The first cohort of graduates of Romanian photographed with Institute leaders and their teachers (first row from the left: Zhao Shen, Yang Shunxi, Zhang Gaoduo, Li Dihua, Liu Ke, Zhang Xichou, Yang Ganchun)

　　从 1959 年到 1966 年"文革"前，学校规模有所扩大，专业大量增加，在继续培养一批英、俄、德、法、西等语种毕业生的同时，非通用语种的人才培养也初见成效。

From 1959 to the eve of "Cultural Revolution" in 1966, the Institute grew in size and the number of foreign language programmes increased enormously. While students of English, Russian, German, French and Spanish were continuously graduating from the Institute year after year, initial success was achieved in teaching students of minor languages.

1

2

3

4

1. 匈牙利语专业第一届毕业生

2. 阿尔巴尼亚语专业第一届毕业生

3. 塞尔维亚语专业第一届毕业生

4. 保加利亚语专业第一届毕业生

1. The first cohort of graduates of Hungarian

2. The first cohort of graduates of Albanian

3. The first cohort of graduates of Serbian

4. The first cohort of graduates of Bulgarian

5. 1961 年留苏预备部学员合影

6. 1964 年斯瓦希里语专修班及第一届本科生
   与亚非语系领导及斯瓦希里语教师合影

5. A group photo of students from the Training
   Division for Studying in the Soviet Union
   graduating in 1961

6. The students of a Swahili Training Class and the
   first intake of undergraduate students of Swahili
   photographed with heads of the Department of
   Asian and African Languages and teachers of
   the Swahili programme in 1964

5

6

1965 年全体毕业生合影

A group photo of all the students graduating in 1965

第六章

"文革"十年　举步维艰

（1966年5月—1976年10月）

Chapter Six
A decade of "Cultural Revolution" and hardships
(May 1966–October 1976)

1966 年 5 月，"无产阶级文化大革命"爆发，高等院校首当其冲，接着全国陷入混乱。持续 10 年的"文革"使北京外国语学院遭到严重破坏，其间还曾一度迁至湖北沙洋办学。在"十年动乱"中，周恩来总理十分关注北京外国语学院，关心外语教育改革，使学院师生受到极大的教育和鼓舞。全校教职工在逆境中艰苦奋斗，努力办学。

In May 1966, "the Great Proletariat Cultural Revolution" broke out. Institutions of higher learning were the first to be affected and the whole nation was thrown into chaos. This 10-year long "Cultural Revolution" inflicted heavy damage on Beijing Foreign Languages Institute, which for a time was relocated to Shayang, Hubei. During the decade of turmoil, Premier Zhou Enlai paid a great deal of attention to the Institute and in particular its foreign language education reform, which proved to be very instructive and encouraging to the teachers and students of the Institute. Despite the adverse conditions and hardships, the faculty and staff of the whole Institute tried their best to go about business as usual.

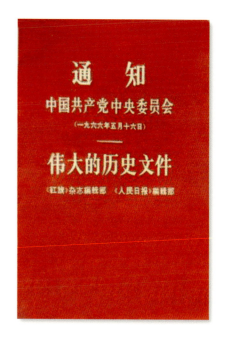

中共中央《五·一六通知》

The CPC Central Committee's "May 16th Notification"

1966

1966 年 5 月 16 日，中共中央政治局扩大会议通过了《中国共产党中央委员会通知》（即《五·一六通知》），要求"高举无产阶级文化革命大旗，彻底揭露反动学术权威的资产阶级立场；彻底批判文化领域的资产阶级反动思想，夺取各文化部门的领导权"。6 月 1 日，《人民日报》发表社论，号召群众起来"横扫一切牛鬼蛇神"。全国高校开始"停课闹革命"。北京外国语学院的青年学生被煽动起来成立"红卫兵组织"，张贴大字报，批判、揪斗学院党政领导人以及所谓的"牛鬼蛇神""反动学术权威"。学院党、政、工、团机构全部陷于瘫痪。群众组织一边在校内"踢开党委闹革命"，一边走向社会，并在 1967 年春、夏参加了外交部"夺权""围困中南海""火烧英国驻华代办处"等活动。

On 16th May 1966, the enlarged meeting of the Politburo of the Communist Party of China approved "Notification of the Central Committee of the Communist Party of China", more commonly known as "May 16th Notification", which asked the whole Party to "hold high the great banner of the proletarian cultural revolution, thoroughly expose the bourgeois stance of reactionary academic authorities, thoroughly criticize the reactionary ideology of the bourgeoisie, and seize power of all cultural departments and institutions". On 1st June, the *People's Daily* carried an editorial calling on the masses to rise up and get rid of all "devils and demons". All colleges and universities in China "suspended lessons and started to join the revolution". Young students from Beijing Foreign Languages Institute were instigated to form the rebellious organization called "red guards", who put up big-character wall posters, held denunciation meetings against and verbally and often physically abused the Institute's CPC and administrative leaders, the so-called "devils and demons", and "reactionary academic authorities". As a result, the Institute's Party organization, administrative body, trade union and Communist Youth League were all paralyzed. The mass organizations not only "kicked away the CPC Committee to wage a revolution" on campus, but also took to the streets. In the spring and summer of 1967, they took part in "seizing power" at the Ministry of Foreign Affairs, besieging Zhongnanhai, which housed the State Council and the families of some top Party and state leaders, and setting the British Embassy ablaze.

《北京外国语学院无产阶级文化革命委员会筹委会成立声明》

"Declaration of the establishment of the Preparatory Committee of Beijing Foreign Languages Institute's Proletarian Cultural Revolutionary Committee"

1

2

1. 红卫兵组织"北外红旗战斗大队"印发的刊物《外语红旗》

2. 校园内的大字报

1. *Foreign Language Red Flag*, a serial printed by a "red guard" organization called BFLI Red Flag Brigade

2. Big-character wall posters on campus

1968 年欢迎"首都工人、解放军毛泽东思想宣传队"进校。

"The capital city's workers and PLA Mao Zedong Thought propaganda team" being welcomed into the Institute in 1968

1968

1968 年 8 月，根据毛泽东主席批示"照发"的《中共中央、国务院、中央军委、中央文革小组关于派工人宣传队进学校的通知》，由北京市第五建筑公司的工人和海军某部干部战士组成的"首都工人、解放军毛泽东思想宣传队"进校。9 月，各派群众组织实现"大联合"，成立"北京外国语学院革命委员会"（简称"革委会"），其主要成员是宣传队和群众组织的负责人。革委会成立后，学校"复课闹革命"，继续在"左"的理论、方针指导下，对学院原党政领导干部、知名教授等进行批斗，并且开展了"清理阶级队伍"的活动，错误地迫害了一大批人。

In August 1968, in accordance with "Notification from the CPC Central Committee, the State Council, the Central Military Commission, and the Central Cultural Revolution Group on sending workers' propaganda teams into schools", which was approved by Chairman Mao Zedong with the directive "have it issued as it is", "the capital city's workers and the People's Liberation Army Mao Zedong Thought propaganda team" composed of workers from Beijing No. 5 Construction Company and officers and men from a certain unit of the Navy entered the Institute. In September, all factions of the mass organizations formed "a broad coalition" and set up "Beijing Foreign Languages Revolutionary Committee", with heads of the propaganda team and the mass organizations serving as its major members. After the revolutionary committee was set up, the Institute "resumed classes while waging the revolution"; under the guidance of "Leftist" theories and principles, it continued organizing denunciation meetings against the Institute's former CPC and administrative leaders and well-known professors, carried out the campaign to "clean up the ranks in accordance with class lines", and wrongly persecuted a large number of people.

1968 年庆祝院、系革委会成立

Celebration of the establishment of Institute and department-level revolutionary committees in 1968

1969 年在唐山某军垦农场劳动、学习的三排女生与解放军战士合影

The female students of the third platoon working and studying on an army reclamation farm in Tangshan photographed with PLA soldiers in 1969

　　1968 年底，根据周恩来总理指示，为了保护和储备外语人才，六七、六八两届学生由外交部统一组织到唐山地区北京部队的几个农场劳动锻炼，同时派出教师进行教学和辅导。由于当时情况混乱，这批学生在 1970 年大多数被分配到县以下厂矿和学校。1970 年初，解放军八三四一部队"毛泽东思想宣传队"（也就是"军宣队"）进校。4 月，学院迁往湖北沙洋办"五七"干校，边劳动边继续搞运动。

　　At the end of 1968, in accordance with a directive issued by Premier Zhou to protect and preserve foreign language professionals, students who would have graduated in 1967 and 1968 were assigned by the Ministry of Foreign Affairs to a number of farms around Tangshan owned by the PLA Beijing Command to undergo the test of manual labour, with teachers sent out to teach and supervise the students. Because of the confusion at the time, this cohort of students were mostly assigned to factories, mines and schools in different counties in 1970. At the beginning of 1970, the PLA Unit 8341 "Mao Zedong Thought propaganda team" (commonly referred to as "Army propaganda team") entered the Institute. In April, the Institute relocated to Shayang, Hubei, to run a "May Seventh" Cadre School, an idea endorsed by Chairman Mao in a directive he issued on 7th May that year, where they did farm work while continuing waging the "cultural revolution".

1. 1970 年欢迎解放军八三四一部队"毛泽东思想宣传队"进校。

2. 师生在湖北汉江码头搬运修建校舍的建筑材料。

3. 师生自己动手修建的沙洋校舍

1. The PLA Unit 8341 "Mao Zedong Thought propaganda team" being welcomed into the Institute in 1970

2. Teachers and students of the Institute unloading building material for the new campus at a wharf of River Han in Hubei

3. Teachers and students building the Shayang campus with their own hands

4

5

6

7

4. 学生宿舍内部

5. 在水田中劳动

6. 军宣队召开干部大会。

7. 粮食入仓

4. Interior of the students' dormitory

5. Students working in rice paddies

6. Army propaganda team holding a meeting of the cadres

7. Students storing the grain

1

3

4

2

---

1. 部分干部和军宣队合影

2. 搭建猪舍

3. 学生在户外就餐。

4. 教师在收获冬瓜。

1. Some of the cadres photographed with the Army propaganda team

2. Students building a pigsty

3. Students eating outdoors

4. Teachers harvesting winter melons

杨伯箴（1919—1989），贵州镇远人。1936年加入中国共产党。曾任中共北京市委宣传部、教育部副部长，北京师范学院党委书记兼院长，驻瑞典大使，中国联合国教科文组织全国委员会副主任等职务。1973年1月至1975年4月任北京外国语学院临时领导小组组长，1975年4月至1980年3月任北京外国语学院党委书记。

Yang Bozhen (1919-1989), born in Zhenyuan, Guizhou, joined the CPC in 1936. He was in Propaganda Department and then the Department of Education under the CPC Committee of Beijing Municipal, Secretary of the CPC Beijing Normal College Committee and President of the College, Ambassador to Sweden, and Deputy Director of China's National Committee for UNESCO Affairs. He was Leader of Beijing Foreign Languages Institute Provisional Leading Group from January 1973 to April 1975, and Secretary of Party Committee from April 1975 to March 1980.

1975年4月，学院在距上届党代会12年之后，召开了第三届党代会。会议选举产生了新的党委会，杨伯箴为党委书记，胡叔度、汪家荣、王一兵、刘柯为副书记。

In April 1975, 12 years after its last Party Congress, the Institute held its 3rd CPC Congress, which elected a new committee, with Yang Bozhen as Secretary, Hu Shudu, Wang Jiarong, Wang Yibing, and Liu Ke as Vice Secretaries.

▌ 1976年10月，党中央粉碎"四人帮"，21日至23日，学校师生员工参加北京市百万人游行。

In October 1976, the CPC Central authorities arrested the "Gang of Four" composed of Jiang Qing and three other radical top leaders within the Party; from 21st to 23rd, teachers, students and staff from the Institute took part in the million-man parade in Beijing.

1972

1972年7月，学院奉命从湖北沙洋迁回北京。1973年1月17日，根据中央指示，宣传队全部撤出学院。外交部派杨伯箴、浦寿昌、胡叔度三人小组进校主持日常工作。2月，中央派廖承志兼任北京外国语学院院长。

In July 1972, the Institute was ordered to return to Beijing from Shayang, Hubei. On 17th January 1973, in accordance with a directive from the central authorities, the propaganda team was completely withdrawn from the Institute. The Ministry of Foreign Affairs sent a three-member group composed of Yang Bozhen, Pu Shouchang and Hu Shudu into the Institute to preside over the everyday work of the Institute. In February, the central authorities appointed Liao Chengzhi as President of Beijing Foreign Languages Institute while retaining his other positions.

1971 年，学员在沙洋
"五七"干校宿舍中学习。

Students studying in their
dormitory in Shayang "May
Seventh" Cadre School in 1971

在"文革"期间，周恩来总理十分珍惜外语人才，关心外语教育改革。1970 年 11 月 6 日到 20 日，周恩来总理先后 5 次接见北京外国语学院和其他几所高校（北京大学、清华大学参加 3 次接见）的宣传队及师生代表，着重谈外语教育改革问题。周恩来总理反对外语教学中片面强调政治的绝对化做法，要求正确处理政治与业务、理论与实践、教与学等各种关系，并对培养目标、办学方针、学制和教材编写、教学方法等方面作了许多指示。周恩来总理特别提出，学习外语要天天练，要打好政治思想、语言本身和各种文化知识三方面的基本功。周恩来总理关于三个基本功的指示，成为北京外国语学院抵制极"左"路线、坚持正确的外语教育方向的有力武器。

1970 年 4 月，学院迁到湖北沙洋后不久，周恩来总理就派人帮助军宣队研究外语教学改革和准备恢复招生的工作。1971 年恢复招生。8、9 月，我校从北京、河北、山西、内蒙古、黑龙江、吉林、江苏、浙江、湖北等九省区招收学员 800 人，其中由工厂、农村、军队"推荐""保送"的工农兵学员 760 人，另有根据周恩来总理指示在北京市招收的在校高中学生 40 人。

During the "Cultural Revolution", Premier Zhou cherished foreign language professionals and showed great concern about foreign language education reforms. From 6th to 20th November 1970, he met with the propaganda teams and representatives of teachers and students from Beijing Foreign Languages Institute and a few other universities on five occasions (three of those including Peking University and Tsinghua University), mainly talking about issues concerning foreign language education reforms. He was against emphasizing only political indoctrination in foreign language teaching and learning, called for correctly dealing with the relationship between politics and subjects, theory and practice, teaching and learning, and gave many directives concerning the aim of education, guidelines for running the university, duration of study, teaching material development, teaching methodology, etc. He especially pointed out that one needed to practise every day when learning a foreign language, and that students had to lay a good foundation in terms of their political ideology, language proficiency, and all kinds of cultural knowledge. His directive about the "three foundations" became a powerful weapon for the Institute to resist extreme "Leftist" tendencies and stay on the right path in developing foreign language education.

Shortly after the Institute moved back to Beijing from Shayang, Hubei, Premier Zhou sent his subordinates to help the army propaganda team understand the foreign language teaching reforms and prepare for the resumption of admitting students. Student admission resumed in 1971. In August and September of that year, the Institute admitted 800 students from Beijing, seven provinces including Hebei, Shanxi, Heilongjiang, Jilin, Jiangsu, Zhejiang, Hubei, and the Inner Mongolian Autonomous Region; of these, 760 were "recommended" or "guarantee"worker-peasant-soldier students from factories, countryside villages and military forces, the other 40 were senior high school students from Beijing, who were admitted following Premier Zhou's directive.

▌1974 年北京外国语学院首届工农兵学员代表大会

The 1st Beijing Foreign Languages Institute's Worker-Peasant-Soldier Students Congress in 1974

1973

1973 年 2 月，廖承志担任院长后，注重教学工作。2 月 8 日，他主持临时领导小组会议，听取教学改革工作情况的汇报，就恢复教学秩序、提高教学水平提出了许多重要意见。

After he was appointed President of the Institute in February 1973, Liao Chengzhi placed emphasis on teaching. On 8th February, he presided over a meeting of the provisional leaders' group, listening to reports about teaching reforms, and voicing many important opinions about restoring normal teaching order and raising teaching standards.

▌**廖承志担任院长期间提出的办学指导思想及措施**

Remarks made by Liao Chengzhi concerning how the Institute should be run while he was its President

学校定位 Orientation	"要把学校办成又红又专的外国语学院。"
	"We must turn this institution into a foreign languages institute that is both politically correct and professionally competent."
机构与教学 Structure	"要把系恢复起来。"
	"The various departments must be restored."
学制 Duration of study	"增设一年制的预科，给学生补习文化知识。"
	"A one-year foundation programme should be added so as to provide the students with extra tuition in cultural knowledge."
语种设置 Bilingualism	"不能单打一，要开设第二外语。"
	"We cannot teach the students just one foreign language. A second foreign language is necessary."
教材建设 Teaching materials	"要搞好教材建设。教材是政治业务的统一体，不能分开。"
	"We must do a good job in teaching materials development. Teaching materials must integrate political ideology and professional learning; the two cannot be separated."
教学方法 Teaching methods	"要让学生听外语广播，看外报外刊，《圣经》也不妨看看，不要怕。"
	"We should let the students listen to foreign language broadcast and read foreign newspapers and magazines. Even the Bible is worth reading. Don't be afraid."
师资队伍 Teaching staff	"现在教师力量相当不强，是否考虑聘请外国专家或采取大胆地加强教师队伍的措施。"
	"The teaching ability of the faculty is seriously lacking and bold measures to bolster the faculty or the employment of foreign experts should be considered."

1973 年 5 月，在华北五省市区教材改革经验交流会上，我校代表在《改革外语教材的几点体会和设想》的发言中提出："外语教材必须遵循语言规律和语言教学的规律。""外语教材必须始终坚持革命的思想内容和语言规律、语言教学规律的统一。一部违反语言规律和语言教学规律的教材，无论从哪方面看，都不能说是一部好教材。"

学校在"文革"的动乱期间仍努力参与社会服务，如 1969 年派出小分队为首都机场等单位开办英语、俄语培训班，1970 年在沙洋举办中学英语教师短训班。从 1973 年起，英语系教师承担了北京人民广播电台业余英语广播教学的任务。

At a meeting for exchanging experience on teaching materials reform in five provinces and municipalities in North China held in May 1973, representatives from the Institute pointed out: "Foreign language textbooks must follow the law of languages and language teaching", "foreign language teaching materials must embody the unity of revolutionary thoughts and the law of languages and language teaching. A textbook that goes against the law of languages and language teaching cannot be considered a good textbook from whatever point of view."

During the chaotic period of the "Cultural Revolution", the Institute still managed to provide services to the society. In 1969, for example, it sent groups to the Capital Airport and other places to run English and Russian training classes; in 1970 it ran short-term training classes for secondary school teachers of English; starting from 1973, teachers from the English Department undertook the task of running the afterhours English language teaching programme at Beijing People's Broadcasting Corporation.

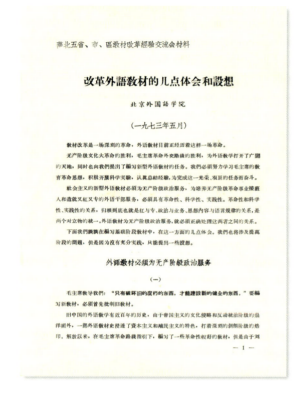

《改革外语教材的几点体会和设想》

"Some discoveries and proposals for reforming foreign language teaching materials"

从 1971 年到 1976 年的 6 年中，学院招收了五届工农兵学员，共 2,190 人。学校注意保证一定的教学时间，在编写教材、制订教学方法等方面根据他们的实际水平，采取了一些措施，使他们学到必要的外语和文化知识。在当时"开门办学""教育革命"等违背教学规律的错误方针指导下，学院也组织师生走出校门"学军""学农""学工"，但在选点时尽可能注意有利于开展外语教学活动，并在"三学"中保证了一定的外语学习时间，从而在一定程度上减少了"开门办学"对教学的影响和损失，在当时的困难条件下为国家培养了一批具有一定水平的外语人才。

1975 年第 53 期《教育革命通讯》

Newsletter of Educational Revolution (No. 53, 1975)

In the six years between 1971 and 1976, the Institute enrolled 2,190 worker-peasant-soldier students through five intakes. The Institute made sure that there were enough teaching hours and, by adapting the teaching materials and teaching methods to the students' actual abilities, ensured that they acquired the necessary foreign language skills and cultural knowledge. Although the Institute had to follow misguided principles such as "open-door schooling" and "educational revolution", which were contrary to natural teaching principles, and sent teachers and students out of campus to "learn from soldiers, peasants and workers", it did everything it could in choosing venues that were most conducive to foreign language teaching and guaranteed a certain amount of time for foreign language learning during the "three-learn" period. As a result, the adverse influence of "open-door schooling" on teaching was somewhat mitigated. Under those circumstances, the Institute still managed to produce a cohort of students with some foreign language proficiency.

第七章

拨乱反正　万象更新

（1977—1993年）

Chapter Seven
From chaos back to order—an
all-round revival
(1977-1993)

1977年8月，中共十一大召开，大会宣布"文革"结束。1981年6月，中共十一届六中全会通过《关于建国以来党的若干历史问题的决议》，对"文革"给予了彻底否定。以1978年12月召开的中共十一届三中全会为起点，中国人民进入了改革开放和社会主义现代化建设的新时期。在这前所未有的良好外部环境下，从1977年至1993年，北京外国语学院拨乱反正、除旧布新，在整顿调整中加快发展步伐。

In August 1977 the Communist Party of China held its 11th National Congress, which declared the end of "the Great Cultural Revolution". Then in June 1981 the 6th Plenary Session of the CPC's 11th Central Committee approved the "Resolution Concerning a Number of Historical Issues of the Party Since the Founding of the People's Republic", in which "the Great Cultural Revolution" was completely repudiated. Following the 3rd Plenary Session of the CPC's 11th Central Committee held in December 1978, China entered a new era of reform as the nation started on a path of socialist modernisation. In this extraordinarily favourable environment from 1977 to 1993, Beijing Foreign Languages Institute put an end to the chaos, returned to the right path, and started a series of renovations, speeding up its pace of development in the course of reform and restructuring.

1977

1977年至1980年，学校拨乱反正，平反冤、假、错案，落实知识分子政策，努力清除"文革"对学校工作造成的影响。"文革"期间受到迫害和错误批判处分的575人得到平反，1957年"反右"运动中被错划为"右派"的253人和因为所谓右派言论受到错误处理的340人全部得到纠正。

1978年12月举行的中共十一届三中全会决定"把全党工作的着重点和全国人民的注意力转移到社会主义现代化建设上来"。在这一政治路线的指引下，从1979年起，学校对教学工作进行了调整和整顿。

刘 柯

1981年2月至1984年4月任北京外国语学院院长。

Liu Ke, President of Beijing Foreign Languages Institute from February 1981 to April 1984.

During the period between 1977 and 1980, the new governing body of the Institute rectified the miscarriages of justice, annulled the fabricated and misjudged cases in the "Cultural Revolution", and implemented the Communist Party's policies concerning intellectuals. All of the 575 people who had been persecuted or wrongly criticised and punished during the "Cultural Revolution" were rehabilitated, and all 253 people who had been wrongly branded "Rightist" in the campaign against "right wings" and all 340 people who had been wrongly punished because of their so-called right-wing remarks were vindicated.

To implement the decision to shift the focus of the Communist Party's work and the attention of the nation to China's socialist modernisation, which had been made by the 3rd Plenary Session of CPC's 11th National Congress, the Institute restructured and readjusted its teaching in 1979.

1980年，学校由原属外交部领导转为直属教育部的重点大学。院一级恢复了党委领导下的院长负责制，1981年教育部任命刘柯为院长，同时派来孙萍任党委书记，尹企卓任常务副院长，王振稼为党委副书记，并先后任命秦思平、王佐良、王福祥为副院长。1984年4月，教育部再次调整了学院领导班子：院长王福祥，副院长胡文仲、刘政权，党委副书记（代理书记）王振稼，副书记刘毓缧。1984年12月，王振稼调离外国语学院，李宜今来校任党委书记。此后，又增调曹小先为副书记。1992年曹小先任党委书记。

In 1980 the governance of the Institute was transferred from the Ministry of Foreign Affairs to the Ministry of Education and the Institute became a key national institution of higher learning under the direct governance of the MOE. With the Institute once again managed by its President under the leadership of the CPC Committee, the MOE appointed Liu Ke as President, Sun Ping as Secretary of CPC Committee, Yin Qizhuo as Executive Vice President, Wang Zhenjia as Vice Secretary of CPC Committee, and successively appointed Qin Siping, Wang Zuoliang and Wang Fuxiang as Vice Presidents. In April 1984 the MOE reappointed the governing body of the Institute, with Wang Fuxiang as President, Hu Wenzhong and Liu Zhengquan as Vice Presidents, Wang Zhenjia as Acting Secretary of CPC Committee, Liu Yuxiang as Vice Secretary. In December 1984, Wang Zhenjia was transferred out of the Institute and Li Yijin succeeded him as the Secretary of CPC Committee. Later Cao Xiaoxian was appointed as Vice Secretary. In 1992 Cao was appointed as Secretary.

孙 萍

（1916—2001），浙江新昌人，1935年加入中国共产党。曾任少共上海区委宣传部部长、上海法南区委书记、中共吉林省委党校校务处处长等职务。中华人民共和国成立后，曾任中共北京市委党校第二书记兼副校长、北京第二外国语学院党委书记等职务。1981年2月至1984年4月任北京外国语学院党委书记。

Sun Ping (1916-2001), was born in Xinchang, Zhejiang, Sun joined the CPC in 1935, and was appointed successively as Head of Propaganda Department of Shanghai Regional Committee of Young Communist Party of China, Secretary of CPC Fa'nan District in Shanghai, and Director of School Affairs Department at the Party School of the CPC Jilin Provincial Committee. After the founding of the People's Republic, he was appointed as Second Secretary of the CPC Committee and Vice President of the Party School of the CPC Beijing Municipal Committee, and Secretary of the CPC Committee of Beijing Second Foreign Languages Institute. He was Secretary of the CPC Committee of Beijing Foreign Languages Institute from February 1981 to April 1984.

李宜今

（1928—2013），河北永年人，1945年加入中国共产党，曾就读于华北大学工学院。曾任北京光电技术研究所所长、党委书记，北京工业学院副院长、副书记。1984年12月至1991年12月任北京外国语学院党委书记。

Li Yijin (1928-2013), was born in Yongnian, Hebei. He joined the CPC in 1945 and studied at North China University in its School of Technology. He served as Director and Secretary of the CPC Committee at the Beijing Institute of Photo-electric Technology, Vice President and Vice Secretary of the CPC Committee at Beijing Institute of Technology. He was Secretary of the CPC Committee of Beijing Foreign Languages Institute from December 1984 to December 1991.

王福祥

1934年生于山东寿光，中共党员，曾就读于哈尔滨外国语专门学校、莫斯科语言大学（获副博士学位）。1982年6月至1984年4月任北京外国语学院副院长，1984年4月至1997年2月先后任北京外国语学院院长、北京外国语大学校长。第八、九届全国政协委员。

Wang Fuxiang (1934-), was born in Shouguang, Shandong. A member of the CPC, he studied at Harbin School of Foreign Languages and received a PhD from Moscow State Linguistic University. He was Vice President of Beijing Foreign Languages Institute from June 1982 to April 1984, President of Beijing Foreign Studies University from April 1984 to February 1997. He was also a member of the National Committee of the 8th and 9th CPPCC.

曹小先

1934 年生于江苏无锡，中共党员，毕业于清华大学物理系。曾任清华大学物理系分党委书记、教务处副处长。1985 年 6 月调任北京外国语学院党委副书记，1992 年 1 月至 1996 年 5 月任校党委书记。

Cao Xiaoxian (1934-), born in Wuxi, Jiangsu, is a member of CPC and a Physics graduate from Tsinghua University. She served as Secretary of CPC Committee of the Physics Department at Tsinghua University and the Deputy Registrar. She was appointed as Vice Secretary of the CPC Committee of Beijing Foreign Languages Institute in June 1985, Secretary of the CPC Committee from January 1992 to May 1996.

1986 年 12 月 16 日，学校召开第四次党员代表大会，李宜今代表党委作题为《团结办学、开拓前进，为把我院建设成为社会主义精神文明的坚强阵地而奋斗》的工作报告。大会选举了新一届党委会和纪律检查委员会。

On 16th December 1986 the Institute held its 4th CPC Congress. On behalf of the CPC Committee, Li Yijin made a report entitled "Unite to make headways and strive to build the Institute into a stronghold of socialist civilisation". The congress elected a new committee and a new Commission for Discipline Inspection.

党委书记 Secretary	李宜今 Li Yijin
党委副书记 Vice Secretaries	王福祥 刘毓缰 Wang Fuxiang, Liu Yuxiang
党委常委 Standing Committee members	王福祥 申春生 刘政权 刘毓缰 陈乃芳 李宜今 赵申 胡文仲 曹小先 Wang Fuxiang, Shen Chunsheng, Liu Zhengquan, Liu Yuxiang, Chen Naifang, Li Yijin, Zhao Shen, Hu Wenzhong, Cao Xiaoxian
纪委书记 Secretary of the Commission for Discipline Inspection	赵申 Zhao Shen

1991 年 12 月 28 日至 30 日，学校召开第五次党员代表大会，李宜今代表党委作题为《加强党的建设，坚持社会主义办学方向，为培养德才兼备的外语人才而努力》的工作报告。大会选举了新一届党委会和纪律检查委员会。

From 28th to 30th December 1991 the Institute held its 5th CPC Congress. On behalf of the CPC Committee, Li Yijin made a report entitled "Strengthen the leadership of the Party, hold onto the direction of socialism in running the Institute, and strive to train foreign language professionals that are both able and politically correct". The Congress elected a new CPC Committee and a new Commission for Discipline Inspection.

党委书记 Secretary	曹小先 Cao Xiaoxian
党委副书记 Vice Secretary	陈乃芳 Chen Naifang
党委常委 Standing Committee members	王福祥 申春生 余章荣 陈乃芳 赵申 曹小先 穆大英 Wang Fuxiang, Shen Chunsheng, Yu Zhangrong, Chen Naifang, Zhao Shen, Cao Xiaoxian, Mu Daying
纪委书记 Secretary of the Commission for Discipline Inspection	赵申 Zhao Shen

1

2

1982

1982年，学校公布新的教学方案，明确其指导思想是"从实际出发，扬长避短"，要坚持和发扬外语基本功的训练，把提高学生的口笔语实践水平作为"传家宝"，不可须臾忽视与削弱。除英语和日语两个专业为四年制外，其他通用语种为五年制。培养目标进一步确定为培养外事、中外文化交流、语言文学及社会科学研究、高校师资等四个方面的外语人才。

1982年成立了院学术委员会，由院长刘柯任主任委员，接着成立了院学位委员会，由副院长王佐良教授任主任委员。各系也分别成立了系一级学术委员会和学位委员会，并恢复了教研室和教学小组的建制。

---

1. 院学术委员会会议

2. 院学位评定委员会会议

1. The Institute's Academic Committee in session

2. The Institute's Academic Degree Evaluation Committee in session

In 1982 the Institute announced a new teaching plan, specifying that the guiding principle was "be practical, bring out our advantages and avoid our disadvantages", that it was necessary to persist in and reinforce the training of students' basic foreign language skills, and that raising the students' proficiency in speaking and writing should be regarded the cherished tradition of the Institute that must never be neglected or weakened at any time. Apart from those studying English and Japanese whose courses were four years long, the schooling of all other languages was to be five years. The aim of the Institute was specified as educating foreign language professionals specializing in foreign affairs, international cultural exchange, studies of language, literature and social sciences, and higher education.

In 1982 the Academic Committee of the Institute was established, with Institute President Liu Ke as its Chairman; followed by the establishment of the Institute's Degree Evaluation Committee, with Vice President Wang Zuoliang as its Chairman. Academic Committees and Academic Degree Evaluation Committees at the department-level were also established, and teaching and research divisions and teaching groups were reinstituted.

1

2

3

1977 年全国恢复高考，学校积极参加了 1977 年和 1978 年的全国统一招生。1977 年 9 个语种招生 256 人，1978 年有 10 个语种招生 277 人。同时，为了适应国家进入新的历史时期对建设人才的迫切需要，按照北京市的部署开办了北京外国语学院分院，1978 年在北京地区招收英语专业新生 200 名，日语和法语专业新生各 50 名。

Following the reintroduction of the national college entrance examination in 1977, the Institute took active part in nationally unified student recruitment in 1977 and 1978, admitting 256 students majoring in nine separate languages in 1977, and 277 students majoring in ten separate languages in 1978. At the same time, to meet the needs of the local government for college graduates in a new and historical period of development, the Institute set up a branch campus, admitting 200 students of English and 50 students of Japanese and French each from the Beijing area in 1978.

1. 英语系恢复高考后招收的第一届学生
   （1977 级 5 班）毕业前和教师合影留念
2. 英语系恢复高考后招收的第一届学生
   （1977 级 7 班）毕业前和教师合影留念
3. 西班牙语系 1977 级毕业生合影

1. A graduation photo of the first intake of students (class 5, intake of 1977) of the English Department together with their teachers after the reintroduction of college entrance examination
2. A graduation photo of the first intake of students (class 7, intake of 1977) of the English Department together with their teachers after the reintroduction of college entrance examination
3. A graduation photo of the students of the Spanish Department from the intake of 1977

周珏良教授

Professor Zhou Jueliang

王佐良教授

Professor Wang Zuoliang

许国璋教授

Professor Xu Guozhang

余章荣教授

Professor Yu Zhangrong

白春仁教授

Professor Bai Chunren

谢莹莹教授

Professor Xie Yingying

祝彦教授

Professor Zhu Yan

1978 年恢复招收研究生，1982 年国务院学位委员会批准我校英语、法语、德语、俄语、西班牙语、阿拉伯语 6 个专业有权授予硕士学位，英语系被批准为有权授予博士学位的单位。王佐良、许国璋为博士生导师，王佐良、祝彦被任命为国务院学位委员会委员；1984 年批准周珏良为博士生导师。1990 年 10 月，国务院学位委员会批准我校俄语语言文学、德语语言文学、阿拉伯语语言文学三个专业为博士授予点，白春仁、谢莹莹和余章荣教授为博士生导师。

In 1978 universities in China resumed their programmes for postgraduate studies. In 1982 the State Council's Academic Degree Committee authorised the Beijing Foreign Languages Institute to award MA degrees in English, French, German, Russian, Spanish and Arabic, and the English Department was authorised to award PhD degrees, with Wang Zuoliang and Xu Guozhang appointed as supervisors of PhD students, and Wang Zuoliang and Zhu Yan appointed as members of the State Council's Academic Degree Committee; in 1984, Zhou Jueliang was appointed as a PhD supervisor; in October 1990, the State Council's Academic Degree Committee agreed for the Institute's programmes in Russian Language and Literature, German Language and Literature, and Arabic Language and Literature to have the right to award PhD degrees, with Bai Chunren, Xie Yingying and Yu Zhangrong appointed as PhD supervisors.

第一位博士学位获得者杨国斌在博士论文答辩会后与导师王佐良及答辩委员会其他成员合影。（左起：胡文仲、何其莘、敏泽、吴景荣、丁往道、王佐良、杨国斌）

Yang Guobin (1st from right), the first student who was awarded the degree of Doctor of Philosophy at the Institute, photographed with his supervisor Wang Zuoliang (2nd from right) and the examiners after his viva voce (from left: Hu Wenzhong, He Qixin, Min Ze, Wu Jingrong, and Ding Wangdao)

1. 1978 年"文革"后法语系招收的第一届研究生

2. "文革"后英语系招收的第一届研究生与导师合影

1. A group photo of the French Department's first intake of graduate students after the "Cultural Revolution" began in 1978

2. A group photo of the English Department's first intake of graduate students with their supervisors after the "Cultural Revolution"

1

2

3. 1980 年春李莎与俄语系研究生合影（左起：
   刘泰莱、王伟、纽英丽、张建华、李莎、王君）

4. 1983 年秋，世界著名语言学家韩礼德（穿皮
   夹克者）在我校举办语法讲习班，与王佐良、
   许国璋以及我校和来自其他大学的学员合影。

5. 周珏良教授主持研究生论文答辩。

3

4

3. A photograph of Li Sha (Elizabeth Kishkina) with the Russian
   Department's graduate students taken in the spring of 1980
   (from the left: Liu Tailai, Wang Wei, Niu Yingli, Zhang Jianhua,
   Li Sha and Wang Jun)

4. In the autumn of 1983, the world famous linguist M.A.K
   Halliday (in leather jacket) came to the Institute to give a series
   of lectures on grammar. This photo shows him with Wang
   Zuoliang, Xu Guozhang and students from the Institute and
   other colleges and universities in China.

5. Professor Zhou Jueliang presiding over the viva voce of a
   research student

5

■ 1979 年全国首届法语教师培训班合影

A group photo of the nation's first French teachers training course in 1979

■ 教育部北京外国语学院全国高校英语教师进修班结业合影

A graduation photo of the MOE Beijing Foreign Languages Institute's National College English Teacher Development Programme

自 1980 年起，我校根据教育部要求，进一步加强了全国高等院校培训外语教师的工作。1980 年至 1984 年培训近千人。其中 63 人是根据中英文化协定，由我院和英中文化协会共同培养，并在教师研修班学习，学制两年。这批学生毕业回原校后大都成为业务骨干，发挥了学科带头人的作用。

Starting from 1980, in accordance with the requirement from the Ministry of Education, the Institute strengthened its role in training college foreign language teachers for the nation. From 1980 to 1984 nearly one thousand teachers received training at the Institute; 63 of them were trained in the teacher development class run jointly by the Institute and the British Council in accordance with a cultural agreement between China and the UK. When they returned to their colleges and universities, most of them became important members of faculty staff in their respective work places, playing a lead role in teaching and academic research.

柯鲁克和伊莎白指导英语系青年教师备课。

David Crook and Isabel tutoring the young teachers of the English Department on how to prepare lessons

副院长王佐良教授给本科生上课。

Vice President Wang Zuoliang lecturing in an undergraduate class

1981年，日语、阿拉伯语专业脱离亚非语系各自独立建系，系主任分别为李德、纳忠；德语专业脱离东欧语系再度独立建系（含瑞典语专业），系主任祝彦。1984年11月，成立英语二系，承担全校英语二外教学以及中学师资培训任务。为接纳外国留学生来华学习、进修汉语，1982年设立外国留学生汉语进修部。1985年9月，新设立的对外汉语专业和图书馆信息学专业正式招生。1986年9月，原马列教研室与国际政治教研室合并，成立社会科学部。1991年，汉语部改为中国语言文学系。学校在恢复正常教学管理、教学秩序的同时，下大力气抓教学质量，努力提高人才培养水平。

In 1981, the Japanese language and Arabic language were separated from the Department of Asian and African Languages and became independent departments, with Li De and Na Zhong appointed as Heads of the two departments respectively; German Language was separated from the Department of Eastern European Languages and became an independent department again (containing Swedish), with Zhu Yan appointed as Head of the Department. In November 1984, the Second English Department was established, responsible for teaching English as a second foreign language to all students of the Institute whose majors are not English and for middle school teacher development. To accept overseas students who came to China to learn Chinese, the Overseas Students Chinese Programme was set up in 1982. In September 1985, the two newly established programmes — Chinese as a Foreign Language and Library and Information Studies started accepting students. In September 1986, the former Marxism and Leninism Teaching Section and the International Politics Teaching Section were merged into the Faculty of Social Sciences. In 1991, the Chinese Section was expanded into the Department of Chinese Language and Literature. While restoring normal order in teaching and administration, the Institute made great efforts to enhance the quality of teaching and raise the standards of education.

1

1. 罗马尼亚专家达尼洛夫和1979级罗马尼亚语专业学生在校园里。

2. 德语系祝彦教授给研究生上课。

3. 德语系学生上德国国情研究课。

1. Romanian expert Danilov and students of Romanian from the intake of 1979 walking on campus

2. Professor Zhu Yan lecturing in a postgraduate class

3. Students of German in a class on General Information about Germany

2

3

为纪念我校英籍教师陈梅洁，学校于1986年设立"陈梅洁奖"，专门奖励外语基础阶段教学优秀教师。

In memory of Margaret Turner, whose Chinese name was Chen Meijie, the Institute established Chen Meijie Award in 1986 to reward outstanding teachers teaching first- and second-year students

4

5

6

4. 西班牙语系刘家海老师向学生介绍
　 工具书的使用方法。

5. 英语系中青年教师集体备课。

6. 西班牙语系教师讨论教学。

7. 匈牙利语专家对学生进行语言训练。

4. Mr Liu Jiahai of the Spanish Department
   demonstrating how to use dictionaries

5. Middle-aged and young teachers
   preparing lessons collectively

6. Teachers of the Spanish Department
   discussing teaching

7. A teacher from Hungary giving students
   language training

7

1

2

3

4

1. 阿拉伯语系教师在上课。

2. 法语系学生在语言实验室上听力课。

3. 英语系学生上公共课。

4. 1985 年的图书馆中文阅览室

1. A teacher of Arabic giving a lecture

2. Students of French taking a listening class in the language lab

3. Students of English taking a common required course

4. Chinese reading room of the library in 1985

6

5

8

7

5. 1985 年的图书馆外文阅览室

6. 亚非语系马来语教师吴宗玉组织马来语、越南
   语学生在校园内勤工俭学。

7. 中文系留学生上书法课。

8. 中文系教师交流教学心得。

5. Foreign language reading room of the library in 1985

6. Wu Zongyu, a teacher of Malaysian from Department of the Asian and African
   Languages helping students of Malaysian and Vietnamese find part-time jobs
   to support themselves

7. Overseas students in the Chinese Department taking a calligraphy class

8. Teachers from the Chinese Department exchanging their teaching experience

英语系词典组教师在工作。

The lexicography group of the English Department at work

在调整、整顿工作中，学校积极恢复并大力开展科学研究工作，努力使学校成为教学、科研并重的大学。在这一思想指导下，学校的科学研究工作与"文革"之前相比有了很大发展。

自1980年后，我校参加了教育部领导的全国外语教材编审组的活动和各种外语学会、外语教学研究会的活动。王佐良担任了第一届全国高校外语教材编审委员会主任，许国璋担任副主任兼英语组组长，赵辉担任副主任兼俄语组组长。1982年4月，中国德语教学研究会在杭州举行成立大会，祝彦当选为会长；同年5月，中国英语教学研究会成立大会在昆明举行，王佐良当选为会长。1986年，国家教委聘王佐良任第二届高等学校外语专业教材编审委员会主任委员，王福祥、许国璋、胡文仲任副主任委员。胡文仲兼任英语编审组组长，王福祥兼任俄语编审组组长，董燕生任西班牙语编审组组长，余章荣任阿拉伯语编审组组长。我校编写的大学基础阶段英语、法语、德语、俄语、西班牙语等教材，被推荐给全国高校使用。

In the process of restructuring and reorientation, the Institute encouraged its faculty to resume academic research and undertake research projects so as to turn the Institute into an institution of higher learning, strong in both teaching and research. Following this new guideline, academic research at the Institute made significantly greater progress than the period before the "Cultural Revolution".

After 1980, teachers of the Institute played an important role in the National Foreign Language Textbooks Compilation and Review Group led by the Ministry of Education and took an active part in the various foreign language associations and foreign language teaching and research societies. Wang Zuoliang was appointed as Chairman of the 1st National College Foreign Language Textbooks Compilation and Review Committee, Xu Guozhang as Vice Chairman and Head of the English sub-committee, and Zhao Hui Vice Chairman and Head of the Russian sub-committee. In April 1982, the inaugural meeting for the China-German Language Education Association was held in Hangzhou, at which Zhu Yan was elected President; in May of the same year, the inaugural meeting for the China-English Language Education Association was held in Kunming, at which Wang Zuoliang was elected President. In 1986, the State Education Commission appointed Wang Zuoliang as Chairman of the 2nd National College Foreign Language Textbooks Compilation and Review Committee; Wang Fuxiang, Xu Guozhang and Hu Wenzhong as Vice Chairmen; Hu Wenzhong concurrently as Head of the English sub-committee, Wang Fuxiang concurrently as Head of the Russian sub-committee, Dong Yansheng as Head of the Spanish sub-committee, and Yu Zhangrong as Head of the Arabic sub-committee. The English, French, German, Russian, Spanish textbooks compiled by the Institute and designed for the foundation stage of college foreign language teaching were recommended to all institutions of higher education in China.

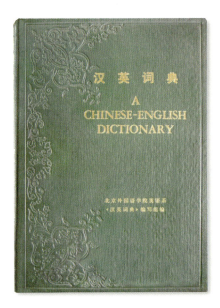

▌20世纪70年代末和80年代初我校教师编纂的部分词典

Dictionaries complied by faculty members during the late 70's and early 80's of the 20th century

　　我校承担了国家出版局交付的十八部外语词典编写任务。1978年出版的《汉英词典》是一部中型外语工具书，收汉语单字条目六千多，多字条目五万多，不但为国内广泛使用，而且很快为英、美、日等国以及中国香港地区所翻印，得到国内外学者的好评。1982年新的中型《西汉词典》问世，《汉德词典》《罗汉词典》《捷汉词典》《波汉词典》《保汉词典》《匈汉词典》等陆续发行。

The Institute undertook to compile 18 foreign language dictionaries commissioned by the State Publication Bureau. *A Chinese-English Dictionary* published in 1978 was a medium-sized dictionary containing over 6,000 Chinese head characters and over 50,000 Chinese headwords. It was not only used extensively within China, but also quickly reprinted in the UK, the USA, Japan and Hong Kong of China, receiving favourable reviews at home and abroad. 1982 saw the publication of the medium-sized *A Spanish-Chinese Dictionary*, which was followed by *A Chinese-German Dictionary*, *A Romanian-Chinese Dictionary*, *A Czech-Chinese Dictionary*, *A Polish-Chinese Dictionary*, *A Bulgarian-Chinese Dictionary*, and *A Hungarian-Chinese Dictionary*.

■ 许国璋教授在《英语学习》征文评比会上讲话。

Professor Xu Guozhang speaking at a jury meeting of *English Language Learning*'s essay writing competition

1. 《外国文学》创刊号

2. 1979 年创刊的《德语学习》是中国第一本德语辅导刊物。

3. 1980 年创刊的《法语学习》是中国第一本法语辅导刊物。

1. The first issue of *Foreign Literature*

2. *German Language Learning*, launched in 1979, is the first German language tutorial magazine in China.

3. *French Language Learning*, launched in 1980, is the first French Language tutorial magazine in China.

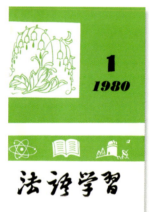

1

2

3

　　1979 年，成立"外语教学与研究出版社"，主要出版各类外语图书，并负责出版《外语教学与研究》《外国文学》《苏联文艺》《英语学习》《法语学习》《德语学习》《课外学习》等刊物。东欧语系和亚非语系 1982 年先后出版了内部发行的《东欧》和《亚非》两个不定期的学术刊物。这些刊物对于推动学校科学研究的发展和繁荣外语教育事业，发挥了重要的作用，得到社会读者和专家的好评。

　　In 1979 Foreign Language Teaching and Research Press was founded, mainly publishing foreign language books and journals such as *Foreign Language Teaching and Research*, *Foreign Literature*, *Arts and Literature of the Soviet Union*, *English Language Learning*, *French Language Learning*, *German Language Learning*, *Extracurricular Learning*. In 1982 Department of Eastern European Languages and the Department of Asian and African Languages published two irregularly issued and internally circulated academic journals — *Eastern Europe* and *Asia and Africa*. These journals have played an important role in promoting the academic research of the Institute and the prosperity of foreign language teaching, and have won a high regard from the public and the academic world.

《北京外国语学院 1983 年科学报告会论文集》

Proceedings of Beijing Foreign Languages Institute's Academic Conference in 1983

王佐良教授在外国文学研究所、英语系举办的"英美文学讲座"上作学术报告。

Professor Wang Zuoliang giving an academic lecture as a part of Lectures on British and American Literature jointly organised by the Research Institute of Foreign Literature and the English Department

1983 年 5 月，我校举行全院科学报告会。这是继 1956 年和 1960 年以后的第三次全校性科研活动。在此之前，各系及教研室分别举行了各自的报告会。全校科学报告会包括大会和 12 个分组会，共提出 70 篇学术报告。会后汇集出版了《北京外国语学院 1983 年科学报告会论文集》（上、下两册），共收入论文 56 篇，另外 14 篇论文分别发表在全国性学术刊物上。

In May 1983 the Institute held an institute-wide academic conference, which was the third of its kind after two previous conferences held in 1956 and 1960. Before that each department and its divisions had held their own academic conferences. The conference of the Institute was divided into 12 sessions, with 70 academic papers presented. After the conference, 56 of the papers were included in the *Proceedings of Beijing Foreign Languages Institute's Academic Conference in 1983* (two volumes), the other 14 papers were published in national academic journals.

1984

1984 年 3 月，经教育部批准，成立"外国语言研究所"和"外国文学研究所"，分别由许国璋教授和王佐良教授担任所长。1989 年 5 月，成立"国际关系与世界文化研究所"，1992 年更名为"国际问题研究所"。

With the approval of the Ministry of Education in March 1984, the Research Institute of Foreign Languages and the Research Institute of Foreign Literature were established, with Professor Xu Guozhang and Professor Wang Zuoliang serving as the respective directors of the two research institutes. In May 1989, the Research Institute of International Relations and World Cultures was created; in 1992 it was renamed Research Institute of International Issues.

1

2

1. 学员上同声传译课。

2. 学员在译员厢内实习。

3. 联合国译员训练班开学典礼合影

4. 学员仕练习听力。

3

1984

1. Trainees taking a simultaneous interpreting class

2. Trainees practising in the interpreters' box

3. A photo taken at the opening ceremony of the UN Interpreter and Translator Training Course

4. Trainee taking a listening exercise class

1979 年 3 月，经国务院批准，我校接受联合国总部委托，为联合国开办同声传译和笔译人员训练班，学制两年，并于同年 9 月开学。英语系副主任张载梁任主任。1984 年，译员训练班改为联合国译员训练部。这是联合国继莫斯科、内罗毕之后在世界上开设的第三个译员培训基地。此后从中国派往纽约、巴黎、日内瓦等地联合国机构担任笔译和同声传译的人员全部出自我校。联合国译员训练部共招收了 12 期学员，共计 227 人，到 1993 年停止招生。

In March 1979, with the approval of the State Council and at the request of the United Nations, the Institute agreed to run a two-year Interpreter and Translator Training Course for the UN. The course started in September of the same year, with Mr Zhang Zailiang from the English Department appointed as its Director. In 1984 the programme was officially named the United Nations Translators and Interpreters Programme, which was the third of such programme in the world after those in Moscow and Nairobi. After that, all the translators and simultaneous interpreters sent from China to the UN headquarters in New York and the other UN organisations in Paris and Geneva were from this Institute. Before it stopped admitting students in 1993, the UN Translators and Interpreters Programme had 12 intake of students, totalling 227 people.

6

8

7

9

5. 胡文仲在考试团最后报告上签字。

6. 联合国译员训练部举行考试团全体会议。

7. 1983 年，由联合国拨款 60 万美元修建的电化教学楼落成，楼内装备了当时先进的同声传译设备和视听设备，为联合国译员训练部及全校的外语教学提供了良好的条件。

8. 联合国译员训练部教学使用的联合国文件

9. 联合国译员训练部教学使用的联合国会议录音带

5. Hu Wenzhong signing his name on the final report of the board of examiners

6. The UN Translators and Interpreters Programme holding its plenary meeting of the board of examiners

7. In 1983 the audio-visual teaching building built with a 600,000 US dollars grant from the United Nations was completed, equipped with highly advanced audio-visual equipment and facilities for simultaneous interpreting, providing excellent conditions for foreign language teaching and learning for the whole institute, as well for the UN Translators and Interpreters Programme. The photo above shows the audio-visual teaching building.

8. The UN documents used by the UN Translators and Interpreters Programme

9. The conference recording tapes used by the UN Translators and Interpreters Programme

■ 1978 年陈琳和吴青主讲电视英语节目，图为录制现场
（原载于 1978 年第四期英文版《中国建设》）。

Chen Lin and Wu Qing in front of TV camera for an English
language teaching programme (Picture featured in the April 1978
edition of *China Reconstructs*)

■ 英文报纸《中国日报》对胡文仲的报道

A report about Hu Wenzhong in the English
language newspaper *China Daily*

　　中共十一届三中全会之后，国家急需大量外语人才。在校大、中学生及社会各界人士对学习外语有极高的热情和强烈的需求。20 世纪 80 年代初，我校参加了电视大学的英语教学，由陈琳主要负责，并主编电视英语课本。1982 年，胡文仲与英语专家 Kathy Flower 一起主持了中央电视台的《跟我学》（*Follow Me*）英语教学节目。1984 年 11 月，按照中法文化协定，中央电视台开办了《法语入门》教学节目，由我校庄元泳主讲。1981 年，经国务院批准，在全国高等教育自学考试委员会下设英语专业委员会，许国璋任主任委员。1983 年 6 月，我校开办了夜大，学制三年，开设的课程有英语、俄语、法语、德语、日语、西班牙语、阿拉伯语。1984 年 10 月，我校开办了函授部，语种设有英语、俄语、法语、德语、日语、阿拉伯语等。电视外语教学和夜大、函授部的开办，为普及外语教育发挥了重要作用。1985 年，我校成立出国人员培训部，主要承担国家教委公派出国人员出国前的外语短期强化培训任务。1992 年 3 月，我校成立成人教育学院，陈琳任院长。

After the Third Plenary Session of the CPC's 11th Central Committee, China needed large numbers of people who were proficient in foreign languages. There was extraordinary enthusiasm in and a strong demand for learning foreign languages among middle school and college students as well as the public. Starting from the early 1980s, the Institute was involved in the English language teaching programmes of the China Central Radio and TV University. Mr Chen Lin was appointed Chief Editor in charge of compiling TV English textbooks. In 1982 Hu Wenzhong and Kathy Flower, an English expert, presented the English learning programme *Follow Me* on China Central Television. In November 1984, in accordance with a cultural agreement between China and France, the China Central Television started the French learning programme *Entrée libre*, which was presented by Zhuang Yuanyong from the Institute. In 1981, with the approval of the State Council, the English Language Board was set up under the National Higher Education Self-Teaching Examination Committee, with Xu Guozhang appointed as its Chairman. In June 1983, the Institute started its Night University, offering three-year programmes in English, Russian, French, German, Japanese, Spanish, and Arabic. In October 1984, the Institute set up its Division of Teaching by Correspondence, offering courses in English, Russian, French, German, Japanese, and Arabic. The foreign language teaching offered by the China Central Radio and TV University, Night University, and the Division of Teaching by Correspondence played an important role in the spread of foreign language education. In 1985, the Institute set up its Division of Foreign Language Training for Studying Abroad, undertaking the task of providing short-term intensive foreign language training for people sent by the State Education Commission to study abroad. In 1992 the School of Adult Education was set up, with Chen Lin appointed as the Dean.

1

2

3

4

5

1. 胡文仲与英语专家 Kathy Flower 在演播室录制英语教学节目《跟我学》（ *Follow Me* ）。

2. 庄元泳和法语专家在录制电视法语教学节目《法语入门》。

3. 英语二系楼光庆为中国电视师范学院录制高级英语语法讲座。

4. 英语系教师李宪生在录制广播英语。

5. 陈琳主持北京高等院校成人教育国际研讨会。

1. Hu Wenzhong and the English language expert Kathy Flower recording the programme *Follow Me* in the studio

2. Zhuang Yuanyong and a French language expert recording the programme *Entrée libre*

3. Lou Guangqing recording an Advanced English Grammar lecture series for the Chinese Television Teacher Training College

4. Li Xiansheng, a teacher from the English Department recording an English radio programme

5. Chen Lin presiding over the 1989 Beijing Symposium on Adult Education at College

1

2

3

1. 1982 年，捷克斯洛伐克对外友协主席接见我校
   《捷汉词典》编辑组成员。

2. 1984 年，王福祥院长和来访的海德堡大学校际协
   作代表签署交流协议。

3. 1986 年 9 月 1 日，授予海德堡大学迪特拉夫教授
   （右三）北京外国语学院荣誉教授称号。

1. In 1982, Chairman of the Czechoslovaki-
   an Association of Friendship with Foreign
   Countries meeting with members of the
   lexicography group of *A Czech-Chinese
   Dictionary*

2. In 1984, Institute President Wang
   Fuxiang signing an exchange agreement
   with an officer from the University of
   Heidelberg on international collaboration

3. On 1st September 1986, Professor
   Diether Raff (3rd from right) from the
   University of Heidelberg was awarded
   the title of Honorary Professor of Beijing
   Foreign Languages Institute.

　　自 20 世纪 80 年代初，国家实行改革开放政策以来，北京外国语学院得风气之先，积极开展国际文化交流活动，提升学校影响力、办学水平和国际化水平。学校和国际上一批大学建立了校际交流关系，邀请外国学者来校任教或研究、讲学，派出我校学者出访交流；学校还举办国际学术会议，接受留学生来校学习，接待外国政要及政府有关代表团来访。

　　In the early 1980s, China implemented reform and opened its door to the outside world. Beijing Foreign Languages Institute took the initiative to carry out international cultural exchange, thereby enhancing its international reputation, quality of teaching and the level of internationalisation. The Institute established inter-institutional relations with a large number of universities abroad; invited scholars from abroad to teach, do research or give public lectures at the Institute; sent its own staff abroad for academic visit; held international academic conferences; accepted overseas students to the Institute; and received foreign dignitaries and government delegations visiting China.

4

5

6

7

4. 1986 年王福祥院长与华沙大学校长签订两校合作协议。

5. 1987 年与阿盟教科文委员会签订文化交流协议书。

6. 1987 年刘政权副院长与约旦雅尔穆克大学副校长签订两校 1987—1989 年执行协议书。

7. 1987 年苏联教育代表团来访。

4. Institute President Wang Fuxiang signing a collaboration agreement with the President of the University of Warsaw in 1986.

5. An agreement on cultural exchange was signed between the Institute and the Arab League Educational, Scientific and Cultural Organisation in 1987.

6. Vice President Liu Zhengquan and Vice President of Yarmouk University of Jordan signing an agreement between the two universities for implementation between 1987-1989 in 1987

7. A Soviet Union educational delegation visiting the Institute in 1987

▌ 1985 年 9 月，经中日两国政府决定，由北京外国语学院和日本国际交流基金共同承办的北京日本学研究中心成立，李德任主任。图为参加北京日本学研究中心成立典礼人员合影。

In September 1985, as a result of a bilateral agreement between the Chinese and Japanese governments, the Beijing Japanese Studies Centre was established by the Institute together with the Japanese International Exchange Fund, with Li De as Director. The photo is attendees at the opening ceremony.

1

2

1. 1986 年 5 月，澳大利亚总理罗伯特·霍克来我校访问，王福祥院长陪同参观校园。

2. 1986 年 11 月，民主德国人民议院议长辛德曼（左二）访问我校并赠书。

1. In May 1986, Australian Prime Minister Robert visited the Institute. Institute President Wang Fuxiang accompanied the Prime Minister on a tour of the campus.

2. In November 1986, the leader of the House of Representatives for the Germen Democratic Republic (2nd from left) visited the Institute and donated some books.

3

4

5

3. 1987年10月，第七届国际俄语杂志编辑会议在我校举行，图为院长王福祥教授在开幕式上讲话。

4. 1989年国际俄罗斯语言文学教师联合会执委会议在我校召开，来自12个国家的25位代表出席会议。左三为苏联科学院院士尼古拉耶夫。

5. 1990年11月，阿联酋总统扎耶德·本·苏尔坦·阿勒纳哈扬向我校阿拉伯语系赠款仪式。赠款数额为661,000美元，用于建造阿拉伯语教学楼。阿联酋驻华使馆临时代办艾哈迈德·侯赛因、我国外交部副部长杨福昌出席仪式。

3. In October 1987, the 7th International Conference for Editors of Russian Language Journals was held at the Institute. Institute President Prof. Wang Fuxiang speaks at the opening ceremony.

4. In 1989, the International Russian Language and Literature Teachers' Conference was held at the Institute, attended by 25 representatives from 12 countries. Third from the left in the photo is Nicolev, Fellow of Soviet Academy of Science.

5. In November 1990, ceremony to mark a donation to the Institute's Arabic Department by the President of United Arab Emirates Zayedbin Sultan AlNahyan. The donation of 661,000 US dollars was used for the construction of the Arabic Teaching Building. The Embassy of UAE to China and Deputy Minister of Foreign Affairs Yang Fuchang attended the ceremony.

第八章

深化改革　追求卓越

（1994—2014年）

Chapter Eight
Deepening the reforms and striving for excellence
(1994-2014)

　　1994 年 2 月，经国家教委批准，北京外国语学院更名为北京外国语大学。自 1994 年至 2014 年，学校坚持"外、特、精"的办学理念，以建设国际一流、特色鲜明的外国语大学为办学目标，以培养高层次国际化人才、研究和传播中外优秀文化、探索新知、推动世界文明多样性发展为办学宗旨。"深化改革，追求卓越"成为这一时期学校发展的主旋律。

　　In February 1994, with the approval of the State Education Commission, Beijing Foreign Languages Institute was renamed Beijing Foreign Studies University. From 1994 to 2014, with "Striving to be strong in foreign languages, unique in characteristics, and high in standards" as its guideline, the University set out to build itself into an internationally recognised first-class university with distinct characteristics. It aimed to cultivate high-calibre international professionals, study and propagate the cultures of China and other countries, explore new horizons of knowledge, and promote the diversified development of civilisations around the world. Deepening reforms and striving for excellence became the development theme for the University during this period.

1994 年至 2014 年期间任职的主要党政领导

（其间王福祥任校长至 1997 年 2 月，曹小先任党委书记至 1996 年 5 月）

The Secretaries of CPC Committee and the Presidents of the University from 1994 to 2014

(During this period Wang Fuxiang's presidency lasted until February 1997, and Cao Xiaoxian's tenure as Party Secretary lasted until May 1996)

陈乃芳

1940 年生，江苏南通人，毕业于北京外国语学院英语系，教授。中共十六大代表，第九、十届全国政协委员。1996 年 5 月至 2002 年 7 月任校党委书记兼校长，2002 年 7 月至 2005 年 6 月任校长。

Chen Naifang, professor, born in Nantong, Jiangsu in 1940, graduated from the English Department of Beijing Foreign Languages Institute. She was a delegate to the CPC's 16th Congress, and a member of National Committee of the 9th and 10th Chinese People's Political Consultative Conference; Secretary of the CPC Committee of BFSU and President from May 1996 to July 2002, President from July 2002 to June 2005.

杨学义

1951 年生，河北三河人，毕业于北京外国语学院英语系，教授。曾任副校长、校党委副书记。第十二届全国政协委员。2002 年 7 月至 2014 年 2 月任校党委书记。

Yang Xueyi, professor, born in Sanhe, Hebei in 1951, graduated from the English Department of Beijing Foreign Languages Institute. He served as Vice President and Deputy Secretary of the CPC Committee of BFSU, and was a member of National Committee of the 12th Chinese People's Political Consultative Conference. He was Secretary of the CPC Committee of BFSU from July 2002 to February 2014.

郝 平

1959 年生，山东青岛人，毕业于北京大学，法学博士，教授。曾任北京大学副校长。2005 年 6 月至 2009 年 4 月任北京外国语大学校长。2009 年 4 月任教育部副部长（兼任北京外国语大学校长至 2010 年 3 月）。

Hao Ping, professor, born in Qingdao, Shandong in 1959, graduated from Peking University. He served as Vice President of Peking University before being appointed as President of Beijing Foreign Studies University in June 2005. He served in this post until April 2009, when he was appointed Deputy Minister of Education, but he retained the presidency until March 2010.

陈雨露

1966 年生，河北藁城人，毕业于中国人民大学，经济学博士，教授。曾任中国人民大学副校长。2010 年 3 月至 2012 年 8 月任北京外国语大学校长，2011 年 11 月调任中国人民大学校长。

Chen Yulu, PhD in Economics, professor, born in Gaocheng, Hebei in 1966, graduated from Renmin University of China. He was a Vice President of Renmin University before serving as President of Beijing Foreign Studies University between March 2010 and August 2012. He was appointed as President of Renmin University in November 2011.

韩 震

1958 年生，山东阳谷人，毕业于北京师范大学，哲学博士，教授。曾任北京师范大学副校长。2012 年 8 月至 2014 年 2 月任北京外国语大学校长，自 2014 年 2 月起任北京外国语大学党委书记。

Han Zhen, Doctor of Philosophy, professor, born in Yanggu, Shandong in 1958, graduated from Beijing Normal University. He was a Vice President of Beijing Normal University before serving as President of Beijing Foreign Studies University from August 2012 to February 2014. He has been Secretary of the CPC Committee of BFSU since February 2014.

彭 龙

1964 年生，安徽无为人，毕业于中国科学院系统科学研究所，理学博士，教授。2007 年 8 月至 2014 年 2 月任北京外国语大学副校长，自 2014 年 2 月起任北京外国语大学校长。

Peng Long, Doctor of Science, professor, born in Wuwei, Anhui in 1964, graduated from Institute of System Science, Chinese Academy of Sciences. He served as Vice President of Beijing Foreign Studies University from August 2007 to February 2014. He has been President of Beijing Foreign Studies University since February 2014.

1994

1994年2月，经国家教委批准，北京外国语学院更名为北京外国语大学。同年10月，国务院副总理李岚清来校视察，就我校的办学方针、培养目标、教学改革作了指示，指出："对北京外国语大学的培养方向是什么要进行研究。北外主要是培养外交、外贸人才，不能只靠外语，要加大内容，增加外交、外贸方面的知识，要培养复合型的人才。基础研究不能丢，但外语教学也要适应新形势的需要。"

2011年9月22日，中共中央政治局委员、国务委员刘延东在北京外国语大学70周年校庆期间，在教育部部长袁贵仁的陪同下来校视察，亲切看望师生员工。刘延东对北外建校70周年表示祝贺，她指出，北京外国语大学成立70年来，坚持贯彻党的教育方针，培养了大批高素质专门人才，为我国的外交事业做出了重要贡献。刘延东强调，要把提高质量作为高等教育改革发展的核心任务，还应科学合理定位，突出办学特色，弘扬优秀传统，创新教育模式，推动高等教育科学发展，为现代化建设提供强有力的人才和智力支撑。

After Beijing Foreign Languages Institute was renamed Beijing Foreign Studies University in February 1994, Vice-Premier Li Lanqing inspected the University in October of the same year. He gave a number of instructions concerning the University's management, the kind of graduates it should aim to educate, and the teaching reforms the University was carrying out. He pointed out: "It is necessary to study what the direction of development should be for Beijing Foreign Studies University. Your university should mainly cultivate talented professionals for international diplomacy and foreign trade. You can't depend on foreign languages alone. You should expand your academic horizon, increase your students' knowledge in international diplomacy and foreign trade, and turn them into graduates with more than one type of expertise. The basics should never be abandoned, but foreign language teaching should also adapt to new situations."

On 22nd September 2011, during the 70th anniversary of Beijing Foreign Studies University, Ms Liu Yandong, a member of the Politburo and a State Councillor, accompanied by Minister of Education Yuan Guiren, inspected the University and expressed her kind regards to the staff of the University. Liu congratulated BFSU on its 70th anniversary, pointing out that for 70 years after its founding, it had followed the CPC's educational guidelines, graduated a large number of highly qualified specialists and made important contributions to the diplomatic endeavours of the People's Republic. She stressed that the University should place enhancement of teaching quality at the core of its higher educational reform and development, orient itself scientifically, enhance its characteristics, carry forward its fine tradition, create new models of education, promote the scientific development of higher education and provide a continuous stream of human and intellectual resources for the nation's modernisation.

1996 年，在《北京外国语大学"211 工程"建设项目可行性研究报告》中，学校提出新的建设目标："从现在起到 2010 年，经 15 年的努力，将以教授外国语言为主的单科型大学建成一所多语种、多学科、多层次，培养复合型、复语型的高质量外语专门人才，具有重要国际影响的社会主义外国语大学。届时，学校将拥有一支以国内外知名学者为首的，以教授、副教授为主体的高水平学术梯队，建立起外语与外交、国际经贸、文学、语言学、法律、新闻等学科相复合的教学和科研体系，成为全国外语教学、科研、进修、信息和国际学术交流的中心，在办学模式、教学理论、教学方法、教材和工具书等建设方面为北京及全国提供高质量的成果。"同年，学校通过国家教委"211 工程"部门预审，成为国家重点建设的 100 所重点大学之一。

1. 1996 年 6 月 20 日，北京外国语大学"211 工程"部门预审会上，王福祥校长作汇报发言。

2. "211 工程"预审组专家参观校史展览。

1. President Wang Fuxiang reporting the progress the university has made at a preliminary review meeting of Beijing Foreign Studies University's "211 Project" held on 20th June 1996

2. The "211 Project" Review Panel visiting an exhibition of the history of the University

In "Report on the Feasibility Study of Beijing Foreign Studies University's '211(short for 21st century's 100 top universities) Project'" written in 1996, the new aim of the University's development was set as follows: "Through the next 15 years, from now until 2010, this single-disciplinary university that offers mainly foreign language teaching shall be transformed into an internationally renowned and socialist-oriented university that is not only multilingual but also multi-disciplinary and multi-level, able to cultivate multilingual high-qualified foreign language specialists with more than one type of expertise. By that time the University shall have a high-calibre team of academic staff led by internationally renowned scholars and composed mainly of professors and associate professors, have built up a teaching and research system that combines foreign languages with international relations, international trade, literature, linguistics, law, journalism, and have become a national centre for foreign language teaching, research, continuing education, information and international exchange, yielding high-quality results for Beijing and the whole nation in terms of university management, theories of teaching and learning, methods of teaching, and development of teaching materials and reference works." In the same year, the university successfully passed the review of the Department for the "211 Project" at the State Education Commission and became one of the 100 key universities granted priority funding.

3

4

5

3. 2001 年 6 月 14 日，"211 工程""九五"期间建设项目验收专家组来校进行项目验收。

4. 2002 年 10 月 17 日，陈乃芳校长在"十五""211 工程"建设可行性报告论证会上向专家组汇报。

5. 2006 年 6 月 21 日，教育部"十五""211 工程"验收专家组来校进行项目验收。

3. On 14th June 2001, the review board came to the University to assess the progress of the "211 Project" completed during the period of the ninth five-year plan.

4. At the meeting about the feasibility study of the University's "211 Project" of the 10th five-year plan period held on 17th October 2002, University President Chen Naifang made a report to the review board.

5. On 21st June 2006, leaders of the University introducing the University's campus planning to the review board assessing the University's "211 Project" during the 10th five-year plan period

2001 年国际商学院成立大会

The meeting marking the establishment of the School of International Business in 2001

为逐步实现改革的总体目标，学校调整、组建了一批教学机构。1994 年在联合国译员训练部的基础上组建了高级翻译学院。同年组建了国际经贸学院。1998 年将中文学院与国际交流学院合并，组成新的国际交流学院。1999 年建立外交系。2000 年，学校建立网络教育学院。2001 年，应用英语学院更名为大学英语部，英语系更名为英语学院，国际经贸学院更名为国际商学院。2006 年，西班牙语系更名为西班牙语葡萄牙语系，国际交流学院更名为中国语言文学学院，法律系和外交系从英语学院分离出来，成立法学院和国际关系学院。2007 年，亚非语系更名为亚非学院，欧洲语言系更名为欧洲语言文化学院，社会科学部更名为哲学社会科学学院。2008 年，在大学英语部与国际商学院的英语教学部的基础上，组建成立了专门用途英语学院，在原计算机中心的基础上，成立计算机系。2011 年成立艺术研究院。2014 年，在原英语学院国际新闻与传播系基础上成立国际新闻与传播学院，此外还成立了全球史研究院和国际教育集团／国际教育学院，哲学社会科学学院更名为马克思主义学院。2002 年，学校恢复、重建了 1984 年停办的北京外国语大学附属学校。

To realise the overall aim of the reform step by step, the University restructured the old faculties and departments and created a number of new ones. In 1994, the Graduate School of Translation and Interpretation was set up on the basis of the former UN Translators and Interpreters Programme; in the same year the School of International Business and Trade was established. In 1998 the School of Chinese and the Institute of International Exchange were merged to form a new Institute of International Exchange. In 1999 the Department of International Relations and Diplomacy was established. In 2000 the University set up its School of Online Education. In 2001 the School of Applied English Studies was renamed Division of Teaching English to Non-English-Major Students, the English Department was renamed School of English and International Studies, and the School of International Business and Trade was renamed School of International Business. In 2006, the Spanish Department was renamed Department of Spanish and Portuguese, the Institute of International Exchange was renamed School of Chinese Language and Literature, and the Department of Law and the Department of International Relations and Diplomacy separated from the School of English and International Studies and became School of Law and School of International Relations and Diplomacy respectively. In 2007, the Department of Asian and African Languages was renamed School of Asian and African Studies, the Department of European Languages was renamed School of European Languages and Cultures, and the Faculty of Social Sciences was renamed School of Philosophy and Social Sciences. In 2008, the School of English for Specific Purposes was formed on the basis of the former Division for Teaching English to Non-English-Major Students and the English Language Unit of the School of International Business; and the Computer Department was established on the basis of the former Computer Centre. In 2011 the Institute of Arts was created. In 2014, the School of International Journalism and Communication was established on the basis of the former Department of International Journalism and Communication, the Institute of Global History and School of International Education was created, and the School of Philosophy and Social Sciences was renamed School of Marxism. Additionally, in 2002 the University reopened Beijing Foreign Studies University Affiliated School, which was rebuilt on a new site.

北京外国语大学教学科研机构（至 2014 年）

Teaching and research institutions of BFSU (up to 2014)

◆ 英语学院	School of English and International Studies
◆ 俄语学院	School of Russian
◆ 欧洲语言文化学院	School of European Languages and Cultures
◆ 亚非学院	School of Asian and African Studies
◆ 高级翻译学院	Graduate School of Translation and Interpretation
◆ 中国语言文学学院	School of Chinese Language and Literature
◆ 国际商学院	International Business School
◆ 国际关系学院	School of International Relations and Diplomacy
◆ 法学院	School of Law
◆ 国际新闻与传播学院	School of International Journalism and Communication
◆ 马克思主义学院	School of Marxism
◆ 专门用途英语学院	School of English for Specific Purposes
◆ 网络与继续教育学院	School of Online and Continuing Education
◆ 日语系	Department of Japanese
◆ 德语系	Department of German
◆ 法语系	Department of French
◆ 西班牙语葡萄牙语系	Department of Spanish and Portuguese
◆ 阿拉伯语系	Department of Arabic
◆ 计算机系	Department of Computer Science
◆ 体育教研部	Unit of Physical Education

教育部人文社科重点研究基地	MOE key humanities and social sciences research centre
◆ 中国外语教育研究中心	National Research Centre for Foreign Language Education

教育部区域和国别研究培育基地	MOE probationary centre for regional and national studies
◆ 中东欧研究中心	Central and Eastern European Studies Centre
◆ 日本学研究中心	Japanese Studies Centre
◆ 英国研究中心	British Studies Centre
◆ 加拿大研究中心	Canadian Studies Centre

国家语委科研中心	State Language Commission research centre
◆ 国家语言能力发展研究中心	National Language Capacity and Development Research Centre

北京市哲学社会科学重点研究基地	Beijing key philosophy and social sciences research centre
◆ 北京对外文化交流与世界文化研究基地	Beijing Centre for the Study of International Cultural Exchanges and World Cultures

校级研究机构	University-level research units
◆ 北京日本学研究中心	Beijing Japanese Studies Centre
◆ 中国文化"走出去"协同创新中心	Centre for the Propagation of Chinese Culture through Collaborative Innovation
◆ 中国外语测评中心	China Foreign Language Assessment Centre
◆ 中国海外汉学研究中心	National Research Centre for Overseas Sinology
◆ 外国文学研究所	Institute of Foreign Literature
◆ 外国语言研究所	Institute of Linguistics and Foreign Languages
◆ 国际问题研究所	Institute of International Affairs
◆ 公共外交研究中心	Public Diplomacy Research Centre
◆ 联合国与国际组织研究中心	Centre for the Study of United Nations and International Organizations
◆ 中外廉政法制建设研究中心	Centre for the Studies of Clean Government and Legal System Development in China and Abroad
◆ 世界语言与文化研究中心	Centre for the Study of World Languages and Cultures
◆ 世界亚洲研究信息中心	Information Centre for Global Asian Studies
◆ 高等教育研究所	Institute of Higher Education
◆ 中外教育法研究中心	Centre for the Study of Education Law in China and Abroad
◆ 非洲语言与文化研究中心	Centre for the Study of African Languages and Cultures
◆ 北京外国语大学知识产权研究中心	Beijing Foreign Studies University International Property Rights Research Centre
◆ 艺术研究院	Institute of Arts
◆ 丝绸之路研究院	Institute of Silk Road Studies
◆ 全球史研究院	Institute of Global History

1. 2001年7月6日，钟美荪副校长在英语学院成立大会上讲话。

2. 2006年国际关系学院、法学院揭牌仪式

3. 2006年11月5日，国际关系学院教师与校领导及参加建院庆祝大会的来宾合影。

1. University Vice President Zhong Meisun speaking at the meeting marking the establishment of the School of English and International Studies on 6th July 2001

2. The unveiling ceremony of the School of International Relations and Diplomacy and the School of Law held in 2006

3. Teachers of the School of International Relations and Diplomacy photographed with leaders of the University and guests attending the meeting celebrating the establishment of the school on 5th November 2006

1. 2007 年亚非学院、诗琳通语言文化学院成立仪式（左二为泰国公主诗琳通）

2. 2007 年 9 月 21 日，我校举行欧洲语言文化学院成立大会。中国人民对外友好协会会长、中国欧盟协会会长陈昊苏（中）受聘为名誉院长。

3. 2007 年 9 月 27 日，我校举行哲学社会科学学院成立仪式，著名经济学家厉以宁（左二）受聘为名誉院长。

4. 2011 年 6 月 11 日，我校举行艺术研究院成立仪式。

1. Ceremony marking the establishment of the School of Asian and African Studies and the Sirindhorn School of Language and Culture in 2007, with Princess Maha Chakri Sirindhorn standing in the middle

2. On 21st September 2007, the University held a meeting celebrating the founding of the School of European Languages and Cultures, with Mr Chen Haosu, President of Chinese People's Association of Friendship with Foreign Countries and President of the China-EU Association, appointed as its honorary dean.

3. On 27th September 2007, the University held a ceremony marking the founding of the School of Philosophy and Social Sciences, with the well-known economist Li Yining appointed as its honorary dean.

4. The ceremony marking the founding of the Institute of Arts on 11th June 2011

5. 2014 年 5 月 23 日北京外国语大学附属苏州湾外国语学校奠基仪式

6. 2014 年 5 月 28 日，学校举行国际教育学院揭牌仪式。

7. 2014 年 7 月 7 日，我校举行国际新闻与传播学院揭牌仪式，原新华社副社长兼常务副总编辑马胜荣受聘为院长（从左至右：马胜荣、韩震、彭龙、许戈辉）。

8. 2014 年 12 月 10 日，全球史研究院成立。

5. Ceremony for laying the foundation for BFSU Affiliated Suzhou Bay Foreign Language School held on 23rd May 2014

6. The plaque unveiling ceremony was held for the University's School of International Education on 28th May 2014.

7. The unveiling ceremony of the University's School of International Journalism and Communication was held on 7th July 2014, with Mr Ma Shengrong, former Vice President and Executive Deputy Chief Editor of Xinhua News Agency appointed as Dean of the School (from left to right: Ma Shengrong, Han Zhen, Peng Long, and Xu Gehui, a BFSU alumnus and a well-known presenter at Phoenix TV).

8. Institute for Global History founded on 10th December 2014

▍博士学位授权点（一级学科）

Doctor's degree programmes (Academic disciplines of the first order)

外国语言文学	Foreign languages and literature

▍博士学位授权点（二级学科）

Doctor's degree programmes (Academic disciplines of the second order)

英语语言文学	English language and literature	欧洲语言文学	European languages and literature
俄语语言文学	Russian language and literature	亚非语言文学	Asian and African languages and literature
法语语言文学	French language and literature	外国语言学及应用语言学	Linguistics and applied linguistics (foreign languages)
德语语言文学	German language and literature	比较文学与跨文化研究	Comparative literature and cross-cultural studies
日语语言文学	Japanese language and literature	翻译学	Translation studies
西班牙语语言文学	Spanish language and literature	语言政策与规划学	Language policy and planning
阿拉伯语语言文学	Arabic language and literature		

▍国家重点学科

National key academic disciplines

英语语言文学	English language and literature	外国语言学及应用语言学	Linguistics and applied linguistics (foreign languages)
德语语言文学	German language and literature	日语语言文学（培育）	Japanese language and literature (probationary)

▍硕士专业学位授权点

Specialized Master's programmes

翻译硕士	Translation studies	金融硕士	Finance
汉语国际教育硕士	Teaching Chinese to students of other languages	国际商务硕士	International business

▍北京市重点学科

Key academic disciplines of Beijing

俄语语言文学	Russian language and literature	阿拉伯语语言文学	Arabic language and literature
法语语言文学	French language and literature	欧洲语言文学	European languages and literature
日语语言文学	Japanese language and literature	比较文学与跨文化研究	Comparative literature and cross-cultural studies
西班牙语语言文学	Spanish language and literature		

▍硕士学位授权点（一级学科）

Master's degree programmes (Academic disciplines of the first order)

外国语言文学	Foreign languages and literature	政治学	Political science
中国语言文学	Chinese language and literature	管理科学与工程	Management science and engineering
法学	Law	新闻传播学	Journalism and communication

▍硕士学位授权点（二级学科）

Master's degree programmes (Academic disciplines of the second order)

英语语言文学	English language and literature	比较文学与世界文学	Comparative literature and world literature
俄语语言文学	Russian language and literature	民商法学	Civil and commercial law
法语语言文学	French language and literature	国际法学	International law
德语语言文学	German language and literature	知识产权法	Intellectual property law
日语语言文学	Japanese language and literature	中外政治制度	Political systems in China and abroad
西班牙语语言文学	Spanish language and literature	科学社会主义与国际共产主义运动	Scientific socialism and international communist movement
阿拉伯语语言文学	Arabic language and literature	国际政治	International politics
欧洲语言文学	European languages and literature	国际关系	International relations
亚非语言文学	African languages and literature	外交学	Diplomacy
外国语言学及应用语言学	Linguistics and applied linguistics (foreign languages)	公共外交管理	Public diplomacy management
比较文学与跨文化研究	Comparative literature and cross-cultural studies	金融工程与风险管理	Financial engineering and risk management
翻译学	Translation studies	国际贸易与投资管理	International trade and investment management
语言政策与规划学	Language policy and planning	国际物流与供应链管理	International logistics and supply line management
语言学及应用语言学	Linguistics and applied linguistics (Chinese)	跨国经营与信息管理	Multinational business operation and information management
汉语言文字学	Chinese language and graphology	新闻学	Journalism
中国古代文学	Ancient Chinese literature	传播学	Communication

本科专业（至2014年）

阿尔巴尼亚语	拉脱维亚语	西班牙语
阿拉伯语	老挝语	希伯来语
阿姆哈拉语	立陶宛语	希腊语
爱尔兰语	罗马尼亚语	匈牙利语
爱沙尼亚语	马耳他语	意大利语
巴利语	马来语	印地语
保加利亚语	孟加拉语	印尼语
冰岛语	缅甸语	英语
波兰语	尼泊尔语	约鲁巴语
波斯语	挪威语	越南语
朝鲜语	普什图语	祖鲁语
丹麦语	葡萄牙语	
德语	日语	电子商务
俄语	瑞典语	法学
法语	塞尔维亚语	翻译
梵语	僧伽罗语	工商管理
菲律宾语	斯洛伐克语	国际经济与贸易
芬兰语	斯洛文尼亚语	汉语国际教育
哈萨克语	斯瓦希里语	汉语言文学
豪萨语	索马里语	计算机科学与技术
荷兰语	泰米尔语	金融学
吉尔吉斯语	泰语	会计学
加泰罗尼亚语	土耳其语	外交学
柬埔寨语	土库曼语	新闻学
捷克语	乌尔都语	信息管理与信息系统
克罗地亚语	乌克兰语	政治学与行政学
拉丁语	乌兹别克语	

Undergraduate programmes (by 2014)

Albanian	Japanese	Swedish
Amharic	Kazakh	Tamil
Arabic	Kirghiz	Thai
Bengali	Korean	Turkish
Bulgarian	Laotian	Turkmen
Burmese	Latin	Ukrainian
Cambodian	Latvian	Urdu
Catalan	Lithuanian	Uzbek
Croatian	Malay	Vietnamese
Czech	Maltese	Yoruba
Danish	Nepali	Zulu
English	Norwegian	
Estonian	Pali	Accounting
Dutch	Pashto	Business management
Filipino	Persian	Chinese language and literature
Finish	Polish	Computer science and technology
French	Portuguese	Diplomacy
German	Romanian	E-commerce
Greek	Russian	Finance
Hausa	Sanskrit	Information management & information system
Hebrew	Serbian	International economy and trade
Hindi	Sinhala	Journalism
Hungarian	Slovakian	Law
Icelandic	Slovenian	Politics and Administration
Indonesian	Somali	Teaching Chinese to speakers of other languages
Irish	Spanish	Translation
Italian	Swahili	

学校在逐步推进非外语类学科建设的同时，始终坚持巩固优势、强化特色的战略方针，不断加强外国语言文学学科建设：重点学科注重内涵发展，不断增强学科影响力和领先地位；优势学科不断提高教学科研水平，巩固优势；非通用语种特色学科主动并具有前瞻性地适应国家发展战略，不断扩大学科覆盖范围。全校学科布局更为均衡合理，协调发展，特色与优势更加突出。

While steadily pushing forward the development of academic disciplines other than foreign languages, the University has always followed the strategy of further consolidating its advantages and enhancing its characteristics in strengthening its position in the field of foreign languages and literature. For key national academic disciplines, the focus has been on intensive development by constantly strengthening its disciplinary influence and leadership position; for the University's characteristic academic disciplines, the emphasis has been on raising the standards of teaching and research and consolidating the University's advantage in such disciplines; and for minor languages, which also constitute one of the University's unique characteristics, the approach has been to take the initiative to adapt foresightedly to the nation's development strategy and continuously expand the coverage of this discipline. Now the disciplinary composition of the University is more balanced and logical, with all disciplines developing in a concerted manner and the characteristics and advantages of the University standing out more prominently.

1. 1997 年 6 月 20 日，马来语中心成立大会，国家教委主任朱开轩（右）讲话。
2. 马来西亚教育部部长纳吉布在成立大会上致辞。
3. 2000 年 11 月 3 日，陈乃芳校长与刘润清教授为教育部人文社科重点研究基地中国外语教育研究中心揭牌。

1. Mr Zhu Kaixuan, State Commissioner for Education, speaking at the meeting marking the establishment of the Malay Centre on 20th June 1997
2. Malaysian Minister of Education Najib Razak speaking at the meeting
3. University President Chen Naifang and Professor Liu Runqing unveiling the plaque for the National Research Centre for Foreign Language Education on 3rd November 2000. The Centre is one of the MOE's key humanities and social sciences research centres.

学校发挥自身优势，不断拓展学术研究领域，建立了一批研究机构，为学科建设提供了有力支撑，同时大大加强了与语言对象国之间的交流与合作。

The University has played to its advantages, constantly extended its field of academic research, and established a number of research institutions, which have provided strong support to the development of academic disciplines and also greatly strengthened the exchange and collaboration with countries whose languages are taught at the University.

4. 2001年5月18日，俄罗斯教育代表团出席俄语中心成立大会，俄罗斯教育部部长菲利波夫向中心赠送礼品。

5. 教育部专家组考察中国外语教育研究中心。

6. 2006年6月30日中国海外汉学研究中心成立大会

4. A Russian educational delegation attending the meeting marking the establishment of the Russian Centre on 18th May 2001. The photograph shows Mr Vladimir Filippov, Russian Minister of Education, presenting a gift to the centre.

5. An assessment panel from the MOE inspecting the National Research Centre for Foreign Language Education

6. The meeting marking the establishment of the National Research Centre for Overseas Sinology on 30th June 2006

1. 2006 年 6 月 10 日北京外国语大学德意志文化中心成立大会

2. 2011 年 12 月 9 日美国信息中心揭牌仪式

3. 2011 年 12 月 20 日，教育部副部长郝平和波兰来宾为欧语学院波兰研究中心揭牌。

1. The meeting marking the establishment of the Deutsche Cultural Centre at BFSU on 10th June 2006

2. The plaque unveiling ceremony for the American Information Centre on 9th December 2011

3. Vice Minister of Education Hao Ping and a distinguished Polish guest unveiling the plaque for the Polish Studies Centre at the School of European Languages and Cultures on 20th December 2011

4. 2012 年 3 月 23 日印度尼西亚中心揭牌仪式

5. 2014 年 9 月 29 日，我校举行中国外语测评中心成立大会暨中国外语人才评价标准高端论坛。

6. 2014 年 5 月 16 日中葡语言文化合作交流联合体成立仪式

4. The plaque unveiling ceremony for the Indonesian Centre on 23rd March 2012

5. On 29th September 2014, the University held a meeting marking the founding of the China Foreign Language Assessment Centre as well as a Forum on the Assessment of China's Foreign Language Talents

6. The inauguration ceremony of the Consortium for Cooperation and Exchange between Portuguese and Chinese Cultures and Languages

学校极其注重与国内外学术界的对话与交流。通过举办或承办各类学术会议或其他学术活动，推动我校乃至全国相关领域学术研究的活跃与繁荣，加强与国内外学术界的交往交流，不断提高学校影响力。

The University pays great attention to dialogues and exchanges between Chinese academics and their foreign counterparts. By holding or organizing various academic conferences or other academic activities and strengthening the interaction and exchange between its faculty and the academic world at home and abroad, it has led to an increase in academic research in the University and the whole country, and has enhanced the University's academic influence.

1. 1997 年 11 月 1 日，国际翻译学术研讨会在我校举行。

2. 1999 年 2 月 9 日《国际论坛》首发式暨国际问题研究座谈会

3. 1999 年 4 月 17 日，我校举办巴尔扎克诞辰二百周年纪念会，法国驻华大使毛磊先生在大会上讲话。

1. An international symposium on translation was held at the University on 1st November 1997.

2. The launch of *International Forum* and a symposium on international affairs was held on 9 February 1999.

3. French Ambassador Pierre Morel speaking at a meeting commemorating the 200th birthday of Balzac held at the University on 17th April 1999

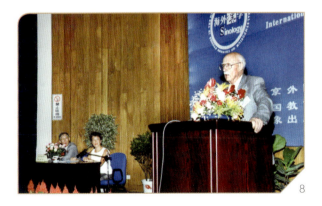

4. 1999年6月28日，第一届东方葡萄牙语言暨文化研讨会在我校举行。

5. 1999年7月16日第十八届庞德国际学术研讨会

6. 1999年9月11日，第十一届意大利文学研讨会，意大利驻华大使致辞。

7. 1999年11月11日，中国俄罗斯文学研究会20周年年会，俄罗斯驻华大使（左二）讲话。

8. 2001年9月6日，世界著名大学汉学系主任在国际学术研讨会上讲话。

4. The First Seminar on Portuguese Language and Culture in the East was held at the University on 28th June 1999.

5. The 18th International Conference on Ezra Pound held on 16th July 1999

6. The Italian Ambassador addressing the 11th Conference on Italian Literature held on 11th September 1999

7. The Russian Ambassador speaking at the annual meeting marking the 20th anniversary of the Chinese Society for the Study of Russian Literature held on 11th November 1999

8. International Seminar for Heads of Chinese Departments at World-famous Universities held on 6th September 2001

1. 2002 年 9 月 28 日，日本学研究中心国际学术研讨会在我校举行，教育部副部长章新胜致辞。

2. 2002 年 10 月 18 日，第五届全国国际商务英语研讨会在我校举行。

3. 2002 年 10 月 19 日，中国第九届当代语言学研讨会在我校举行。

4. 2004 年 5 月 22 日，第四届中国英语教学国际研讨会，胡文仲教授致辞。

5. 2005 年 12 月 2 日首届德语区汉学国际研讨会开幕式

1. Vice Minister of Education Zhang Xinsheng addressing an international conference held in the University's Japanese Studies Centre on 28th September 2002

2. The 5th National Conference on International Business English held at the University on 18th October 2002

3. The 9th National Symposium on Contemporary Linguistics held at the University on 19th October 2002

4. Professor Hu Wenzhong addressing the 4th International Conference on ELT in China held on 22nd May 2004

5. The opening ceremony of the 1st International Symposium on Sinology in German-Speaking Areas held on 2nd December 2005

6. 2006 年 5 月 22 日，张建华教授在
中俄作家论坛上演讲。

7. 2006 年 5 月 26 日，我校承办中
国—欧盟高等教育合作研讨会。

8. 2006 年 9 月 21 日 亚太地区外语教
育高端论坛

9. 2007 年 10 月 20 日日本学学术国
际研讨会

6. Professor Zhang Jianhua speaking at
a symposium of Chinese and Russian
writers on 22nd May 2006

7. The Seminar on EU-China Cooperation
on Higher Education was held at the
University on 26th May 2006.

8. The Asia-Pacific Region Foreign
Language Education Summit held on 21st
September 2006

9. An international conference on Japanese
studies held on 20th October 2007

1. 2008 年，美国著名华裔作家汤亭亭访问英语学院并做学术讲座。

2. 2008 年 10 月 31 日，全国外语院校 2008 年发展规划与高教研究工作研讨会在我校举行。

3. 2010 年，第七届亚洲西班牙语学者协会国际研讨会在我校举行。

4. 2011 年 8 月，我校主办第 16 届世界应用语言学大会。

1. Maxine Hong Kingston, a famous Chinese American author, visiting the School of English and International Studies and giving a public lecture in 2008

2. A symposium on the 2008 development plan for China's foreign language institutions of higher education and on research work at institutions of higher education held at the University on 31st October 2008

3. The 7th International Conference of the Association of Asian Scholars of Spanish was held at the University in 2010.

4. The 16th AILA (Association Internationale de Linguistique Appliquée) was held at the University in August 2011.

5. 文秋芳教授在世界应用语言学大会上演讲。

6. 2011年9月23日70周年校庆学者选集
   首发式

7. 2011年10月29日，彭龙教授在商学院
   院长论坛演讲。

8. 2011年12月1日纪念联合国前秘书长哈
   马舍尔德国际研讨会

5. Professor Wen Qiufang speaking at the
   AILA conference

6. The launch of selected works by the
   University's scholars marking the 70th
   anniversary of the University was held
   on 23rd September 2011.

7. Professor Peng Long speaking at the
   forum for business school deans on
   29th October 2011

8. An international conference was held on
   1st December 2011 to commemorate
   Dag Hammarskjöld, former Secretary
   General of the UN.

1. 2011 年 12 月 5 日，阿拉伯语系举办阿拉伯语国际研讨会。

2. 2011 年，高级翻译学院举办翻译教育发展国际研讨会。

3. 2012 年 10 月 18 日韩震教授《社会主义核心价值观五讲》新书首发式暨座谈会

4. 2012 年 12 月 1 日，我校主办中国非通用语教学研究会第七次代表大会。

1. An international conference was organized by the Department of Arabic on 5th December 2011.

2. An international conference on the development of translation education was held at the Graduate School of Translation and Interpretation in 2011.

3. The launch of *Five Lectures on the Core Values of Socialism* by Professor Han Zhen and a symposium about the book was held on 18th October 2012.

4. The 7th Congress of the Chinese Society for the Teaching of Less Widely Used Languages was held at the University on 1st December 2012.

5. 2012年12月1日，我校承办2012中欧语言
   合作研讨会，韩震校长在开幕式上致辞。

6. 中欧语言合作研讨会代表考察德语系课堂教学。

7. 2014年4月26日，我校法学院主办中国第三
   届比较法论坛"知识产权司法制度：比较与借鉴"
   学术研讨会。

8. 2014年5月17日，西葡语系举行纪念加西
   亚·马尔克斯研讨会。

5. University President Han Zhen addressing the 2012 EU-China Conference on Multilingualism
   held at the University on 1st December 2012

6. Participants of the 2012 EU-China Conference on Multilingualism observing classroom teaching
   at the Department of German

7. The 3rd National Comparative Law Forum on "Intellectual Property Rights Legislations: Compari-
   son and Mutual Learning" was held by the School of Law at the University on 26th April 2014.

8. The Department of Spanish and Portuguese holding a symposium commemorating Gabriel
   García Márquez on 17th May 2014

1

2

3

1. 1996 年 12 月 7 日，学校召开本科高年级课程体系改革研讨会。

2. 2005 年 11 月，学校召开 2005 年本科教学工作会议。

3. 2005 年本科教学工作会议分组讨论会会场

1. The University holding a seminar on reforming the syllabus for 3rd-year and 4th-year undergraduates on 7th December 1996

2. The University holding a meeting in November 2005 on undergraduate teaching for that year

3. A group session during the 2005 undergraduate teaching meeting

保持并不断提高教学质量，始终坚持培养高级外语人才和复合型人才，是北京外国语大学的优良传统，也是学校核心竞争力一个极其重要的方面。学校对提高教学质量常抓不懈，广大教师积极参与教学改革，为人才培养工作奠定了牢固基础。

It has always been a fine tradition to maintain and continuously raise teaching standards and persevere to cultivate highly qualified foreign language professionals and graduates with expertise in multiple disciplines, which also constitutes an extremely important element of the University's core competitive power. The University's close attention to enhancing teaching quality and its faculty's active participation in teaching reform have laid a solid foundation for high quality teaching.

4

4. 北京外国语大学2005年本科教学工作
   会议，教育部副部长章新胜及校党政领
   导与部分资深教授合影。

5. 2008年，我校以优秀的成绩通过教育
   部本科教学评估。

6. 2011年，我校举行日语本科教学国际
   学术研讨会。

7. 2012年6月21日，北京外国语大学
   研究生院成立。

8. 2014年2月18日增列硕士学位专业
   授权点专家评审会

5

6

8

7

4. Vice Minister of Education Zhang Xinsheng photographed with CPC leaders, presidents, and some senior professors of the University at the 2005 BFSU Undergraduate Teaching Meeting

5. The University passed the MOE undergraduate teaching assessment with excellent marks in 2008

6. The University holding an international conference on undergraduate teaching of Japanese in 2011

7. The School of Graduate Studies, BFSU, was established on 21st June 2012.

8. A meeting for reviewing the addition of new Master's degree programmes held on 18th February 2014

1. 20 世纪 90 年代英语系部分教授合影

2. 20 世纪 90 年代法语系部分教授合影

3. 20 世纪 90 年代阿拉伯语系部分教授合影

1. Some of the professors from Department of English photographed in the 1990s

2. Some of the professors from Department of French photographed in the 1990s

3. Some of the professors from Department of Arabic photographed in the 1990s

　　高素质、高水平的教师队伍是北京外国语大学最为宝贵的财富，也是培养优秀人才的最基本保障。各院系教师继承和发扬学校长期以来形成的优良学风，教学相长，为学校的改革发展和人才培养提供了保障与活力。

A high-calibre faculty is the University's most valuable asset, and also its best guarantee for producing outstanding talent. Teachers across the University have inherited and carried on the University's excellent scholarly traditions and have developed themselves academically while teaching, providing a solid basis for the University's future development and continuing excellence in teaching.

4. 20 世纪 90 年代德语系部分教授合影

5. 20 世纪 90 年代初俄语系部分教授合影

6. 20 世纪 90 年代初日语系部分教授合影

7. 20 世纪 90 年代东欧研究室成员、《东欧》
   季刊编委合影

8. 20 世纪 90 年代中期东欧语系部分教授合影

4. Some of the professors from Department of German photographed in the 1990s

5. Some of the professors from Department of Russian photographed in the early 1990s

6. Some of the professors from Department of Japanese photographed in the early 1990s

7. Members of the Eastern European Studies Group and editorial board members of *Eastern Europe* photographed together in the 1990s

8. Some of the professors from the Department of Eastern European Languages photographed in the mid 1990s

1. 20 世纪 90 年代英语系丁往道教授指导青年教师备课。

2. 20 世纪 90 年代英语系青年教师集体备课。

3. 20 世纪 90 年代阿拉伯语系教授在指导博士研究生。

4. 东欧语系青年教师进行硕士论文答辩。

1. Professor Ding Wangdao advising young teachers from the Department of English on how to prepare lessons in the 1990s

2. Young teachers from the Department of English preparing lessons collectively in the 1990s

3. Professors from the Department of Arabic supervising PhD students in the 1990s

4. A young teacher from the Department of Eastern European Languages during the viva voce on his MA thesis

5. 2008年，剑桥大学副校长艾莉森·理查德（左二）与我校三位剑桥博士陈国华（左一）、吴一安（左三）、金利民（左四）合影。

6. 东欧语系获得硕士学位的青年教师与导师合影。

7. 20世纪90年代社会科学部教师为本科生上公共课。

8. 20世纪90年代体育教研室全体教师参加统计课学习。

9. 2013年5月，德语系吴江（左三）在北京高校第八届青年教师教学基本功比赛中获文史类一等奖、最佳教案奖、最佳演示奖。

5. Cambridge University's Vice Chancellor Alison Richard (2nd left) photographed with Chen Guohua (first left), Wu Yi'an (3rd left) and Jin Limin (4th left) from BFSU, all three having received their PhD degrees from Cambridge

6. Young teachers from the Department of Eastern European Languages who have received their MA degrees photographed with their supervisors

7. A teacher from the Faculty of Social Sciences giving a lesson of a common required course to undergraduate students in the 1990s

8. All the teachers of the Physical Education Unit taking a lesson on Statistics in the 1990s

9. Ms Wu Jiang (3rd left) from the Department of German won First Prize in the Arts and History category, the Award for Best Teaching Plan, and the Award for Best Demonstration at the 8th Beijing Higher Education Basic Teaching Skills Competition for Young Teachers in May 2013

1. 2006 年罗马尼亚总统和我校罗马尼亚语专业师生合影。

2. 僧伽罗语专业学生赴斯里兰卡访问时与总统马欣达·拉贾帕克萨合影。

3. 马来语专业学生在马来西亚做田野调查。

4. 我校学生暑期赴美国加州大学伯克利分校学习。

1. Romanian President photographed with teachers and students of Department of Romanian from the University in 2006

2. Students of Sinhala photographed with Sri Lanka President Mahinda Rajapaksa when they visited Sri Lanka

3. Students of Malay doing fieldwork in Malaysia

4. Students of BFSU studying at UC Berkley during their summer break

学校利用与外国高校广泛的交流关系，派出学生到语言对象国学习交流，在学习语言文化的同时，增强对语言对象国的直接了解，增进相互间的友谊。

Through its extensive network of partnership universities, the University sends its students abroad so that they can gain firsthand knowledge of the countries whose languages they have been learning and build up friendship with the people there while learning their languages and cultures.

5. 僧伽罗语专业学生在斯里兰卡学习。

6. 豪萨语专业学生在尼日利亚学习。

7. 保加利亚语专业学生在保加利亚学习。

8. 冰岛语专业学生在冰岛学习。

5. Students of Sinhala studying in Sri Lanka

6. Students of Hausa studying in Nigeria

7. Students of Bulgarian studying in Bulgaria

8. Students of Icelandic studying in Iceland

1. 我校学生暑期赴英国剑桥大学学习。

2. 波斯语专业学生在伊朗学习。

3. 朝鲜语专业学生赴韩国交流。

4. 老挝语专业学生在老挝实习。

1. BFSU students studying at a summer school of Cambridge University

2. Students of Persian studying in Iran

3. Students of Korean studying in Republic of Korea on an exchange programme

4. Students of Laotian on an internship programme in Laos

5. 泰语专业学生在泰国学习。

6. 土耳其语专业学生在土耳其学习。

7. 乌尔都语专业学生在巴基斯坦学习。

8. 希伯来语专业学生在以色列学习。

9. 印尼语专业学生在印度尼西亚学习。

5. Students of Thai studying in Thailand

6. Students of Turkish studying in Turkey

7. Students of Urdu studying in Pakistan

8. Students of Hebrew studying in Israel

9. Students of Indonesian studying in Indonesia

1. 1994 年"五四"青年节校园节目主持人大赛获奖
   选手合影。

2. 1997 年 6 月,我校主办京沪粤港大学生迎香港回
   归英语演讲比赛。

3. 2004 年 5 月 16 日,阿拉伯语系举行阿拉伯语诗
   歌朗诵会,阿拉伯国家驻华使节在朗诵会上致辞。

4. 学生朗诵阿拉伯语诗歌。

1. Winners of the Campus Show Presenters Contest
   photographed at the May 4th Youth Festival in 1994

2. English Speech Contest of University Students from
   Beijing, Shanghai, Guangzhou and Hong Kong to
   Celebrate the Return of Hong Kong to China, held in June
   1997

3. A representative of the diplomatic missions of Arab
   countries addressing a poetry reading organized by the
   Department of Arabic on 16th May 2004

4. Students reading an Arabic poem

　　学校注重全面提高学生能力与素质。学生
通过参与各种校园文体活动及社会实践活动,
在丰富课余生活的同时,陶冶情操,培养社会
责任感及团队精神,开阔视野,锻炼能力,为
日后发展奠定坚实基础。

　　The University places great emphasis on the comprehensive improvement
of its students' abilities and personal qualities. Through various cultural activities
on campus and in the outside world, students have not only enriched their extracurricular life, but also refined their character and personality, cultivated a sense
of social responsibility and team spirit, broadened their field of vision, and tested
their abilities, thereby laying a solid foundation for their future development.

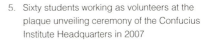

5. 2007年，我校60名学生承担孔子学院总部揭牌仪式志愿服务工作。

6. 2010年，由西葡语系、法语系、德语系5名学生组成我校第一批世博会志愿者。

7. 2013年3月26日，财政部前副部长、亚行副行长金立群校友来校演讲。

8. 我校志愿者参加2014年APEC工商领导人峰会服务工作。

5. Sixty students working as volunteers at the plaque unveiling ceremony of the Confucius Institute Headquarters in 2007

6. Five students from the University's Department of Spanish and Portuguese, Department of French and Department of German serving as the University's first group of volunteers at the World Expo in Shanghai in 2010

7. Mr Jin Liqun, an alumnus, former Deputy Minister of Finance and Deputy Governor of the Asian Development Bank giving a speech at the University on 26th March 2013

8. Volunteers from the University working at the APEC CEO Summit 2014

1. 2009 年，我校留学生申秀容（右三）在北京市教委举办的北京外国留学生"汉语之星"大赛中获奖。

2. 2010 年，我校承办全国高校俄语大赛。

3. 2010 年，马来西亚总理纳吉布向荣获国际马来语演讲比赛冠军的我校学生张颂颁奖。

4. 2011 年 9 月 29 日中欧青年辩论赛闭幕式

1. Mr Shen Xiurong (3rd from the right), an overseas student at the University, won a prize at the Beijing Chinese Star Contest for Overseas Students in 2009.

2. The National University Russian Contest was held at the University in 2010.

3. Malaysian Prime Minister Najib awarding a trophy to BFSU student Miss Zhang Song, champion of the International Malay Speech Contest in 2010

4. The closing ceremony of the EU-China Youth Debate Tournament on 29th September 2011

■ 学校 2006 年启动"歆语工程"，通过向偏远地区提供外语师资培训和支教服务，促进外语教育的均衡发展。2010 年 11 月，"歆语工程"荣获联合国教科文组织亚太地区"文晖教育创新奖"。图为"文晖教育创新奖"证书。

In 2006 the University launched its Xin Yu Project, which aimed to promote a balanced development of foreign language education by providing foreign language teacher training and teaching support to former revolutionary base areas, regions with ethnic groups or close to the frontier regions and poor areas. The project won the UNESCO APEID (Asia-Pacific Programme of Educational Innovation for Development) Wenhui Award for Educational Innovation in November 2011. The photo shows the Certificate for the award.

1. 参与"歆语工程"的湖南民族地区中小学英语教师
2. "歆语工程"赴新疆和田支教队
3. 学生志愿者在进行英语教学。

1. Primary and secondary school English teachers from Hunan ethnic groups' regions taking part in the Xin Yu Project
2. A teaching support unit of the Xin Yu Project working in Hetian, Xinjiang
3. Student volunteers doing English language teaching

2008 年，学校 2,765 名师生担任奥运会志愿者，1,054 人担任残奥会志愿者，分布在北京市的 46 个竞赛及非竞赛场馆，出色地完成了志愿服务任务。我校的北京奥运会多语言服务中心为奥林匹克大家庭、竞赛场馆、非竞赛场馆、训练场馆和服务场所通过电话翻译方式提供 10 个语种 24 小时值守热线、34 个语种 18 小时值守热线的语言服务。在北京残奥会期间，提供 9 个语种 24 小时电话值守热线，共完成电话翻译服务 3,000 余次，使北京奥运会成为历届奥运会提供语言服务种类最多最全的一届奥运会。

In 2008, 2,765 teachers and students from the University worked as Olympic volunteers, 1,054 worked as Paralympic volunteers. Assigned to 46 event and non-event venues, they did an outstanding job. Via telephone, the Beijing Olympic Multilingual Service Centre run by the University provided the Olympic Family, event venues, non-event venues, training venues, and service providers with round-the-clock hot-line translation service for 10 languages, and 18-hour hot-line translation service for 34 languages. During the Paralympic Games, the Centre offered round-the-clock hot-line service for 9 languages, providing telephone translation more than 3,000 times, making the Beijing Olympic Games the best Games in terms of the range of foreign language support on offer.

1. 2007 年奥运会志愿者演讲活动

2. 北京奥运会期间，我校学生冯宇则担任国际奥委会名誉主席萨马兰奇的陪同。

3. 北京奥运会期间，我校学生担任国际奥委会主席罗格的陪同。

4. 2008 年 6 月 4 日，我校举行 2007—2008 年度"奥运先锋"五四评优表彰大会。

1. BFSU students taking part in an Olympic volunteer public speaking activity in 2007

2. During the Beijing Games, Miss Feng Yuze, a student from the University, served as the facilitator for Mr Samaranch, Honorary President of the International Olympic Committee.

3. During the Beijing Games, another student from the University served as the facilitator for the IOC President Jacques Rogge.

4. The University's Commendation Ceremony for Olympic Pioneers for the year 2007-2008 held on 4th June 2008

5. 2004年5月23日，日本和泉流狂言二十世宗家来校演出。

6. 2007年5月第十届北京外国语大学日本文化节

7. 2009年，我校举办中俄大学生艺术联欢节。

5. The 20th soke of the Izumi School of Japanese Kyogen performing at the University on 23rd May 2004

6. The 10th BFSU Japanese Culture Festival in May 2007

7. The China-Russia University Arts Festival held at the University in 2009

1. 庆祝新中国与东欧国家建交 60 周年文艺晚会

2. 我校与科威特驻华使馆共同举办"科威特文化周之夜"。

1. Evening Gala celebrating the 60th anniversary of the establishment of diplomatic relations with Eastern European countries

2. The Kuwait Culture Night held jointly with the Kuwaiti Embassy to China

建校 70 周年文艺晚会

The University's 70th Anniversary Evening Gala

1996 年全体毕业研究生与部分导师合影

All the graduating research students photographed together with some of their supervisors in 1996

学校在人才培养方面坚持"保证质量，提高层次，控制规模，适度增长"的方针，在不断拓展学科领域的同时，拓宽人才培养口径，提高人才培养规格与层次，培养出了大批高级外语人才和具有扎实外语基础的复合型人才，为国家的改革开放事业和经济文化建设提供了优秀的人才资源。学校不断提高国际化办学水平，截至 2014 年，各类在校外国留学生数量达到 1,300 余人。

2013 年本科生毕业典礼暨学士学位授予仪式

The graduation and BA degree ceremony for students graduating in 2013

The University has always followed its guidelines of "assuring teaching quality, cultivating academic excellence, and growing at a controlled and modest pace". By continuously expanding its range of academic disciplines, it has increased the number of subjects the students can take, and raised their academic level and ability. The University has provided the country with a large number of high-qualified foreign language professionals and gifted interdisciplinary professionals with solid foreign language skills to help implement its reforms and economic and cultural development. The University is also becoming increasingly internationalised. In 2014 the total number of various overseas students studying at the University numbered over 1,300.

▌ 2010 届优秀本科毕业生合影

A group photo of outstanding students graduating with a Bachelor's degree in 2010

▌ 2012 年春季、夏季研究生毕业典礼暨学位授予仪式

The graduation and degree-awarding ceremony for research students graduating in the spring and summer of 2012

▌ 2013 年春季研究生毕业典礼暨学位授予仪式

The graduation and degree-awarding ceremony for research students graduating in the spring of 2013

1. 2013年本科生毕业典礼暨学士学位授予仪式，韩震校长为毕业生拨穗。
2. 2014年春季研究生毕业典礼暨学位授予仪式，彭龙校长为毕业生拨穗。

1. University President Han Zhen awarding BA degree certificates to students graduating in 2013
2. University President Peng Long awarding PhD and MA degree certificates to students graduating in 2014

▌2014届本科生毕业典礼

Graduation ceremony in 2014

　　校办产业是学校事业的一个重要组成部分。成立于 1979 年的外语教学与研究出版社（简称"外研社"），伴随着学校的改革发展而成长，为学校的教材及工具书建设提供了有力保障，为全国的外国语言文学研究者的学术成果提供了广阔的出版平台，为推动和普及我国的外语教育提供了全方位支持，为推动中外文化交流、传播中华文化发挥了积极作用。经过 30 余年的努力奋斗，外研社已发展成为一家拥有 2,500 名员工、10 大出版分社、13 个全资子公司和多个参股公司的综合性国际教育出版集团。自创建以来，外研社出版了 47 种语言的万余种图书，社长蔡剑峰于 2014 年荣获出版界最高荣誉——韬奋奖，并入选"中国十大出版人物"；外研社荣获"出版政府奖"，入选"首届首都文化企业三十强"。

The University-owned businesses are an important component of the University. Founded in 1979, the University's Foreign Language Teaching and Research Press (or FLTRP) has grown along with the reform and development of the University, providing not only firm guarantee for the University's development of teaching materials and reference books, but also a broad platform for scholars of foreign languages and literature of the whole nation to publish their academic works. It has also provided all-round support for promoting and popularizing China's foreign language education and has played a positive role in facilitating cultural exchanges between China and foreign countries and propagating Chinese culture in the world. After over 30 years of hard work, the Foreign Language Teaching and Research Press has grown into a comprehensive international education publisher, with 2,500 employees, 10 subsidiary publishing houses, 13 wholly-owned subsidiary companies and many joint stock companies. Since its founding, FLTRP has published over 10,000 titles of books in 47 languages. In 2014 its president Mr Cai Jianfeng won the Taofen Award, the highest honour in the world of publishing in China, and was named one of the Ten Major Publishers in China; FLTRP won the Government Award for Publishing and was named one of the first batch of Top 30 Cultural Enterprises in the capital.

1. 外研社创建之初的办公场所（左侧第二个楼房，楼前平房为库房）

2. 第一代社领导合影（左起姚金中、梁克家、林易、熊健、林学洪、靳平妥）

3. 1997 年，外研社大厦落成，社长李朋义致辞。

4. 2004 年外研社国际会议中心落成

1. The premises of FLTRP when it was founded (the 2nd building from left; the bungalow on its right was its storage unit)

2. First generation leaders of the publishing house (from left: Yao Jinzhong, Liang Kejia, Lin Yi, Xiong Jian, Lin Xuehong, Jin Pingtuo)

3. President Li Pengyi speaking at the ceremony marking the completion of the FLTRP Building in 1997

4. FLTRP International Conference Centre completed in 2004

■ 外研社出版的部分精品图书

Some of the best-selling academic books,
textbooks and dictionaries published by FLTRP

■ 外研社承办 AILA 2011（第 16 届世界应用语言学大会）

FLTRP hosting AILA 2011 (the 16th World Congress of Applied Linguistics)

　　近10余年来，外研社每年在全国各地举办免费教师培训活动、国际学术会议，累计培训大学英语教师10余万人次、中小学英语教师60余万人次，承办数百场学术会议，为语言教学改革和学术发展做出了贡献。

　　In the past ten years and more, FLTRP has been running free teacher-training programmes in all parts of China, providing training for over 100,000 university teachers and over 600,000 primary and secondary school English teachers; it has also sponsored or held hundreds of national and international academic conferences, making its contribution to language teaching reform and academic development.

1. 外研社连续 5 年承办"国培计划",并承接教育部"中小学英语教师培训课程标准研制"项目。

2. 外研社连续 16 年举办"全国高等大学英语教学研修班"。

3. 外研社举办第四届中国英语教学国际研讨会。

1. For five years in succession, FLTRP has hosted the National Teacher-Training Programme and has undertaken the MOE's project "the Development of Standards for Primary and Secondary School English Teachers Training Courses".

2. FLTRP has run National College English Teaching Workshops for 16 years in a row.

3. FLTRP holding the 4th International Conference on ELT in China

外研社连续 10 余年举办全国性大型公益赛事,覆盖上千所高校,成为数千万学子展示风采的舞台,并于 2013 年成立"外研文化教育基金",积极投身公益、回馈社会。

For over ten years, FLTRP has been holding large-scale public competitions and contests covering more than 1,000 institutions of higher education nationwide, providing a stage for millions of students to showcase their talents. It also set up the FLTRP Cultural and Educational Fund in 2013 to fund public service activities to contribute to society.

1997 年,首届外研杯英语辩论赛举行。

The 1st "FLTRP Cup" National English Debating Competition held in 1997

1. 2012年外研社杯全国英语演讲大赛

2. 2013年全国新概念英语技能大赛

3. 中国宋庆龄基金会外研文化教育基金成立

4. 外研社"助学筑梦"全国公益赠书活动

5. "我是书虫"阅读漂流活动吸引了数百所中小学学生参与。

1. The 2012 "FLTRP Cup" English Public Speaking Contest

2. 2013 New Concept English Ability Competition

3. China Soong Ching Ling Foundation FLTRP Cultural and Educational Fund created

4. FLTRP's "School Aid for Realizing a Dream", a national initiative to donate books to schools

5. "I am a bookworm", a reading competition attracting students from hundreds of primary and secondary schools

▍外研社杯全国大学生英语辩论赛，每年有千余所院校组织参与，是中国规模最大、水平最高的英语口语赛事。

The "FLTRP Cup" National English Debating Competition held every year, with participation from over 1,000 universities and colleges, is the largest and highest-level English speaking contest in China.

学校主动融入国家的改革开放和建设事业中，发挥自身优势，利用优质资源，为国家和北京市提供高水平服务，推动了我国外语教育事业的发展。与此同时，学校与社会各界加强联系，开拓资源渠道，积极争取社会力量参与办学，提高社会关注度，增强办学实力与活力。

The University has actively participated in the nation's reforms and social and economic development. It has been able to make full use of its advantages and utilise its high-quality resources to push forward the nation's foreign language education; at the same time, it does everything it can to strengthen its links with all sectors of society in order to find new sources of funding, encourage societal participation in the running of the University, improve its visibility in society, and increase its strengths and competitiveness.

1. 1999年至2003年，我校举办多期欧盟青年经理培训项目。

2. 2002年1月10日第一期部级干部英语培训试点班第二阶段开学仪式

3. 2003年9月17日，部级干部英语培训班结业典礼在我校举行。

4. 2006年11月21日，许戈辉校友设立奖助金签约仪式。

5. 2008年与国家外文局合作建立教学实习基地。

6. 2010年与中国日报社举行合作共建签字仪式。

7. 2013年8月30日，与北京师范大学签署战略合作协议。

1. The University ran the EU Junior Managers Training Programme from 1999 to 2003

2. The opening ceremony of Phase Two of the 1st English Training Pilot Class for Ministerial Cadres on 10th January 2002

3. The graduation ceremony of the English Training Programme for Ministerial Cadres held on 17th September 2003

4. Agreement signing ceremony marking the establishment of the Xu Gehui Scholarship and Student Grant on 21st November 2006. Ms Xu, the benefactor, is an alumnus of the University.

5. Establishing a work experience base for students of the University in collaboration with China Foreign Language Bureau in 2008

6. Agreement signing ceremony marking the University's collaboration with China Daily in 2010

7. BFSU and Beijing Normal University signing a strategic collaboration agreement on 30th August 2013

1. 2014年3月28日，与中国电力国际有限公司签订战略合作框架协议。

2. 2014年4月25日，与中国电信集团签订战略合作框架协议。

3. 2014年5月19日，北京外国语大学中晨欧洲语种群和亚非语种群教育发展基金捐赠暨董事会聘任仪式。

4. 2014年5月22日，鞍山中奥投资有限公司捐赠暨董事会聘任仪式。

5. 2014年5月28日，天昊师资队伍培养和人才引进教育发展基金捐赠暨董事会聘任仪式。

1. BFSU and China Power International signing a strategic collaboration framework agreement on 28th March 2004

2. BFSU and China Telecom Group signing a strategic collaboration framework agreement on 25th April 2014

3. Ceremony marking a donation to the BFSU Sinorise European Languages and Asian and African Languages Educational Development Fund and the appointment of its Board of Directors on 19th May 2014

4. Ceremony marking the donation made by Anshan Zhong'ao Investment Company Ltd and the appointment of Board of Directors on 22nd May 2014

5. Ceremony marking a donation to the Tianhao Educational Development Fund for Teacher Education, Development and Introduction, and the appointment of its Board of Directors on 28th May 2014

6. 2014年6月5日，与上海外国语大学签署合作协议。

7. 2014年7月7日，与首都师范大学签署战略合作协议。

8. 2014年10月24日，中富展望丝绸之路研究基金捐赠暨董事会聘任仪式。

9. 2014年10月30日，合生珠江教育发展基金捐赠暨框架合作协议签署仪式。

6. BFSU and Shanghai University of International Studies signing a collaboration agreement on 5th June 2014

7. BFSU and Capital Normal University signing a strategic collaboration agreement on 7th July 2014

8. Ceremony marking a donation to the Prospect Silk Road Studies Fund and the appointment of its Board of Directors on 24th October 2014

9. Ceremony marking a donation to Hopson Zhujiang Educational Development Fund and the signing of a framework collaboration agreement on 30th October 2014

1996 年 5 月 15 日，学校召开第六次党员代表大会，曹小先作题为《团结进取，扎实工作，为把我校建成具有重要国际影响的社会主义外国语大学而奋斗》的报告。图为大会选举新一届党委会。

The 6th BFSU CPC Congress was held on 15th May 1996, during which Cao Xiaoxian made a report entitled "Unite to make progress, work in a practical manner, and strive to build the University into a socialist foreign language university with significant international influence". The photo shows delegates electing a new party committee.

2002 年 7 月，中国共产党北京外国语大学第七次党员代表大会召开，党委书记陈乃芳代表第六届党委作题为《解放思想，实事求是，与时俱进，扎实工作，全面推进学校在新世纪的改革与发展》的工作报告。

The 7th BFSU CPC Congress was held in July 2002. On behalf of the 6th Party Committee, Secretary Chen Naifang made a report entitled "Liberate our thinking, seek truth from facts, keep abreast with the times, work in a practical manner, so as to comprehensively push forward the reform and development of the University in the new century".

学校在办学过程中始终坚定执行党的教育方针，坚持党委对办学方向和大政方针的把握，长期注重加强党组织建设和思想政治工作，使学校的改革发展和人才培养工作得到了有力保障。

In running the University, the University's leadership has always followed the CPC's education guidelines, upheld the BFSU CPC Committee's guidance on the University's future and its fundamental policies, and strengthened the Party's presence and its ideological and political work in the University, ensuring that the University's reforms, its development and its teaching activities receive sufficient support.

中国共产党北京外国语大学第六届党委常委名单（按姓氏笔画为序）

List of members of the Standing Committee of the 6th BFSU CPC Committee

申春生　何其莘　杨学义　陈乃芳
金传豪　钟美荪　裴玉芳

Shen Chunsheng, He Qixin, Yang Xueyi, Chen Naifang, Jin Chuanhao, Zhong Meisun, Pei Yufang

党委书记	党委副书记
Committee Secretary	Deputy Secretaries
陈乃芳	杨学义　裴玉芳
Chen Naifang	Yang Xueyi, Pei Yufang

中国共产党北京外国语大学第七届党委
常委名单（按姓氏笔画为序）

List of members of the Standing Committee of the 7th
BFSU CPC Committee

何其莘　杨学义　陈乃芳
周　烈　钟美荪　曹文泽

He Qixin, Yang Xueyi, Chen Naifang,
Zhou Lie, Zhong Meisun, Cao Wenze,

党委书记	党委副书记
Committee Secretary	Deputy Secretary
杨学义	曹文泽
Yang Xueyi	Cao Wenze

1. 2007 年 9 月 18 日，北京市委教工委党建和思想政治
   工作评估专家组莅临我校，就我校的党建和思想政治工
   作进行检查指导。

2. 专家组走访日语系，了解基层党组织建设情况。

3. 2010 年 10 月，北京市党的建设和思想政治工作先进
   普通高等学校评选专家组到校，对学校党建和思想政治
   工作进行全面检查评估。图为考察组走访亚非学院。

4. 2010 年，我校荣获北京市党的建设和思想政治工作先
   进高等学校称号。

1. A review board from the Educational Work Commission of the
   CPC Beijing Municipal Committee reviewing the University's
   organisational, ideological and political work of the Party on 18th
   September 2007

2. The review board holding a hearing at the Japanese Department
   about the Party's work at the grass roots level

3. A panel from the CPC Beijing Municipal Committee for Reviewing
   and Selecting Institutions of Higher Education carried out a
   comprehensive review and assessment of the BFSU Party's work
   in October 2010. The photo shows the panel visiting the School of
   Asian and African Studies.

4. The University was awarded the title of Advanced Institution
   of Higher Education for Party Organisational, Ideological and
   Political Work in Beijing in 2010.

**中国共产党北京外国语大学第八届党委
常委名单（按姓氏笔画为序）**

List of members of the Standing Committee of the 8th
BFSU CPC Committee

| 文　君　孙有中　杨学义　周　烈　姜绪范 |
| 郝　平　钟美荪　曹文泽　彭　龙 |

Wen Jun, Sun Youzhong, Yang Xueyi, Zhou Lie, Jiang Xufan,
Hao Ping, Zhong Meisun, Cao Wenze, Peng Long

党委书记	党委副书记
Committee Secretary	Deputy Secretaries
杨学义	周　烈　曹文泽
Yang Xueyi	Zhou Lie, Cao Wenze

2007 年 12 月，中国共产党北京外国语大学第八次党员代表大会召开，提出"高举中国特色社会主义伟大旗帜，以邓小平理论和'三个代表'重要思想为指导，深入贯彻落实科学发展观，同心同德，振奋精神，求真务实，开拓进取，为把我校建设成为一所多语种、多学科、高层次、特色鲜明，国内一流，具有重要影响的教学研究型外国语大学而奋斗"的奋斗目标。

The 8th BFSU CPC Congress was held in December 2007, setting the following as the goal of the University: "Holding high the great banner of socialism with Chinese characteristics, with Deng Xiaoping's Theory and the 'Three Represents' as important guidelines, thoroughly implementing the idea of developing the country scientifically, let's work with a unified heart and mind, lift our morale, seek truths, be practical and creative, forge ahead to build the University into a multilingual, multi-disciplinary, academically advanced and domestically first-class teaching-research foreign language university with distinct characteristics and important influence."

**中国共产党北京外国语大学第九届党委
常委名单（按姓氏笔画为序）**

List of members of the Standing Committee of the 9th
BFSU CPC Committee

| 孙有中　闫国华　姜绪范　赵　旻 |
| 贾文健　贾德忠　彭　龙　韩　震 |

Sun Youzhong, Yan Guohua, Jiang Xufan, Zhao Min,
Jia Wenjian, Jia Dezhong, Peng Long, Han Zhen

党委书记	党委副书记
Committee Secretary	Deputy Secretaries
韩　震	姜绪范　赵　旻
Han Zhen	Jiang Xufan, Zhao Min

2014 年 9 月，中国共产党北京外国语大学第九次党员代表大会召开。党委书记韩震代表学校党委作了题为《坚持内涵发展，深化综合改革，全面推进特色鲜明高水平外国语大学建设》的报告。报告提出，今后五年学校事业发展的总体目标是：立足国家战略和社会发展需要，完善现代大学制度，坚持立德树人，进一步树立以学生为中心、以教师为主体，服务基层、服务一线的意识。将北外建设成为培养和造就具有"祖国情怀、世界眼光、时代精神"的复合型、复语型、高层次国际化人才的摇篮，成为世界语言文化研究、国际区域研究和中国文化"走出去"战略的智库，成为中外文化交流、文化传承与创新的重要基地，成为引领中国外语教育发展的探路者。大会选举产生了中国共产党北京外国语大学第九届党委委员会。

党委书记韩震代表学校党委作题为《坚持内涵发展，深化综合改革，全面推进特色鲜明高水平外国语大学建设》的报告。

On behalf of the Party Committee, Secretary Han Zhen making a report entitled "Persisting in qualitative development, deepening integrated reform, and comprehensively pushing forward the building of a high-standard foreign language university with distinct characteristics"

彭龙校长在大会开幕式上讲话。

University President Peng Long speaking at the opening ceremony

2014 年 9 月，中国共产党北京外国语大学第九次代表大会召开。

The 9th BFSU CPC Congress was held in September 2014.

In September 2014 the 9th BFSU CPC Congress was held. On behalf of the University's Party Committee, Secretary Han Zhen made a report entitled "Persisting in qualitative development, deepening integrated reform, and comprehensively pushing forward the building of a high-standard foreign language university with distinct characteristics". The report set the overall goal of the University's development in the next five years as: Serving the needs of the nation's strategy and social development, perfecting the institution as a modern university, steadfastly cultivating the virtues of students, and further fostering the awareness that a university should regard its students as its focus of attention and its faculty as its main force and everything should be done to serve the grass roots and frontline teaching, and building BFSU into a multi-disciplinary, multilingual, academically advanced cradle of internationalised professionals with patriotic sentiment, global vision and contemporary spirit; a think tank for the study of world languages and cultures, for international regional studies, and for forming strategies to propagate Chinese culture abroad; an important base for cultural exchanges between China and foreign countries and for cultural inheritance and innovation, and an explorer leading the development of China's foreign language education. The Congress elected the 9th BFSU CPC Committee.

第九章
立德立言　滋兰树蕙

Chapter Nine
A distinguished faculty excelling in teaching and research

北京外国语大学的历史，是几代北外人同心同德、奋发图强的历史。全校教师员工敬业爱校，满腔热忱，立言垂范，立德树人，将光荣传统薪火相传并不断发扬光大。高水平、高素质的教师队伍是学校进行人才培养和学术研究的最根本条件，是学校最宝贵的财富和资源。

The history of Beijing Foreign Studies University shows the commitment of several generations of its people as they worked together with the single goal of building the university into a first-class educational institution. With their enthusiasm and zeal, and with their instructive words and exemplary deeds, the faculty and staff of the whole university have exhibited great dedication to their work and great love for the university, cultivating moral integrity in the students and turning them into people of virtue. Through their efforts, the glorious traditions of BFSU have been handed down from one generation to the next, steadily expanding in the process. At the root of all this is the university's high-calibre faculty, which has been the university's most valuable assets and resources, and its professionalism is the most essential precondition for the university to fulfil its mission of educating foreign language professionals and to attain excellence in academic research.

2004 年，波兰驻华大使向程继忠颁发"波兰教育委员会勋章"。

Polish Ambassador to China bestowing Polish Education Commission Medal on Cheng Jizhong in 2004

1

2

自 20 世纪 80 年代末以来，由于我校教师在外国语言文学、文化的教学、研究以及译介等方面所做出的杰出成绩，在推动与有关国家友好交流中所发挥的积极作用，一些国家的政府或组织对其中成就最为突出的学者教师给予了表彰、奖励。这些国际荣誉的获得体现了国际社会对我校教师的关注与尊敬，同时也提高了北京外国语大学的国际知名度与影响力。

Since the late 1980s, for their outstanding achievements in teaching, research, translation and other aspects of foreign languages, literature and culture and in promoting China's friendly communication and exchange with other countries, some governments and organisations have honoured some scholars and teachers who have made the most prominent contributions with awards and prizes. These international honours represent the international community's acknowledgement and respect for what the faculty of the University has done, and have helped to enhance its international reputation and influence.

1. 1989 年，庄元泳荣获"法国棕榈叶教育勋章"，法国驻华大使馆文化参赞为庄元泳佩戴勋章。

2. 1990 年，胡文仲被澳大利亚墨尔本大学授予名誉博士学位。左一为澳中理事会主席、澳大利亚前总理惠特拉姆。

3. 1992 年，严安生（左三）的著作《日本留学精神史》荣获日本第四届"亚洲·太平洋奖大奖"及日本第十九届"大佛次郎奖"。

4. 1995 年，司徒双荣获"法国棕榈叶教育勋章"，法国驻华大使馆文化参赞为司徒双（前排左二）授勋。

5. 2010 年，沈萼梅荣获意大利"仁惠之星骑士勋章"。

1. Zhuang Yuanyong won the Order of French Academic Palms in 1989. The photo shows the French Cultural Counsellor to China pinning the medal on Zhuang's suit.

2. Hu Wenzhong was bestowed an Honorary Doctorate by the University of Melbourne in 1990. The man on the left was Chairman of Australia-China Council and former Australian Prime Minister Gough Whitlam.

3. *An Intellectual History of Chinese Students Studying in Japan* by Yan Ansheng (3rd left) won the Fourth Asia-Pacific Prize and the 19th Osaragi Jirō Prize in Japan in 1992.

4. Situ Shuang (2nd left in the front row) won the Order of French Academic Palms in 1995.

5. Shen Emei won the Order of the Star of Italian Solidarity in 2010.

1. 2000 年，冯志臣荣获艾米内斯库诞辰 150 周年荣誉证书。

2. 2000 年，波兰驻华大使代表波兰总统授予易丽君"波兰共和国十字骑士勋章"。

3. 2000 年，董燕生荣获"伊莎贝尔女王勋章"，西班牙王储（中）出席授勋仪式。

4. 2001 年，纳忠荣获联合国教科文组织颁发的"沙迦阿拉伯文化奖"。

1. Feng Zhichen won a Certificate of Merit in honour of the 150th anniversary of the Romanian poet Mihai Eminescu in 2000.

2. Yi Lijun being bestowed the Knight Commander's Cross of the Order of Merit of the Republic of Poland by the Polish Ambassador on behalf of the Polish President in 2000

3. Dong Yansheng won the Order of Isabella the Catholic, Commander's neck badge in 2000. The badge bestowing ceremony was attended by the Crown Prince of Spain (in the middle).

4. Na Zhong was bestowed the Sharjah Prize for Arab Culture by UNESCO.

5. 2002年，泰国王储授予陈乃芳校长泰国清迈皇家师范大学名誉教育博士学位。

6. 2004年5月29日，马来西亚总理阿卜杜拉向亚非学院吴宗玉颁发"马中友谊贡献奖"。

7. 2006年11月，薛建成在法国驻华大使馆接受"法国棕榈叶教育勋章"。

8. 2006年，武文侠荣获印尼驻华大使馆颁发的"印尼中国友好突出贡献奖"。

5. University President Chen Naifang being bestowed an Honorary Doctorate in Education by the Crown Prince of Thailand on behalf of Chiang Mai Rajabhat University in 2002

6. Malaysian Prime Minister Abdullah Badawi bestowing a Prize for Contribution to Malaysia-China Friendship on Wu Zongyu from the School of Asian and African Studies on 29th May 2004

7. Xue Jiancheng receiving the Order of French Academic Palms at the French Embassy in November 2006

8. Wu Wenxia being bestowed a Prize for Outstanding Contribution to Indonesia-China Friendship by the Indonesian Embassy to China in 2006

1. 2008 年，傅荣被授予"法国棕榈叶教育勋章"。

2. 2009 年，捷克驻华大使代表捷克外交部向丛林（右一）颁发"杨·马萨里克银质奖章"。

3. 2009 年 9 月 8 日，捷克驻华大使代表捷克外交部向李梅颁发"杨·马萨里克银质奖章"。

4. 2010 年，邱苏伦被泰国清迈皇家大学授予名誉博士学位。

5. 2012 年 5 月 31 日，比利时驻华大使向王炳东颁发"利奥波德二世国王勋章"。

6. 2013 年，缅甸司法部官员代表登盛总统向粟秀玉（右）颁发"弘善贤德楷模奖"。

1. Fu Rong being bestowed the Order of French Academic Palms in 2008

2. The Czech Ambassador to China, on behalf of the Czech Ministry of Foreign Affairs, bestowing the Silver Jan Masaryk Honorary Medal on Xiang Conglin (1st right) in 2009

3. The Czech Ambassador to China, on behalf of the Czech Ministry of Foreign Affairs, bestowing the Silver Jan Masaryk Honorary Medal on Li Mei on 8th September 2009

4. Professor Qiu Sulun being bestowed an Honorary Doctorate by Chiang Mai Rajabhat University of Thailand in 2010

5. The Belgian Ambassador bestowing the Order of Leopold II Badge on Wang Bingdong on 31st May 2012

6. On behalf of President Thein Sein, a Ministry of Justice official of the Myanmar awarding Su Xiuyu with the title of "Model for Promoting Good Deeds and Cultivating Virtuous Behaviour" in 2013

北京外国语大学教师获得国际荣誉一览表（按姓氏拼音排序）

姓名	所获国际荣誉奖项
白春仁	◆ 2006 年获国际俄语教师联合会颁发的"普希金奖章"
曹　勤	◆ 1997 年获坦桑尼亚国家斯瓦希里语委员会颁发的"杰出贡献奖"
陈乃芳	◆ 2002 年被泰国王储授予泰国清迈皇家师范大学名誉教育博士学位
	◆ 2003 年被英国兰卡斯特大学授予荣誉法学博士学位
陈　瑛	◆ 2013 年 12 月获"保加利亚议会奖"
陈远志	◆ 1989 年获波兰文化部"波兰文化功勋奖章"
陈振尧	◆ 1992 年获"法国棕榈叶教育勋章"
程继忠	◆ 1985 年获波兰文化部"波兰文化功勋奖章"
	◆ 1997 年获波兰文化部"波兰文化功勋奖章"
	◆ 2000 年获波兰总统授予的"波兰共和国十字骑士勋章"
	◆ 2004 年获波兰教育部授予的"波兰教育委员会勋章"
丛　林	◆ 2009 年获捷克外交部颁发的"杨·马萨里克银质奖章"
丁　超	◆ 2009 年获罗马尼亚外交部颁发的"罗中友好杰出贡献奖"
	◆ 2012 年被波兰斯皮鲁·哈雷特大学授予荣誉博士学位
董燕生	◆ 2000 年获"伊莎贝尔女王勋章"
	◆ 2006 年获西班牙外交部颁发的"中西交流贡献奖"
	◆ 2009 年获西班牙文化部颁发的"西班牙艺术文化奖章"
杜学增	◆ 2002 年获澳大利亚"澳中理事会政府图书奖"
冯玉培	◆ 1997 年获坦桑尼亚国家斯瓦希里语委员会颁发的"杰出贡献奖"

姓名	所获国际荣誉奖项
冯志臣	◆ 2000 年获艾米内斯库诞辰 150 周年荣誉证书
	◆ 2009 年获罗马尼亚外交部颁发的"罗中友好杰出贡献奖"
傅　荣	◆ 2008 年获"法国棕榈叶教育勋章"
葛志强	◆ 2013 年 12 月获"保加利亚议会奖"
顾宗英	◆ 1988 年获匈牙利"杰出工作奖章"
	◆ 1989 年获匈牙利"为了社会主义文化奖章"
国少华	◆ 2005 年获埃及高教部嘉奖
胡文仲	◆ 1990 年被澳大利亚悉尼大学授予名誉文学博士学位
	◆ 1996 年获澳大利亚"澳中理事会文学翻译奖"
	◆ 1999 年获"澳中理事会特殊贡献奖"
	◆ 2003 年被澳大利亚墨尔本大学授予名誉教授级研究员头衔
贾淑敏	◆ 1990 年获匈牙利政府颁发的"为了匈牙利文化奖章"
李　梅	◆ 2009 年获捷克外交部颁发的"杨·马萨里克奖章"
李　莎	◆ 1998 年获国际俄语教师联合会颁发的"普希金奖章"
	◆ 1999 年获俄中友协"为友谊做出贡献奖章"
	◆ 2005 年获"卫国战争胜利六十周年国家奖章"
	◆ 2005 年获"为二次大战做出贡献奖章"
	◆ 2010 年获"卫国战争胜利六十五周年国家奖章"
	◆ 2013 年获"法国共和国荣誉军团（军官勋位）勋章"

姓名	所获国际荣誉奖项
李英男	◆ 2006 年获俄罗斯外交部颁发的"友谊贡献奖章"
	◆ 2009 年获俄罗斯世界基金会颁发的"俄语教育突出贡献奖"
	◆ 2009 年获"俄罗斯国家金质奖章"
	◆ 2010 年获国际俄语教师联合会颁发的"普希金奖章"
林温霜	◆ 2013 年 12 月获"保加利亚议会奖"
刘知白	◆ 1999 年获保加利亚共和国总统颁发的"马达拉骑士一级勋章"
罗慎仪	◆ 1989 年获法国荣誉军团骑士提名，并收入世界妇女名人录
苗春梅	◆ 2007 年获韩国文化观光部颁发的"韩文日总统表彰奖"
纳　忠	◆ 2001 年获联合国教科文组织首届"沙迦阿拉伯文化奖"
庞激扬	◆ 2009 年获罗马尼亚外交部颁发的"罗中友好杰出贡献奖"
邱苏伦	◆ 2010 年被泰国清迈皇家大学授予名誉博士学位
	◆ 2012 年获泰国翻译家协会"优秀翻译家奖"
沈大力	◆ 1991 年获"法国共和国艺术与文学骑士勋章"
	◆ 1995 年获法国"敬业金红十字勋章"
沈萼梅	◆ 1998 年获"意大利文学翻译奖"
	◆ 2010 年获意大利"仁惠之星骑士勋章"
沈志英	◆ 1995 年获坦桑尼亚国家斯瓦希里语委员会颁发的"杰出贡献奖"
史铁强	◆ 2006 年获俄罗斯外交部颁发的"友谊贡献奖章"
	◆ 2009 年获俄罗斯世界基金会颁发的"俄语教育突出贡献奖"
	◆ 2009 年获国际俄语教师联合会颁发的"普希金奖章"

姓名	所获国际荣誉奖项
司徒双	◆ 1995 年获"法国棕榈叶教育勋章"
	◆ 2002 年获摩洛哥国王颁发的"阿勒维王朝勋章"
粟秀玉	◆ 2013 年获缅甸总统登盛颁发的"弘善贤德楷模奖"
田建军	◆ 2013 年 12 月获"保加利亚议会奖"
王炳东	◆ 2006 年获"比利时法语文学翻译奖"
	◆ 2012 年获比利时王国"利奥波德二世国王勋章"
王福祥	◆ 1987 年获国际俄语教师联合会颁发的"普希金奖章"
	◆ 1994 年获泰国清迈皇家师范大学颁发的教育工作者荣誉证书
王 军	◆ 2011 年获意大利"仁惠之星骑士勋章"
文 铮	◆ 2011 年获意大利"仁惠之星骑士勋章"
吴宗玉	◆ 2004 年获马来西亚总理授予的"马中友谊贡献奖"
	◆ 2011 年获马来西亚政府首次颁发的"国际马来语杰出贡献奖"
武文侠	◆ 2006 年获印尼驻华大使馆颁发的"印尼中国友好突出贡献奖"
徐 哲	◆ 2009 年获捷克外交部颁发的"杨·马萨里克银质奖章"
许衍艺	◆ 2005 年获匈牙利"新闻奖"
薛建成	◆ 2006 年获"法国棕榈叶教育勋章"
杨晓京	◆ 2011 年获"斯中友谊突出贡献奖"
杨学义	◆ 2011 年获"斯中友谊突出贡献奖"
	◆ 2013 年获"秘鲁高校联盟会荣誉奖章"

姓名	所获国际荣誉奖项
杨燕杰	◆ 1990 年获保加利亚翻译家协会奖状和"基里尔奖章"
	◆ 1999 年获保加利亚共和国总统颁发的"马达拉骑士一级勋章"
易丽君	◆ 1984 年、1997 年获波兰文化部"波兰文化功勋奖章"
	◆ 2000 年获波兰总统颁发的"波兰共和国十字骑士勋章"
	◆ 2004 年获波兰教育部授予的"波兰教育委员会勋章"
	◆ 2005 年获波兰罗兹大学校长奖
	◆ 2007 年获波兰格但斯克大学名誉博士
	◆ 2007 年获波兰外交部"在世界普及波兰语杰出成就奖"
	◆ 2007 年获波兰著作者协会"ZAiKS 波兰文学翻译杰出成就奖"
	◆ 2008 年获波兰外交部授予的"波兰文学文化传播奖"
	◆ 2008 年获波兰科学院波兰语协会授予的"波兰文化大使"称号
	◆ 2008 年获波兰华沙大学"Polonicum 奖"
	◆ 2009 年获波兰罗兹大学校长奖一等奖
	◆ 2011 年获"波兰共和国军官十字勋章"
	◆ 2012 年获波兰图书协会"穿越大西洋翻译大奖"
	◆ 2014 年获"波中建交 65 周年纪念勋章"
张 宏	◆ 2003 年获亚非作协常设局颁发的"穆巴拉克世界和平竞赛"二等奖
张建华	◆ 2006 年获俄罗斯作家协会颁发的"高尔基文学奖"
	◆ 2009 年获俄罗斯世界基金会颁发的"翻译贡献奖"

姓名	所获国际荣誉奖项
张龙妹	◆ 2001 年获日本第八届"关根奖"
赵 刚	◆ 2005 年获波兰罗兹大学校长奖
	◆ 2009 年获波兰罗兹大学校长奖一等奖
	◆ 2010 年获波兰文化部"波兰文化功勋奖章"
	◆ 2010 年获波兰格但斯克大学奖章
赵鸿玲	◆ 1997 年获葡萄牙政府颁发的"葡萄牙绅士与功绩勋章"
郑于中	◆ 2007 年获"斯中友谊贡献奖"
庄元泳	◆ 1989 年获"法国棕榈叶教育勋章"

Table of International honours that teachers from Beijing Foreign Studies University have received

Name	International honours and awards awarded	Year
Bai Chunren	◆ Medal of Pushkin bestowed by the International Association of Teachers of Russian	2006
Cao Qin	◆ Prize for Outstanding Contribution bestowed by the National Swahili Council of Tanzania	1997
Chen Naifang	◆ Honorary Doctorate in Education bestowed by the Crown Prince of Thailand on behalf of Chiang Mai Rajabhat University	2002
	◆ Honorary Doctorate in Law bestowed by the University of Lancaster	2003
Chen Ying	◆ Bulgarian Parliament Award	December 2013
Chen Yuanzhi	◆ Medal for Merit to Culture bestowed by the Ministry of Culture and National Heritage of Poland	1989
Chen Zhenyao	◆ Order of French Academic Palms bestowed by the Ministry of Education of France	1992
Cheng Jizhong	◆ Medal for Merit to Culture bestowed by the Ministry of Culture and National Heritage of Poland	1985
	◆ Medal for Merit to Culture bestowed by the Ministry of Culture and National Heritage of Poland	1997
	◆ Knight Commander's Cross of the Order of Merit of the Republic of Poland bestowed by the Polish President	2000
	◆ Polish Education Commission Medal bestowed by the Ministry of National Education of Poland	2004
Cong Lin	◆ Silver Jan Masaryk Honorary Medal bestowed by the Czech Ministry of Foreign Affairs	2009
Ding Chao	◆ Prize for Outstanding Contribution to Romania-China Friendship bestowed by the Ministry of Foreign Affairs of Romania	2009
	◆ Honorary Doctorate awarded by Spiru Haret University in Romania	2012
Dong Yansheng	◆ Order of Isabella the Catholic, Commander's neck badge	2000
Dong Yansheng	◆ Prize for Contribution to East-West Exchange bestowed by the Spanish Ministry of Foreign Affairs and Cooperation	2006
	◆ Order of Arts and Letters of Spain bestowed by the Ministry of Culture of Spain	2009
Du Xuezeng	◆ Australian Studies Book Prize bestowed by the Australia-China Council	2002
Feng Yupei	◆ Prize for Outstanding Contribution bestowed by the National Swahili Council of Tanzania	1997
Feng Zhichen	◆ Certificate of Merit in honour of the 150th anniversary of Mihai Eminescu	2000
	◆ Prize for Outstanding Contribution to Romania-China Friendship bestowed by the Ministry of Foreign Affairs of Romania	2009
Fu Rong	◆ Order of French Academic Palms	2008
Ge Zhiqiang	◆ Bulgarian Parliament Award	2013
Gu Zongying	◆ Hungarian Outstanding Service Medal	1988
	◆ Hungarian Medal for Socialist Culture	1989
Guo Shaohua	◆ Commendation Award by the Ministry of Higher Education of Egypt	2005
Hu Wenzhong	◆ Honorary Doctorate of Letters bestowed by the University of Sydney in Australia	1990
	◆ Prize for Literary Translation bestowed by the Australia-China Council	1996
	◆ Prize for Special Contribution bestowed by the Australia-China Council	1999
	◆ Honorary Professorial Fellow appointed by the University of Melbourne	2003
Jia Shumin	◆ Medal for Hungarian Culture bestowed by the Hungarian government	1990
Li Mei	◆ Jan Masaryk Honorary Medal bestowed by the Czech Ministry of Foreign Affairs	2009
Li Sha	◆ Medal of Pushkin bestowed by the International Association of Teachers of Russian	1998
Li Sha	◆ Medal for Contribution to Friendship bestowed by Russia-China Friendship Association	1999
	◆ Jubilee Medal 60 Years of Victory in the Great Patriotic War 1941-1945	2005
	◆ Medal for Contribution to the Victory of the Second World War	2005
	◆ Jubilee Medal 65 Years of Victory in the Great Patriotic War 1941-1945	2010
	◆ French Medal for Legion of Honour Officer	2013
Li Yingnan	◆ Medal of Contribution to Friendship bestowed by the Russian Ministry of Foreign Affairs	2006
	◆ Prize for Outstanding Contribution to Russian Language Education bestowed by the Russian World Foundation	2009
	◆ Russian State Gold Medal	2009
	◆ Medal of Pushkin bestowed by the International Association of Teachers of Russian	2010
Lin Wenshuang	◆ Bulgarian Parliament Award	December 2013
Liu Zhibai	◆ First Order of the Madara Horseman bestowed by the President of the Bulgarian Republic	1999
Luo Shenyi	◆ Nomination for the French Medal for Legion of Honour	1989
Miao Chunmei	◆ Presidential Citation on the Hangeul (Korean Alphabet) Day bestowed by the Korean Ministry of Culture, Sports and Tourism	2007
Na Zhong	◆ Sharjah Prize for Arab Culture bestowed by UNESCO	2001
Pang Jiyang	◆ Prize for Outstanding Contribution to Romania-China Friendship bestowed by the Romanian Ministry of Foreign Affairs	2009
Qiu Sulun	◆ Honorary Doctorate bestowed by Chiang Mai Rajabhat University	2010
	◆ Excellent Translator Prize awarded by the Association of Thai Translators	2012
Shen Dali	◆ Knight of the Order of Arts and Letters of the French Republic	1991

Name	International honours and awards awarded	Year
Shen Dali	◆ French Gold Cross of Devotion	1995
Shen Emei	◆ Prize for the Translation of Italian Literature	1998
	◆ Order of the Star of Italian Solidarity	2010
Shen Zhiying	◆ Prize for Outstanding Contribution bestowed by the National Swahili Council of Tanzania	1995
Shi Tieqiang	◆ Medal for Contribution to Friendship bestowed by the Russian Ministry of Foreign Affairs	2006
	◆ Prize for Outstanding Contribution to Russian Language Education bestowed by the Russian World Foundation	2009
	◆ Medal of Pushkin bestowed by the International Association of Teachers of Russian	2009
Situ Shuang	◆ Order of French Academic Palms	1995
	◆ Knight of the Order of Ouissan Alaouite Medal bestowed by the King of Morocco	2002
Su Xiuyu	◆ Title of "Model for Promoting Good Deeds and Cultivating Virtuous Behaviour" bestowed by Myanmar President	2013
Tian Jianjun	◆ Bulgarian Parliament Award	2013
Wang Bingdong	◆ Prize for the Translation of French Literature in Belgium	2006
	◆ Order of Leopold II Badge of the Kingdom of Belgium	2012
Wang Fuxiang	◆ Medal of Pushkin bestowed by the International Association of Teachers of Russian	1987
	◆ Certificate of Honour for Educators awarded by Chiang Mai Rajabhat University	1994
Wang Jun	◆ Order of the Star of Italian Solidarity	2011
Wen Zheng	◆ Order of the Star of Italian Solidarity	2011
Wu Zongyu	◆ Prize for Contribution to Malaysia-China Friendship bestowed by the Malaysian Prime Minister	2004
	◆ International Prize for Outstanding Contribution to the Malay Language bestowed by the Malaysian government	2011

Name	International honours and awards awarded	Year
Wu Wenxia	◆ Prize for Contribution to Indonesia-China Friendship bestowed by the Indonesian Embassy to China	2006
Xu Yanyi	◆ Hungarian Journalism Prize	2005
Xu Zhe	◆ Silver Jan Masaryk Honorary Medal bestowed by the Czech Ministry of Foreign Affairs	2009
Xue Jiancheng	◆ Order of French Academic Palms	2006
Yang Xiaojing	◆ Prize for Outstanding Contribution to Sri Lanka-China Friendship	2011
Yang Xueyi	◆ Prize for Outstanding Contribution to Sri Lanka-China Friendship	2011
	◆ Medal of Honour awarded by the Association of Peruvian Institutions of Higher Education	2013
Yang Yanjie	◆ Certificate of Merit awarded by the Association of Bulgarian Translators and the Kyrill Medal	1990
	◆ First Order of the Madara Horseman bestowed by the Bulgarian President	1999
Yi Lijun	◆ Medal for Merit to Culture	1984, 1997
	◆ Knight Commander's Cross of the Order of Merit of the Republic of Poland by the Polish Ambassador on behalf of the Polish President	2000
	◆ Medal of the National Commission of Education bestowed by the Polish Ministry of Education	2004
	◆ Prize of the President of the University of Lodz, Poland	2005
	◆ Honorary Doctorate of the University of Gdansk	2007
	◆ Prize for Outstanding Achievements in Promoting the Polish Language Abroad bestowed by the Polish Ministry of Foreign Affairs	2007
	◆ Polish Society of Authors and Composers Prize for Outstanding Achievements in the Translation of Polish Literature	2007
	◆ Prize for Outstanding Achievements in Promoting Polish Literature and Culture Abroad bestowed by the Polish Ministry of Foreign Affairs	2008

Name	International honours and awards awarded	Year
Yi Lijun	◆ Title of Ambassador of Polish Culture awarded by the Polish Language Society of the Polish Academy of Sciences	2008
	◆ Polonicum Award of the University of Warsaw	2008
	◆ First Prize of the President of the University of Lodz	2009
	◆ Commander's Cross of the Order of Merit of the Republic of Poland	2011
	◆ Polish Book Institute Transatlantic Prize	2012
	◆ Medal Commemorating the 65th Anniversary of the Establishment of Diplomatic Relations between Poland and China	2014
Zhang Hong	◆ Second Prize of Mubarak World Peace Contest awarded by the of Afro-Asian Writers Association Standing Committee	2003
Zhang Jianhua	◆ Gorky Prize in Literature awarded by the Union of Russian Writers	2006
	◆ Prize for Contribution to Translation bestowed by the Russian World Foundation	2009
Zhang Longmei	◆ Eighth Sekine Prize, Japan	2001
Zhao Gang	◆ Prize of the President of the University of Lodz, Poland	2005
	◆ First Prize of the President of the University of Lodz, Poland	2009
	◆ Medal for Merit to Culture bestowed by the Polish Ministry of Culture	2010
	◆ Medal of the University of Gdansk, Poland	2010
Zhao Hongling	◆ Medal of the Order of Merit bestowed by the Portuguese government	1997
Zheng Yuzhong	◆ Prize for Contribution to Sri Lanka-China Friendship	2007
Zhuang Yuanyong	◆ Order of French Academic Palms	1989

　　自改革开放以来，学校大力加强师资队伍建设，一大批中青年学者脱颖而出，入选国家或教育部各类优秀人才培养计划。与此同时，学校的一些高水平专家在国家、教育部一些重要咨询机构担任职务，在国家有关思想文化建设、科技发展、外语教育等方面的决策过程中发挥重要作用。学校各院系教师一向注重教材建设和课程建设，将教学实践与科学研究相结合，编写了一大批北外品牌教材，建设了一批国家或北京市精品课程，在提高我国外语教育水平方面发挥了积极作用。

入选国家有关专项人才计划及国家、教育部各类专家（指导）委员会成员名单

国家级有突出贡献的中青年专家	王福祥　钱 青　胡文仲　何其莘　彭 龙
新世纪国家百千万人才工程	韩 震　彭 龙　孙有中
国家"四个一批"人才	韩 震
国家"万人计划"哲学社会科学领军人才	韩 震
中央马克思主义理论研究与建设工程咨询委员会委员	韩 震
教育部高等学校哲学类专业教学指导委员会主任委员	韩 震
教育部学科发展与专业设置专家委员会委员	韩 震　钟美荪
国务院学位委员会学科评议组成员	金 莉　陈国华
教育部社会科学委员会委员	王福祥　韩 震
教育部科学技术委员会委员	彭 龙
教育部高等学校外国语言文学类专业教学指导委员会主任委员	钟美荪
教育部高等学校外国语言文学类专业教学指导委员会副主任委员、德语专业教学指导委员会主任委员	贾文键
教育部高等学校外国语言文学类专业教学指导委员会秘书长	孙有中

新世纪优秀人才培养（支持）计划

韩 震　韩瑞祥　戴桂菊　刘 建　张继红　李雪涛　彭 龙　武育楠　施建军　孙文莉　陶家俊　谢 韬　王文华
马会娟　顾 钧　熊文新　丛立先　许家金　杨鲁新　刘 琛　尹继武　陈 福　李莉文　杨慧玲

Since China started its reform, the University has made great efforts in strengthening its faculty. A large number of young and middle-aged scholars have become more prominent, having been accepted into various national or MOE programmes for cultivating academic excellence. At the same time, a considerable number of senior faculty members at the University have been appointed to a number of important national or MOE advisory bodies, playing key roles in the decision-making process in China's ideological and cultural undertakings, scientific and technological development and foreign language education. Teachers of various schools and departments have always paid close attention to teaching material development and course development, and have combined teaching with academic research. A large number of BFSU branded textbooks and quality courses at the national level or Beijing municipal level have played a positive role in raising the standard of China's foreign language education.

Scholars in the nation's academic excellence programmes and members of national or MOE expert (or steering) committees

National-level young and middle-aged experts who have made outstanding contributions	Wang Fuxiang, Qian Qing, Hu Wenzhong, He Qixin, Peng Long
National Project for Cultivating One Hundred, One Thousand and. Ten Thousand Experts in the New Century	Han Zhen, Peng Long, Sun Youzhong
National Project for Cultivating Four Types of Sector Leaders	Han Zhen
National "Ten-Thousand-Person" Programme for Cultivating Leaders in Philosophy and Social Sciences	Han Zhen
Member of the Central Advisory Committee for the Study and Development of Marxist Theories	Han Zhen
Chairman of the MOE Steering Committee for the Teaching of Philosophy at Institutions of Higher Education	Han Zhen
Members of the MOE Expert Committee for the Development of Academic Disciplines and the Institution of Subjects	Han Zhen, Zhong Meisun
Members of the Academic Discipline Appraisal Board, the Degree Committee of the State Council	Jin Li, Chen Guohua
Members of the MOE Social Sciences Commission	Wang Fuxiang, Han Zhen
Member of the MOE Science and Technology Commission	Peng Long
Chairperson of the MOE Steering Committee for the Teaching of Foreign Languages and Literature at Institutions of Higher Education	Zhong Meisun
Vice Chairman of the MOE Steering Committee for the Teaching of Foreign Languages and Literature at Institutions of Higher Education; Chairman of the Steering Committee for the Teaching of German	Jia Wenjian
Secretary General of the MOE Steering Committee for the Teaching of Foreign Languages and Literature at Institutions of Higher Education	Sun Youzhong

Programme for Cultivating(Supporting) Academic Excellence in the New Century

Han Zhen, Han Ruixiang, Dai Guiju, Liu Jian, Zhang Jihong, Li Xuetao, Peng Long, Wu Yunan, Shi Jianjun, Sun Wenli, Tao Jiajun, Xie Tao, Wang Wenhua, Ma Huijuan, Gu Jun, Xiong Wenxin, Cong Lixian, Xu Jiajin, Yang Luxin, Liu Chen, Yin Jiwu, Chen Fu, Li Liwen, Yang Huiling

教学成果获奖一览表

获奖人		获奖项目	奖项
吴 冰 郭栖庆	丁往道 钟美荪	英语写作基础教程	国家级二等奖
殷桐生 姚晓舟 冷 慧	苑建华 邢爱华	用德语开设的德国经济专业倾向课程系列	国家级二等奖
文秋芳 周 燕 吴一安	陈国华 刘润清	建设研究—教学型导师团队，培养高素质外语教育人才——研究生教育改革探索	国家级二等奖
钱敏汝 王建斌 殷桐生	贾文键 姚晓舟	德语专业复合型、国际化人才培养模式的改革与实践	国家级二等奖
丁往道 钟美荪	吴 冰 郭栖庆	英语写作基础教程	北京市一等奖
殷桐生 姚晓舟 冷 慧	苑建华 邢爱华	用德语开设的德国经济专业倾向课程系列	北京市一等奖
杨立民 梅仁毅 王立礼	徐克容 陆培敏	现代大学英语系列教材（精读）	北京市一等奖
张 宏 齐明敏	王保华	阿拉伯政治外交与中阿关系教材	北京市一等奖
文秋芳 周 燕 吴一安	陈国华 刘润清	建设研究—教学型导师团队，培养高素质外语教育人才——研究生教育改革探索	北京市一等奖
彭 龙 牛华勇 张继红	郭笑文 蔡连侨	跨国经济管理人才培养模式改革	北京市一等奖
钟美荪 孙友忠 张 莲	金利民 李莉文	融合英语教育与人文教育，创新英语本科人才培养模式	北京市一等奖
张 宏 国少华	齐明敏 叶良英	中国阿拉伯语专业精读课程的新开拓——《基础阿拉伯语（精读）》课程建设	北京市一等奖
贾文键 王建斌 殷桐生	钱敏汝 姚晓舟	德语专业复合型、国际化人才培养模式的改革与实践	北京市一等奖
孙有中 谢 韬 王展鹏	金利民 侯毅凌	创建跨学科、跨文化、探究型培养模式 造就英语专业创新型国际化战略人才	北京市一等奖

获奖人		获奖项目	奖项
白 澄 佟伽蒙	杨晓京 孙晓萌	从单纯技能训练到综合全人教育：亚非通用语人才培养模式研究与实践	北京市一等奖
董燕生	刘 建	现代西班牙语教材	北京市二等奖
吴 冰 柯克尔 曾 诚	戴 宁 周 燕	现代汉译英口译教程	北京市二等奖
周 燕 林 岩 周杜娟	龚 雁 俞 露	改革教学内容，创新培养模式——英语口语交际能力课程体系研究	北京市二等奖
陈德彰 王琼琼 梁 昊	吴 青 曾 诚	本科翻译专业系列核心课程建设——用学科最新理念培养 21 世纪翻译人才	北京市二等奖
孙有忠 张淑艳 刘凤鸾	于德社 曹 萍	构建具有北外特色的大学英语教学体系——大学英语教学改革探索	北京市二等奖
丁 超 赵 刚 许衍艺	柯 静 胡唯玲	教循目标，学从规范——《欧洲非通用语种本科教学通用大纲》的研究与编写	北京市二等奖
徐一平 郭连友 宋金文	曹大峰 张龙妹	强化自我发展机制，培养日本学高级人才——研究生教育中日合作机制的改革	北京市二等奖
吴一安 金利民 周 燕	张 莲 孙有中	英语专业课程改革与教师发展良性互动机制的构建	北京市二等奖
彭 龙 蔡连侨 浦令舒	牛华勇 宋泽宁	构建立体化跨文化学习环境培养"领袖型、桥梁式"国际商业人才	北京市二等奖
万 猛 从立先 姚艳霞	王文华 李晓辉	探索复合型、应用型法律人才培养模式，造就卓越涉外法律人才	北京市二等奖
文秋芳 梁茂成 常小玲	周 燕 许家金	创建以"合作—互动—体验"为特色的研修模式 提升大学英语教师专业能力	北京市二等奖
丁 超 柯 静	赵 刚 陈 瑛	瞄准国家战略需求 创新非通用语人才培养——基于开齐欧盟国家语言教学的探索	北京市二等奖

Table of International honours that teachers from Beijing Foreign Studies University have received

Award winners	Items for award	Level of award
Wu Bing, Ding Wangdao, Guo Qiqing, Zhong Meisun	A Handbook of Writing	2nd prize, national
Yin Tongsheng, Yuan Jianhua, Yao Xiaozhou, Xing Aihua, Leng Hui	A series of courses taught in German to students studying German economy as an auxiliary subject	2nd prize, national
Wen Qiufang, Chen Guohua, Zhou Yan, Liu Runqing, Wu Yi'an	Developing a team of research-led teachers for educating high quality foreign language education professionals: an exploration in postgraduate education reforms	2nd prize, national
Qian Minru, Jia Wenjian, Wang Jianbin, Yao Xiaozhou, Yin Tongsheng	Reform and practice in developing a model for educating students of German to develop international vision and expertise in more than one subject	2nd prize, national
Ding Wangdao, Wu Bing, Zhong Meisun, Guo Qiqing	A Handbook of Writing	1st prize, Beijing
Yin Tongsheng, Yuan Jianhua, Yao Xiaozhou, Xing Aihua, Leng Hui	A series of courses taught in German to students studying German economy as an auxiliary subject	1st prize, Beijing
Yang Limin, Xu Kerong, Mei Renyi, Lu Peimin, Wang Lili	Contemporary College English Series (Intensive Reading)	1st prize, Beijing
Zhang Hong, Wang Baohua, Qi Mingmin	Teaching materials for Politics and Diplomacy in Arabic Countries and Arab-China Relations	1st prize, Beijing
Wen Qiufang, Chen Guohua, Zhou Yan, Liu Runqing, Wu Yi'an	Developing a team of research-led teachers for educating high quality foreign language education professionals: an exploration in postgraduate education reforms	1st prize, Beijing
Peng Long, Guo Xiaowen, Niu Huayong, Cai Lianqiao, Zhang Jihong	Reforming the model for educating transnational economic management professionals	1st prize, Beijing
Zhong Meisun, Jin Limin, Sun Youzhong, Li Liwen, Zhang Lian	Integrating English language education with humanistic education and creating a new model for educating English undergraduates	1st prize, Beijing
Zhang Hong, Qi Mingmin, Guo Shaohua, Ye Liangying	Breaking new grounds in the intensive reading course for students of Arabic in China—the development of Elementary Arabic (Intensive Reading)	1st prize, Beijing
Jia Wenjian, Qian Minru, Wang Jianbin, Yao Xiaozhou, Yin Tongsheng	Reform and practice in developing a model for educating students of German to develop an international vision and expertise in more than one subject	1st prize, Beijing
Sun Youzhong, Jin Limin, Xie Tao, Hou Yiling, Wang Zhanpeng	Creating an interdisciplinary, intercultural and exploratory model of education and educating students of English to become innovative international strategists	1st prize, Beijing
Bai Chun, Yang Xiaojing, Tong Jiameng, Sun Xiaomeng	From simple skills training to comprehensive holistic education: research and practice in developing a model for educating students of minor Asian and African languages	1st prize, Beijing
Dong Yansheng, Liu Jian	Modern Spanish	2nd prize, Beijing
Wu Bing, Dai Ning, Ke Keer, Zhou Yan, Zeng Cheng	Contemporary Chinese to English Oral Interpreting: A Course Book	2nd prize, Beijing
Zhou Yan, Gong Yan, Lin Yan, Yu Lu, Zhou Dujuan	Reforming the content of teaching and creating a new model of education: a study of the syllabus for the training of English oral communicative ability	2nd prize, Beijing
Chen Dezhang, Wu Qing, Wang Qiongqiong, Zeng Cheng, Liang Hao	A series of core courses for undergraduate students of translation studies: educating translators in the 21st century with state-of-the-art concepts	2nd prize, Beijing
Sun Youzhong, Yu Deshe, Zhang Shuyan, Cao Ping, Liu FengLuan	Constructing a university English language teaching system with BFSU characteristics: an exploration in university English language teaching reforms	2nd prize, Beijing
Ding Chao, Ke Jing, Zhao Gang, Hu Weiling, Xu Yanyi	Pursuing the set aim in teaching and following the norm in learning: research and compilation of A General Syllabus for Teaching Undergraduate of Minor European Languages	2nd prize, Beijing
Xu Yiping, Cao Dafeng, Guo Lianyou, Zhang Longmei, Song Jinwen	Strengthening mechanisms for self-development, educating high-calibre professionals in Japanese studies: a reform in the mechanism for China-Japan collaboration in postgraduate education	2nd prize, Beijing
Wu Yian, Zhang Lian, Jin Limin, Sun Youzhong, Zhou Yan	Constructing a beneficial interactive mechanism for English syllabus reform and teacher development	2nd prize, Beijing
Peng Long, Niu Huayong, Cai Lianqiao, Song Zening, Pu Lingshu	Constructing a multi-dimensional and multi-cultural learning environment for educating international business professionals with leadership and "bridging" quality	2nd prize, Beijing
Wan Meng, Wang Wenhua, Cong Lixian, Li Xiaohui, Yao Yanxia	Exploring a model for educating law students with combined expertise and practical knowledge	2nd prize, Beijing
Wen Qiufang, Zhou Yan, Liang Maocheng, Xu Jiajin, Chang Xiaoling	Creating a refresher model featuring collaboration, interaction and first-hand experience for enhancing college English teachers' professional ability	2nd prize, Beijing
Ding Chao, Zhao Gang, Ke Jing, Chen Ying	Serving the nation's strategic needs by innovating the education of students of minor languages: an endeavour to set up language programmes for all EU languages	2nd prize, Beijing

北京市教学名师一览表

获奖人	所在院系	获奖人	所在院系
殷桐生	德语系	张中载	英语学院
杨立民	英语学院	张建华	俄语学院
董燕生	西葡语系	刘 建	西葡语系
易丽君	欧语学院	丁 超	欧语学院
史希同	阿拉伯语系	冯玉培	亚非学院
梅仁毅	英语学院	王 军	欧语学院

全国、北京市优秀教师（优秀教育工作者）

获奖人	所在院系	获奖名称
邱苏伦	亚非语系	全国优秀教师
		北京市优秀教师
魏崇新	中文学院	北京市优秀教师
梅仁毅	英语学院	北京市优秀教师
国少华	阿拉伯语系	北京市优秀教师
贾文键	德语系	北京市优秀教师
金利民	英语学院	北京市优秀教师
傅 荣	法语系	北京市优秀教师
王 军	欧语学院	北京市优秀教师
李英桃	国际关系学院	北京市优秀教师
杨学义	校机关	北京市优秀教育工作者
钟美荪	校机关	北京市优秀教育工作者

Renowned Teachers of Beijing

Title holder	School/department
Yin Tongsheng	Department of German
Yang Limin	School of English
Dong Yansheng	Department of Spanish and Portuguese
Yi Lijun	School of European Languages
Shi Xitong	Department of Arabic
Mei Renyi	School of English
Zhang Zhongzai	School of English
Zhang Jianhua	School of Russian
Liu Jian	Department of Spanish and Portuguese
Ding Chao	School of European Languages and cultures
Feng Yupei	School of Asian and African Studies
Wang Jun	School of European Languages

Renowned Teachers of National/Beijing

Title holders	Work place	Title awarded
Qiu Sulun	School of Asian and African Studies	National Excellent Teacher
		Beijing Excellent Teacher
Wei Chongxin	School of Chinese	Beijing Excellent Teacher
Mei Renyi	School of English	Beijing Excellent Teacher
Guo Shaohua	Department of Arabic	Beijing Excellent Teacher
Jia Wenjian	Department of German	Beijing Excellent Teacher
Jin Limin	School of English	Beijing Excellent Teacher
Fu Rong	Department of French	Beijing Excellent Teacher
Wang Jun	School of European Languages	Beijing Excellent Teacher
Li Yingtao	School of International Relations	Beijing Excellent Teacher
Yang Xueyi	University governing body	Beijing Excellent Educationalist
Zhong Meisun	University governing body	Beijing Excellent Educationalist

教育部、北京市优秀教学团队

获奖团队	负责人	所在院系	获奖名称
英语学院英语专业教学团队	杨立民	英语学院	教育部、北京市优秀教学团队
阿拉伯语专业本科教学团队	张 宏	阿拉伯语系	北京市优秀教学团队
西班牙语口笔语实践课教学团队	董燕生	西葡语系	北京市优秀教学团队
金融学专业教学团队	彭 龙	国际商学院	北京市优秀教学团队

MOE/Beijing Excellent Teaching Teams

Team	Leader	School/Department	Title awarded
English-major team, School of English	Yang Limin	School of English	MOE & Beijing Excellent Teaching Team
Arabic-major undergraduate team	Zhang Hong	Department of Arabic	Beijing Excellent Teaching Team
Oral and written Spanish class practicum team	Dong Yansheng	Department of Spanish and Portuguese	Beijing Excellent Teaching Team
Finance-major team	Peng Long	School of International Business	Beijing Excellent Teaching Team

国家级实验教学示范中心

名 称	负责人	所在院系
跨国经济管理人才培养实验教学中心	彭 龙	国际商学院

National Demonstration Centres for Experimental Teaching

Name of centre	Leader	School/Department
Centre for Experimental Teaching of Students of Transnational Economic Management	Peng Long	School of International Business

教育部专业综合改革试点

项　目	负责人	所在院系
英语专业综合改革	**孙有中**	英语学院
德语专业综合改革	**贾文键　吴　江**	德语系
法学专业综合改革	**万　猛**	法学院

Pilot Projects for MOE's Comprehensive Reforms on Subjects

Name of project	Leader	School/Department
Comprehensive reform of English	**Sun Youzhong**	School of English
Comprehensive reform of German	**Jia Wenjian, Wu Jiang**	Department of German
Comprehensive reform of Law	**Wan Meng**	School of Law

教育部卓越法律人才教育培养基地

名称	负责人	所在院系
涉外法律人才教育培养基地	**万　猛**	法学院

MOE Educational Centre for Cultivating Outstanding Law Professionals

Name of centre	Leader	School/Department
Educational Centre for Cultivating Bilingual Law Professionals with International Capacities	**Wan Meng**	School of Law

教育部、北京市精品教材一览表

教材名称	作者	所在院系	获奖名称
西班牙语听力教程（1—3）	刘 建	西葡语系	教育部精品教材
当代大学德语学生用书（3、4）	梁 敏 聂黎曦 任卫东 潘 颖 詹 霞	德语系	教育部精品教材
现代汉译英口译教程	吴 冰等	英语学院	教育部精品教材
现代大学英语系列	杨立民等	英语学院	北京市精品教材
俄罗斯文学史	张建华等	俄语学院	北京市精品教材
阿拉伯语写作	张 宏等	阿拉伯语系	北京市精品教材
日语词汇学教程	朱京伟	日语系	北京市精品教材
俄语专业外交学教程	武瑷华	俄语学院	北京市精品教材
现代日语翻译教程	陶振孝	日语系	北京市精品教材
法国语言与文化	童佩智	法语系	北京市精品教材
语言导论	蓝 纯	英语学院	北京市精品教材
现代语言学及其分支学科	王福祥 吴汉樱	俄语学院	北京市精品教材
高级英语视听说	王镇平	英语学院	北京市精品教材
俄语专业阅读教程（2—4）	史铁强	俄语学院	北京市精品教材
西班牙语口译	常世儒	西葡语系	北京市精品教材
意大利语语法	王 军	欧语学院	北京市精品教材
大学俄语东方新版（1—4）（套书）	史铁强	俄语学院	北京市精品教材
当代大学德语（1—4）（套书）	梁 敏 聂黎曦	德语系	北京市精品教材
西班牙语听力教程（1、2）（套书）	刘 建	西葡语系	北京市精品教材
大学意大利语教程（1—4）（套书）	王 军	欧语学院	北京市精品教材
大学葡萄牙语（1、2）（套书）	叶志良	西葡语系	北京市精品教材
西班牙语阅读教程（3）	史 青 徐 蕾	西葡语系	北京市精品教材
基础日语综合教程（1、2）（套书）	曹大峰	日研中心	北京市精品教材
基础日语综合教程（3、4）	曹大峰	日研中心	北京市精品教材
全媒体时代的法语报刊导读教程	傅 荣	法语系	北京市精品教材
新编斯瓦希里语（3、4）	冯玉培	亚非学院	北京市精品教材
现代西班牙语阅读教程（1）	郑书九 王 磊	西葡语系	北京市精品教材
英语写作教程（4）：批判思维与议论文	张在新	英语学院	北京市精品教材

Quality Teaching Materials recognized by the MOE/Beijing municipal government

Title	Author	School/Department	Awards
Spanish Listening Comprehension Course 1-3	Liu Jian	Department of Spanish and Portuguese	Quality Teaching Materials, MOE
Contemporary College German: Student Book 3-4	Liang Min, Nie Lixi, Ren Weidong, Pan Ying, Zhan Xia	Department of German	Quality Teaching Materials, MOE
Contemporary Chinese to English Oral Interpreting: A Course Book	Wu Bing, etc.	School of English	Quality Teaching Materials, MOE
Contemporary English series	Yang Limin, etc.	School of English	Quality Teaching Materials, Beijing
A History of Russian Literature	Zhang Jianhua, etc.	School of Russian	Quality Teaching Materials, Beijing
Arabic Writing	Zhang Hong, etc.	Department of Arabic	Quality Teaching Materials, Beijing
A Course of Japanese Lexicology	Zhu Jingwei	Department of Japanese	Quality Teaching Materials, Beijing
A Course of Diplomacy Studies for Students of Russian	Wu Aihua	School of Russian	Quality Teaching Materials, Beijing
A Course of Modern Japanese Translation	Tao Zhenxiao	Department of Japanese	Quality Teaching Materials, Beijing
French Language and Culture	Tong Peizhi	Department of French	Quality Teaching Materials, Beijing
Facets of Language	Lan Chun	School of English	Quality Teaching Materials, Beijing
Modern Linguistics and Its Branch Disciplines	Wang Fuxiang, Wu Hanying	School of Russian	Quality Teaching Materials, Beijing
An Advanced Video Course	Wang Zhenping	School of English	Quality Teaching Materials, Beijing
A Reading Course for Students of Russian 2-4	Shi Tieqiang	School of Russian	Quality Teaching Materials, Beijing
Spanish Interpreting	Chang Shiru	Department of Spanish and Portuguese	Quality Teaching Materials, Beijing
A Grammar of Italian	Wang Jun	School of European Languages	Quality Teaching Materials, Beijing
College Russian 1-4 (new edition, a set)	Shi Tieqiang	School of Russian	Quality Teaching Materials, Beijing
Contemporary College German 1-4 (a set)	Liang Min, Nie Lixi	Department of German	Quality Teaching Materials, Beijing
Spanish Listening Comprehension Course 1-2 (a set)	Liu Jian	Department of Spanish and Portuguese	Quality Teaching Materials, Beijing
A Course of College Italian 1-4 (a set)	Wang Jun	School of European Languages	Quality Teaching Materials, Beijing
College Portuguese 1-2 (a set)	Ye Zhiliang	Department of Spanish and Portuguese	Quality Teaching Materials, Beijing
Spanish Reading Course 3	Shi Qing, Xu Lei	Department of Spanish and Portuguese	Quality Teaching Materials, Beijing
Elementary Japanese: A Comprehensive Course 1-2 (a set)	Cao Dafeng	Centre for Japanese Studies	Quality Teaching Materials, Beijing
Elementary Japanese: A Comprehensive Course 3-4	Cao Dafeng	Centre for Japanese Studies	Quality Teaching Materials, Beijing
Introduction to Reading French Newspapers in the Multimedia Age	Fu Rong	Department of French	Quality Teaching Materials, Beijing
New Edition Swahili 3-4	Feng Yupei	School of Asian and African Studies	Quality Teaching Materials, Beijing
Modern Spanish: A Course in Reading 1	Zheng Shujiu, Wang Lei	Department of Spanish and Portuguese	Quality Teaching Materials, Beijing
English Composition 4: Critical Reading and Argumentation	Zhang Zaixin	School of English	Quality Teaching Materials, Beijing

▌ 国家级、北京市精品课程一览表

课程名称	主讲教师	所在院系	获奖级别
专业英语精读	杨立民	英语学院	国家级
西班牙语口笔语实践（精读）	董燕生	西葡语系	国家级
项目设计与论文写作——英语教育	顾曰国	网络学院	国家级
国际经济法	万 猛	法学院	国家级
国际公法	姚艳霞	法学院	国家级
英语文学概论	张 剑	英语学院	国家级、北京市
西班牙语口笔语实践（精读）	董燕生	西葡语系	北京市
阿拉伯文化与中阿文化交流	史希同	阿拉伯语系	北京市
文化透视俄语课程	李英男	俄语学院	北京市
专业英语口语	周 燕	英语学院	北京市
基础阿拉伯语精读	张 宏	阿拉伯语系	北京市
英汉翻译入门	陈德彰	英语学院	北京市
泰语翻译理论与实践	邱苏伦	亚非学院	北京市
基础法语精读	柳 利	法语系	北京市
大学俄语综合课	王凤英	俄语学院	北京市

▌ 教育部精品视频公开课

课程名称	负责人	所在院系
俄罗斯文学的品格与文化特性	张建华	俄语学院
走进俄罗斯	戴桂菊	俄语学院
谈判学	李英桃	国际关系学院

National/Beijing Municipal Assessed Quality Courses

Course name	Chief instructor	School/Department	Level of awards
Intensive reading for students of English	Yang Limin	School of English	National
Spanish speaking and writing practicum (intensive reading)	Dong Yansheng	Department of Spanish and Portuguese	National
Project design and essay writing: English education	Gu Yueguo	Institute of Online Education	National
International economic law	Wan Meng	School of Law	National
International common law	Yao Yanxia	School of Law	National
A general introduction to English literature	Zhang Jian	School of English	National & Beijing
Spanish speaking and writing practicum (intensive reading)	Dong Yansheng	Department of Spanish and Portuguese	Beijing
Arabic culture and China-Arab cultural exchange	Shi Xitong	Department of Arabic	Beijing
Russian course: a cultural perspective	Li Yingnan	School of Russian	Beijing
English speaking for students of English	Zhou Yan	School of English	Beijing
Elementary Arabic intensive reading	Zhang Hong	Department of Arabic	Beijing
Introduction to English-Chinese translation	Chen Dezhang	School of English	Beijing
Thai translation: theory and practice	Qiu Sulun	School of Asian and African Studies	Beijing
Elementary French intensive reading	Liu Li	Department of French	Beijing
College Russian: a comprehensive course	Wang Fengying	School of Russian	Beijing

MOE Assessed Quality Open Classes on Video

Course name	Instructor	School/Department
The character and cultural features of Russian literature	Zhang Jianhua	School of Russian
Entering Russia	Dai Guiju	School of Russian
Negotiation study	Li Yingtao	School of International Relations

北京外国语大学的教师队伍是一支高水平的学术研究队伍。建校七十余年来，经过几代学者的努力，学校形成了深厚的学术积累，在外国语言文学研究、国别与地区研究、外国历史文化研究、外国文学作品译介等领域取得了突出的成绩，形成了自己的研究特色，为学校办学提供了坚实的学术支撑。

北京外国语大学科学研究成果获奖一览表

获奖人	获奖作品	项目名称
王佐良	论契合——比较文学研究集	北京市首届哲社与政策研究优秀成果荣誉奖
		北京市第一届哲社优秀成果荣誉奖
		全国比较文学荣誉奖
		高等学校出版社优秀学术专著——国家教委奖
	英国诗史	教委首届人文社科优秀成果一等奖
	英国浪漫主义诗歌史	北京市第三届哲社优秀成果一等奖
王佐良 丁往道	英语文体学引论	北京市第二届哲社优秀成果一等奖
王佐良 周珏良	英国二十世纪文学史	第二届全国高校出版社优秀学术专著奖特等奖
王佐良 何其莘	英国文艺复兴时期文学史	第十一届中国图书奖
		国家社会科学基金项目优秀成果奖三等奖
王福祥	俄语实际切分句法	北京市首届哲社与政策研究优秀成果一等奖
		北京市第一届哲社优秀成果一等奖
	话语语言学	高等学校出版社优秀学术专著——国家教委奖
		第二届全国高校出版社优秀学术专著奖优秀奖
纳 忠	传承与交融：阿拉伯文化	教委首届人文社科优秀成果二等奖
	阿拉伯通史	北京市第六届哲社优秀成果一等奖
		第三届中国高校人文社科研究优秀成果奖一等奖

获奖人	获奖作品	项目名称
丁树杞等	基础俄语（1—4 册）	北京市首届哲社与政策研究优秀成果一等奖
		北京市第一届哲社优秀成果二等奖
刘世沐等	英汉双解牛津初级学习词典	全国优秀畅销图书奖
洪育沂	1931—1939 年国际关系简史	北京市第一届哲社优秀成果二等奖
许国璋	英语学论文十篇	北京市第一届哲社优秀成果荣誉奖
吴景荣等	汉英词典	北京市第一届哲社优秀成果一等奖
新西汉词典组	新西汉词典	北京市第一届哲社优秀成果中青年奖
杨天戈	"了"字综合研究	北京市第一届哲社优秀成果中青年奖
梁 敏	教学大纲的继承性和时代特征	北京市教育科研优秀成果二等奖
胡文仲等	北京外语学院外语教学基本经验总结	北京市教育科研优秀成果二等奖
胡文仲	关于外语专业教育改革的思考	北京市高等教育学会第五次优秀高等教育科研论文奖二等奖
陈振宜	本科生质量调查报告	北京市教育科研优秀成果四等奖
刘政权	高校领导干部的责任初探	北京市教育科研优秀成果四等奖
刘家泉	宋庆龄传	全国优秀图书奖
	宋庆龄与保卫中国同盟	中国共产党成立 70 周年大会优秀论文一等奖
英语系词典组	现代汉英词典	第四届全国图书"金钥匙"优胜奖
吕 凡 宋正昆	俄语修辞学	北京市第二届哲社优秀成果二等奖
张大可	史记全本新注	北京市第二届哲社优秀成果中青年奖
	中国历史文献学	北京市第三届哲社优秀成果二等奖

获奖人	获奖作品	项目名称
王克非	从中村正直和严复的翻译看日中两国对西方思维的摄取	北京市第二届哲社优秀成果中青年奖
	翻译文化史论	第三届中国高校人文社科研究优秀成果奖三等奖
外研社词典编辑室	现代英汉词典	第五届全国图书"金钥匙"优胜奖
周圣	高尔基文集	首届全国优秀外国文学图书特别奖
李德发	对我校教育改革中的两个问题的思考	北京市教育科研优秀论文成果奖
冯玉培	北京外国语学院研究生教育调查报告	北京市教育科研优秀论文成果奖
周焕凤	针对青年教师流失应采取的措施	北京市教育科研优秀论文成果奖
孙丕池等	形成团结战斗的核心，联系实际做好思想工作	北京市教育科研优秀论文成果奖
沈志英等	北京外国语学院亚非语系调查报告	北京市教育科研优秀论文三等奖
刘润清	西方语言学流派	北京市第四届哲社优秀成果二等奖
刘润清等	高校英语抽样调查报告	北京市第二届哲社优秀成果二等奖
刘润清吴一安等	中国英语本科学生素质调查报告	北京市教育科研优秀论文一等奖
		全国第二届教育科学优秀成果二等奖
		北京市第三届哲社优秀成果二等奖
刘润清戴曼纯	中国高校外语教学改革现状与发展策略研究	北京市第五届教育科学研究优秀成果奖一等奖
殷桐生等	德语专业教学调查报告	北京市第三届哲社优秀成果二等奖
殷桐生	德国外交通论	第六届高等学校科学研究优秀成果奖（人文社科）三等奖

获奖人	获奖作品	项目名称
李书成	中国日本学年鉴	北京市第三届哲社优秀成果二等奖
顾曰国	取效行为的困境	霍英东教育基金会青年教师一等奖
		北京市第三届哲社优秀成果一等奖
丁启阵	秦汉方言	北京市第三届哲社优秀成果中青年奖
张中载	托马斯·哈代：思想和创作	全国高校外国文学教学首届优秀著作奖
张中载	托马斯·哈代：思想和创作	教委首届人文社科优秀成果二等奖
钱青	美国文学名著精选	全国高校外国文学教学首届优秀著作奖
		北京市第四届哲社优秀成果二等奖
马大品	中国佛道诗歌总汇	全国古籍优秀图书奖三等奖
宋柏年	中国古典文学在国外	北京市第四届哲社优秀成果二等奖
陈恕	尤利西斯导读	北京市第四届哲社优秀成果二等奖
李德恩	波波尔·乌	第三届全国优秀外国文学图书奖
	拉美文学流派的嬗变与趋势	普通高等学校第二届人文社科优秀成果奖三等奖
周维宏等	中日农村经济组织比较	孙平化日本学学术奖励基金专著奖
金莉	玛丽亚的传统和夏娃的独立意识	北京市第五届哲社优秀成果二等奖
	20世纪美国女性小说研究	北京市第十二届哲社优秀成果一等奖
张耘	现代西方戏剧名家名著选评	北京市第六届哲社优秀成果二等奖
国少华	阿拉伯语词汇学	北京市第六届哲社优秀成果二等奖

获奖人	获奖作品	项目名称
何其莘	英国戏剧史	第五届全国优秀外国文学图书奖二等奖
董燕生	堂吉诃德	鲁迅文学奖翻译类彩虹奖
戴曼纯	最简方案框架下的广义左向合并理论	北京市第八届哲社优秀成果二等奖
吴一安	英汉空间指示语对比研究语篇与认知	第四届中国高校人文社科研究优秀成果奖二等奖
李永成	霸权的神话：米尔斯海默进攻性现实主义理论研究	北京市第十届哲社优秀成果二等奖
杨燕杰 金丕良 刘知白 葛志强	保加利亚语汉语词典	高等学校科学研究优秀成果奖（人文社科）三等奖
耿力平	沼泽天使权威版及相关研究	高等学校科学研究优秀成果奖（人文社科）三等奖
尹继武	社会认知与联盟信任形成	北京市第十一届哲社优秀成果二等奖
陶家俊	思想认同的焦虑：旅游后殖民理论的对话与超越精神	北京市第十一届哲社优秀成果二等奖
丛立先	网络版权问题研究	辽宁省第十一届哲学社会科学成果奖三等奖
王海华 陈国华	中国学习者使用英语强势词搭配的发展特点	辽宁省第十一届哲学社会科学成果奖三等奖
康敏	"习以为常"之蔽：一个马来村庄日常生活的民族志	北京市第十二届哲社优秀成果二等奖
张晓玲	以"目标协商"为导向的德国高校公法基金会改革——以哥廷根公法基金会大学为例	第六届教育科学研究优秀成果奖三等奖
梁燕主编	齐如山文集（11卷）	第三届中国出版政府奖图书奖
马会娟	汉译英翻译能力研究	北京市第十三届哲社优秀成果二等奖
韩瑞祥	上海，远在何方？	第六届鲁迅文学奖文学翻译类
王家湘	有色人民——回忆录	第六届鲁迅文学奖文学翻译类

获奖人	获奖作品	项目名称
金莉 张朝意 张西平 李雪涛	高校哲学社会科学"走出去"战略规划设计方案（2010—2020）	中国高等教育学会第八次优秀高等教育科研成果优秀奖
		中国高等教育学会高校社科科研管理分会高校社科科研管理优秀成果奖特等奖
贾文键	中国德语本科专业调研报告	中国高等教育学会第八次优秀高等教育科研成果三等奖

The faculty of Beijing Foreign Studies University is composed of a large number of excellent academic researchers. Through the efforts made by several generations of scholars over the past 70 years, the University has established a rich academic heritage and attained remarkable achievements in the studies of foreign language and literature, national and regional studies, foreign history and culture studies, foreign literature translation and introduction, etc. In this process, distinctive research characteristics have emerged and the research undertaken by the faculty has provided a solid academic basis for teaching activities at the University.

Academic research awards won by the faculty members of Beijing Foreign Studies University

Winners	Works	Awards
Wang Zuoliang	Degrees of Affinity---Studies on Comparative Literature and Translation.	First Beijing Award of Honour for Excellence in Studies of Philosophy, Social Sciences and Policies
		First Beijing Award of Honour for Excellence in Studies of Philosophy and Social Sciences
		National Comparative Literature Award of Honour
		State Education Commission Prize for Excellent Academic Monographs Published by University Presses
	A History of English Poetry	First State Education Commission Award for Excellence in Studies of Philosophy and Social Sciences, 1st Prize
	A History of English Romantic Poetry	Third Beijing Award for Excellence in Studies of Philosophy and Social Sciences, 1st Prize
Wang Zuoliang, Ding Wangdao	Introduction to English Stylistics	Second Beijing Award for Excellence in Studies of Philosophy and Social Sciences, 1st Prize
Wang Zuoliang, Zhou Jueliang	A History of 20th-Century British Literature	Second National Award for Excellent Academic Monographs Published by University Presses, Exceptional Prize
Wang Zuoliang, He Qixin	A History of Renaissance British Literature	Eleventh National Book Prize
		State Social Sciences Fund Award for Excellent Projects, 3rd Prize
Wang Fuxiang	A Practical Syntax for the Parsing of Russian	First Beijing Award for Excellence in Studies of Philosophy, Social Sciences and Policies, 1st Prize
		First Beijing Award for Excellence in Studies of Philosophy and Social Sciences, 1st Prize
	Text Linguistics	State Education Commission Prize for Excellent Academic Monographs Published by University Presses
		Second National Award for Excellent Academic Monographs Published by University Presses, Excellence Prize

Winners	Works	Awards
Na Zhong	Heritage and Integration: Arabic Culture	First State Education Commission Award for Excellence in Studies of Philosophy and Social Sciences Prize, 2nd Prize
	A General History of the Arabs	Sixth Beijing Award for Excellence in Studies of Philosophy and Social Sciences, 1st Prize
		Third National Award for Excellence in Studies in Humanities and Social Sciences at Institutions of Higher Education, 1st Prize
Ding Shuqi, etc.	Elementary Russian 1-4	First Beijing Award for Excellence in Studies of Philosophy, Social Sciences and Policies, 1st Prize
		First Beijing Award for Excellence in Studies of Philosophy and Social Sciences, 2nd Prize
Liu Shimu, etc.	Oxford Elementary Learner's English-Chinese Dictionary	National Excellent Bestseller Award
Hong Yuyi	A Brief History of International Relations 1931-1939	First Beijing Award for Excellence in Studies of Philosophy and Social Sciences, 2nd Prize
Xu Guozhang	Ten essays in studies of English	First Beijing Award of Honour for Excellence in Studies of Philosophy and Social Sciences
Wu Jingrong, etc	A Chinese-English Dictionary	First Beijing Award for Excellence in Studies of Philosophy and Social Sciences, 1st Prize
New Spanish-Chinese lexicography group	A New Spanish-Chinese Dictionary	First Beijing Young and Middle-Aged Scholars Award for Excellence in Studies of Philosophy and Social Sciences
Yang Tiange	A Comprehensive study of the character LE (了)	First Beijing Young and Middle-Aged Scholars Award for Excellence in Studies of Philosophy and Social Sciences
Liang Min	Syllabuses: inheritance of tradition and characteristics of the times	Beijing Educational Research Award, 2nd Prize
Hu Wenzhong, etc.	A summary of the basic experiences of foreign language teaching at Beijing Foreign Studies University	Beijing Educational Research Award, 2nd Prize

Winners	Works	Awards
Chen Zhenyi	*A survey report on the quality of undergraduates*	Beijing Educational Research Award, 4th Prize
Liu Zhengquan	*A preliminary exploration into the responsibilities of top leaders of institutions of higher education*	Beijing Educational Research Award, 4th Prize
Liu Jiaquan	*A Biography of Soong Ching Ling (Madame Sun Yat-sen)*	National Excellent Book Prize
	Soong Ching Ling and the China Defence League	First Prize for Excellent Essays awarded at the Conference Commemorating the 70th Anniversary of the Founding of the Communist Party of China
English Lexicography Section	*A Modern Chinese-English Dictionary*	Fourth National Book "Golden Key" Prize
Lexicography Section, FLTRP	*A Modern English-Chinese Dictionary*	Fifth National Book "Golden Key" Prize
Lü Fan, Song Zhengkun	*Russian Rhetoric*	Second Beijing Award for Excellence in Studies of Philosophy and Social Sciences, 2nd Prize
Zhang Dake	*Records of the Historian: A Newly Annotated Edition*	Second Beijing Young and Middle-Aged Scholars Award for Excellence in Studies of Philosophy and Social Sciences
	Chinese Historical Philology	Third Beijing Award for Excellence in Studies of Philosophy and Social Sciences, 2nd Prize
Wang Kefei	*A Comparison of two translations of John S. Mill's On Liberty: one by Nakamura Masanao and one by Yan Fu*	Second Beijing Young and Middle-Aged Scholars Award for Excellence in Studies of Philosophy and Social Sciences
Zhou Sheng	*Collected Works of Gorky*	First National Excellent Foreign Literature Books Special Award
Li Defa	*Reflections on two issues in our Institute*	Beijing Educational Reform Research Award for Excellent Essays
Feng Yupei	*A report on a survey of postgraduate education at Beijing Foreign Studies University*	Beijing Educational Reform Research Award for Excellent Essays

Winners	Works	Awards
Zhou Huanfeng	*Measures that should be taken to counter the drain of junior teachers*	Beijing Educational Reform Research Award for Excellent Essays
Sun Pichi, etc.	*Forming a united core and doing a good job in ideological tutoring in the real world*	Beijing Educational Reform Research Award for Excellent Essays
Shen Zhiying, etc.	*A report on a survey of the Department of Asian and African Languages*	Beijing Educational Reform Research Award for Excellent Essays, 3rd Prize
Liu Renqing	*Schools of Linguistics*	Fourth Beijing Award for Excellence in Studies of Philosophy and Social Sciences, 2nd Prize
Liu Runqing, etc.	*A report on a college English survey*	Second Beijing Award for Excellence in Studies of Philosophy and Social Sciences, 2nd Prize
Liu Runqing, Wu Yi'an, etc.	*A report on a survey of the quality of Chinese undergraduate students of English*	Beijing Educational Reform Research Award for Excellent Essays, 1st Prize
		Second National Education Science Award for Excellence, 2nd Prize
		Third Beijing Award for Excellence in Studies of Philosophy and Social Sciences, 2nd Prize
Liu Renqing, Dai Manchun	*A study of the Current State and Development Strategies of the Reform of Foreign Language Teaching in Institutions of Higher Learning in China*	Fifth Beijing Education Science Award for Excellence, 1st Prize
Gu Yueguo	*The impasse of perlocution*	Fok Ying Tung Education Foundation 1st Prize for Outstanding Young Teachers of Higher Education
		Third Beijing Young and Middle-Aged Scholars Award for Excellence in Studies of Philosophy and Social Sciences, 1st Prize
Yin Tongsheng, etc.	*A report on a survey of the teaching of German to German-major students*	Third Beijing Award for Excellence in Studies of Philosophy and Social Sciences, 2nd Prize
Li Shucheng	*An Almanac of Japanese Study in China*	Third Beijing Award for Excellence in Studies of Philosophy and Social Sciences, 2nd Prize

Winners	Works	Awards
Ding Qizhen	*Dialects of the Qin and Han Dynasties*	Third Beijing Young and Middle-Aged Scholars Award for Excellence in Studies of Philosophy and Social Sciences
Zhang Zhongzai	*Thomas Hardy: His Ideology and Works*	First National Award for Excellent Monographs for Foreign Literature Teaching
		First State Education Commission Award for Excellence in Humanities and Social Sciences, 2nd Prize
Qian Qing	*Highlights of American Literature*	First National Award for Excellent Monographs for Foreign Literature Teaching
		Fourth Beijing Award for Excellence in Studies of Philosophy and Social Sciences, 2nd Prize
Ma Dapin	*An Anthology of Chinese Buddhist and Taoist Poetry*	National Excellent Ancient Books Award, 3rd Prize
Song Bainian	*Chinese Classical Literature Abroad*	Fourth Beijing Award for Excellence in Studies of Philosophy and Social Sciences, 2nd Prize
Chen Shu	*Guide to Ulysses*	Fourth Beijing Award for Excellence in Studies of Philosophy and Social Sciences, 2nd Prize
Li De'en	*Popol Vuh (A Chinese translation)*	Third National Excellent Foreign Literature Books Special Award
	The Evolution and Trend of Literary Schools in Latin America	Second Institutions of Higher Education Award for Excellence in Studies of Humanities and Social Sciences , 3rd Prize
Zhou Weihong, etc.	*A Comparison of Rural Economic Organisations in China and Japan*	Sun Pinghua Japanese Studies Academic Reward Fund Prize for Monographs
Jin Li	*Between Mary and Eve: American women writers and their heroines in the mid-nineteenth century*	Fifth Beijing Award for Excellence in Studies of Philosophy and Social Sciences, 2nd Prize
	A Study of 20th-Century American Feminist Novels	Twelfth Beijing Award for Excellence in Studies of Philosophy and Social Sciences, 1st Prize
Zhang Yun	*On Famous Western Playwrights of Modern Drama and Their Best Works*	Sixth Beijing Award for Excellence in Studies of Philosophy and Social Sciences, 2nd Prize

Winners	Works	Awards
Guo Shaohua	*Arabic Lexicology*	Sixth Beijing Award for Excellence in Studies of Philosophy and Social Sciences, 2nd Prize
Hu Wenzhong	*Reflections on reform in foreign language education in China*	Fifth Beijing Higher Education Association Award for Excellent Higher Education Research Papers, 2nd Prize
He Qixin	*A History of English Drama*	Fifth National Excellent Foreign Literature Books Award, 2nd Prize
Dong Yansheng	*Don Quixote (A Chinese translation)*	Lu Xun Prize for Literature: Rainbow Prize for Translation
Wang Kefei	*A Cultural History of Translation*	Third National Award for Excellence in Studies in Humanities and Social Sciences at Institutions of Higher Education, 3rd Prize
Dai Manchun	*Generalized Leftward Merger Theory: A Minimalist Approach to Adjuncts, Existential, Parasitic Gaps, and Middle Constructions*	Eighth Beijing Award for Excellence in Studies of Philosophy and Social Sciences, 2nd Prize
Wu Yi'an	*Spatial Demonstratives in English and Chinese*	Fourth National Award for Excellence in Studies in Humanities and Social Sciences at Institutions of Higher Education, 2nd Prize
Li Yongcheng	*The Myth of Hegemony: A Study of John Mearsheimer's Theory of Aggressive Realism*	Tenth Beijing Award for Excellence in Studies of Philosophy and Social Sciences, 2nd Prize
Yang Yanjie, Jin Piliang, Liu Zhibai, Ge Zhiqiang	*A Bulgarian-Chinese Dictionary*	Institutions of Higher Education Award for Excellence in Studies of Humanities and Social Sciences, 3rd Prize
Geng Liping	*Swamp Angel: A Critical Edition and related studies*	Institutions of Higher Education Prize for Excellence in Studies of Humanities and Social Sciences, 3rd Prize
Yin Jiwu	*Social Cognition and the Formation of Alliance Trust*	Eleventh Beijing Award for Excellence in Studies of Philosophy and Social Sciences, 2nd Prize
Tao Jiajun	*The Anxiety of Intellectual Identification: The Dialog over and Transcendental Spirit in Travelling Post-Colonial Theory*	Eleventh Beijing Award for Excellence in Studies of Philosophy and Social Sciences, 2nd Prize

Winners	Works	Awards
Cong Lixian	*A Study of Internet Copyright*	Eleventh Liaoning Award for Excellence in Studies of Philosophy and Social Sciences, 3rd Prize
Wang Haihua, Chen Guohua	*An investigation into the developmental features of Chinese EFL learners' use of amplifier collocations: a corpus-based approach*	Eleventh Liaoning Award for Excellence in Studies of Philosophy and Social Sciences, 3rd Prize
Kang Min	*The Drawbacks of Accustomization: The Ethnography of the Everyday Life of a Malay Village*	Twelfth Beijing Award for Excellence in Studies of Philosophy and Social Sciences, 2nd Prize
Yin Tongsheng	*A General Theory of German Diplomacy*	Sixth Institutions of Higher Education Award for Excellence in Studies of Humanities and Social Sciences, 3rd Prize
Zhang Xiaoling	*A goal-oriented approach to German university reforms of public law foundations: a case study of the public law foundation universities in Göttingen*	Sixth Education Science Award for Excellence, 3rd Prize
Liang Yan (Ed.)	*The Collected Works of Qi Rushan (11 Vols)*	Third Chinese Publishing Government Prize for Books
Ma Huijuan	*A Study of Translation Competence from Chinesein to English*	Thirteenth Beijing Award for Excellence in Studies of Philosophy and Social Sciences, 2nd Prize
Han Ruixiang	*Shanghai, Far Away? (A Chinese translation)*	Sixth Lu Xun Prize in Literature for Translation
Wang Jiaxiang	*Coloured People: A Memoir (A Chinese translation)*	Sixth Lu Xun Prize in Literature for Translation
Jin Li, Zhang Chaoyi, Zhang Xiping, Li Xuetao	*The design of the strategic plan for the disciplines of philosophy and social sciences at China's institutions of higher education to "go abroad" (2010-2020)*	China Association of Higher Education Eighth Award for Excellence in Higher Education Research, Excellence Prize
		China Association of Higher Education Social Sciences Research Management Branch Award for Excellence in Social Sciences Research Management, Exceptional Prize
Jia Wenjian	*A Report on China's Undergraduate Study of German*	China Association of Higher Education Eighth Award for Excellence in Higher Education Research, 3rd Prize

第十章
英才辈出　桃李芬芳

Chapter Ten
Generation after generation of highflying graduates

　　北京外国语大学最为世人称道，同时也是学校最引以为傲的成就，是在培养高级外语人才方面对国家所做出的突出贡献。建校七十余年来，学校培养出九万余名毕业生。北外的毕业生一向以外语基本功过硬、综合素质优秀而受到社会的高度赞扬。他们分布在外交、新闻、金融、经贸、教育、法律以及军事等领域，足迹遍布世界各地，其中仅在中华人民共和国外交部、中共中央对外联络部担任副部长以上职务的就有近三十人，驻外大使三百六十余人（不包括大使衔总领事或其他同级外交官）。学校也因此赢得了"共和国外交官摇篮"的美誉。

　　The achievement that Beijing Foreign Studies University is best known for and that the University is most proud of is the contribution it has made to the nation in cultivating high-calibre foreign language professionals. In the past seven decades and more, it has graduated over 90,000 students, who are known for having solid foundations in foreign language skills and excellent overall character. They can be found in foreign service, news media, finance, businesses, foreign trade, education, law, and the military, leaving their footprints all over the world. In the Ministry of Foreign Affairs and the International Liaison Department of the CPC Central Committee alone, nearly 30 BFSU alumni have served as Vice Ministers or above, and over 360 have served as ambassadors to foreign countries (not including those who have served as consul generals at the ambassadorial level or other diplomats of the same rank). For this the University is known as the cradle of diplomats for the People's Republic.

一九四一年抗大三分校俄文大队部分学员

Some of the students enrolled in the Russian Department of the Third Campus of Kangda — the Military and Political University of Chinese People's War of Resistance Against Japanese Aggression — in 1941

白布佳

1923 年生于山西平陆。1938 年参加八路军，1941 年入俄文大队学习，1945 年加入中国共产党。1949 年后历任《东北中苏友好报》和《苏联介绍》编辑部主编，冶金部进出口公司副总经理，冶金部外贸公司董事长、党委书记等职务。

Bai Bujia, born in 1923 in Pinglu, Shanxi, joined the Eighth Route Army in 1938. He enrolled in the Russian Department of Kangda in 1941, and joined the CPC in 1945. After 1949, he served successively as Chief Editor of *Northeast China-USSR Friendship Newspaper* and *Introduction to the Soviet Union*, Deputy General Manager of China Metallurgical Import and Export Corporation, Chairman and Party Secretary of China Metallurgical Foreign Trade Company.

付 克

（1918—2006），河北安平人。1941 年入俄文大队学习。历任教育部高教一司副司长、中国苏联东欧学会副会长、中国外语教学研究会副会长等职务。

Fu Ke (1918-2006), born in Anping, Hebei, joined the Russian Department of Kangda in 1941. He served successively as Deputy Chief of the No.1 Higher Education Division at the Ministry of Education, Vice President of the Chinese Research Association of Soviet Union and Eastern Europe, and Vice President of the Chinese Society for Foreign Language Education.

高 茜

1920 年生于上海。1938 年被抗大录取为学员，1941 年入俄文大队学习。1945 年 10 月在沈阳中共铁西区委宣传部负责俄文翻译工作。1949 年后，历任沈阳市政府交际处处长、文教卫生处处长等职务。

Gao Qian, born in Shanghai in 1920, became a student at Kangda in 1938, and enrolled in its Russian Department in 1941. In October 1945, she started working as a Russian translator for the Propaganda Department of the Tiexi District CPC Committee in Shenyang. After 1949, she served as Head of the Public Relations Department, and then as Head of the Department of Culture, Education and Health of the Shenyang Municipal Government.

高世坤

（1920—2013），山东无棣人。1939
年参加八路军，同年加入中国共产党，
1941年入俄文大队学习。历任外国
语学校俄语部教员、年级主任，外交
部领事司副司长，驻苏联大使馆参赞
等职务。

Gao Shikun (1920-2013), born in Wudi, Shandong, joined the
Eighth Route Army in 1939 and became a member of the CPC in
the same year. He enrolled in the Russian Department of Kangda in 1941 and served successively as teacher and Head of Year
at Institute of Foreign Languages, Deputy Head of the Consulate
Division at the Ministry of Foreign Affairs, and Counsellor at the
Chinese Embassy to the Soviet Union.

高士英

（1919—1976），山西襄汾人。1938
年加入中国共产党，1941年7月入
俄文大队学习，后留校工作。抗战胜
利后随军到东北，先后在东北大学、
东北民主联军总司令部附设外国语学
校、哈尔滨外国语学院工作。其后历
任哈尔滨重型机器厂党委书记、哈尔
滨市农业机械局副局长、哈尔滨市标
准计量局副局长。

Gao Shiying (1919-1976), born in Xiangfen, Shanxi, joined the
CPC in 1938. He enrolled in the Russian Department in July 1941
and stayed at the School after graduation. After the Japanese were
defeated, he followed the military to Northeast China and worked at
the School of Foreign Language Affiliated to Northeastern University
and the General Headquarters of Northeast Democratic Coalition,
and at Harbin School of Foreign Languages. Later, he served as
Party Secretary at Harbin Heavy Machinery Factory, Deputy Director
of the Agricultural Machinery Bureau and then Deputy Director of the
Standard Measurements Bureau in the city of Harbin.

高亚天

（1917—1959），原名高中一，河北
深县人。1941年入俄文大队学习。
1945年毕业后赴东北，先后在东北
大学和哈尔滨外专工作。1950年调
北京俄文专修学校和北京俄语学院任
教务处处长，同时加入高等教育部俄
文教学指导委员会和会刊《俄文教学》
编辑部工作，任委员和副主编。

Gao Yatian (1917-1959), original name Gao Zhongyi, was born
in Shen County, Hebei. He enrolled in the Russian Department in
1941, went to Northeast China after graduation and worked first
at Northeastern University and then at Harbin School of Foreign
Language. He was transferred to Beijing in 1950 and became
Director of Teaching Affairs at Beijing Russian Language School,
which was later renamed Beijing Russian Institute. At the same
time, he was a member of the Russian Language Education
Steering Committee at the Ministry of Higher Education and an
Associate Editor of *Russian Language Education*.

关恩泽

（1919—2010），1941 年进入俄文大队学习。历任东北民主联军总司令部秘书科秘书、绥化铁路局呼兰车站军事站长、哈尔滨铁路局总工会秘书处主任、哈尔滨铁路局计划统计处处长等职务。

Guan Enze (1919-2010) was enrolled in the Russian Department of Kangda in 1941. After graduation, he served successively as a secretary in the Secretariat of the Headquarters of the Northeast Democratic Coalition, the Military Station Master of Hulan Railways Station under the Suihua Railway Branch Bureau, Director of the Secretariat of the General Trade Union for Harbin Railways Bureau, and Head of the Planning and Statistics Division at Harbin Railways Bureau.

何 方

1922 年生于陕西临潼。1939 年加入中国共产党，1941 年入俄文大队学习。1950 年调外交部工作，先后任驻苏联大使馆研究室主任、外交部办公厅副主任。1978 后历任中国社会科学院日本研究所所长、国务院国际问题研究中心副总干事、中苏（中俄）友协副会长。1993 年被俄罗斯科学院远东研究所授予名誉博士学位。为第七、八届全国政协委员。

He Fang, born in Lintong, Shaanxi in 1922, joined the CPC in 1939 and enrolled in the Russian Department at Kangda in 1941. He was assigned to work in the Ministry of Foreign Affairs in 1950 where he held the posts of Director of the Research Office at the Chinese Embassy to the Soviet Union and Deputy Director of the General Office of the Ministry of Foreign Affairs. After 1978, he served as the Director of the Japanese Studies Institute at the Chinese Academy of Social Sciences, Deputy Director General of the International Studies Centre of the State Council, and Vice President of China-USSR (China-Russia) Friendship Association. He received an Honorary Doctorate from the Far East Institute of the Russian Academy of Sciences in 1993 and was a member of the National Committee of 7th and 8th CPPCC.

何 匡

（1915—1983），四川达县人。1939 年加入中国共产党，1941 年入俄文大队学习。历任中共中央东北局翻译局副局长、中央编译局翻译科科长、山东大学党委副书记、人民日报理论部主任等职务。

He Kuang (1915-1983), born in Da County, Sichuan, joined the CPC in 1939, and enrolled in the Russian Department of Kangda in 1941. He served successively as Deputy Head of the Translation Department at CPC Central Government's Northeast Bureau, Head of the Translation Section of the Central Compilation and Translation Bureau, Deputy Party Secretary of Shandong University, and Head of the Theory Unit at the People's Daily newspaper.

何理良

1926 年生于浙江杭州。1941 年入俄文大队学习，1945 年加入中国共产党。1958 年毕业于莫斯科国立国际关系学院历史系。历任驻加拿大大使馆参赞、驻联合国代表团参赞、外交部国际司副司长等职务。自 1977 年至 1997 年任全国政协委员。

He Liliang, born in 1926 in Hangzhou, Zhejiang, enrolled in the Russian Department at Kangda in 1941, joined the CPC in 1945 and graduated from the Department of History at Moscow State Institute of International Relations. She worked as a counsellor in the Chinese Embassy to Canada and then in the Chinese delegation to the United Nations. She served as the Deputy Head of the International Division at the Ministry of Foreign Affairs and was a member of the National Committee of the CPPCC between 1977 and 1997.

蓝 曼

（1922—2002），原名文瑞，河北武强人。1939 年参加八路军，1941 年入俄文大队学习，同年加入中国共产党。曾任装甲兵司令部翻译科科长、《解放军文艺》编辑组组长、解放军第二炮兵政治部文化部部长等职务。有多部诗集及翻译苏联诗集出版。

Lan Man (1922-2002), original name Wen Rui, was born in Wuqiang, Hebei. He joined the Eighth Route Army in 1939, enrolled in the Russian Department at Kangda in 1941 and joined the CPC in the same year. He served successively as Head of the Translation Section of the Armoured Forces Headquarters, Chief Editor of *Arts and Literature of the Liberation Army*, Head of the Culture Division of the Political Department of the Liberation Army Second Artillery. He published a number of collections of personal poetry and Chinese translations of Russian poetry.

李 参

生于 1917 年。1938 年入延安抗日军政大学学习，后转入抗大俄文大队学习，是当时俄文大队的五个区队长之一 。历任中国东北铁路总局副局长、局长，铁道部外事局局长、副部长，中华人民共和国驻东欧铁路协调委员会总代表，中华人民共和国援建坦桑尼亚／赞比亚铁路总指挥，我国第一条地下铁道运营、启动总指挥等职务。

Li Can, born in 1917, enrolled in the Military and Political University of war of Resistance Against Japan in 1938 and was later transferred to its Russian Department and became one of the five class monitors. He served successively as Deputy Head and then Head of Northeast China Railway Bureau, Head of the Foreign Affairs Department and then Vice Minister at the Ministry of Railways, Chief Representative of China's Railway Coordinating Committee posted in Eastern Europe, General Commander of China's aid effort to build the Tanzania-Zambia railway, and General Commander responsible for the start-up and operation of China's first underground railway.

李则望

（1920—1993），山西安泽人。1937 年参加八路军，1939 年加入中国共产党，1941 年入俄文大队学习。1946 年到张家口华北联合大学担任俄语教员。1950 年调外交部工作，历任驻赤塔总领事馆领事、外交部美澳司司长。驻匈牙利、波兰、罗马尼亚、苏联大使。第七、八届全国政协委员。

Li Zewang (1920-1993), born in Anze, Shanxi, joined the Eighth Route Army in 1937, became a member of the CPC in 1939, and enrolled in the Russian Department of Kangda in 1941. He became a Russian language teacher at North China Union University in Zhangjiakou in 1946, was transferred to the Ministry of Foreign Affairs in 1950, and served as the Consul at the Consulate General in Chita, Head of the Americas and Australia Division at the Ministry of Foreign Affairs, and Ambassador to Hungary, Poland, Romania and the Soviet Union. He was a member of the National Committee of the 7th and 8th CPPCC.

梁克昌

（1918—2004），山西介休人。1937 年参加八路军，1940 年加入中国共产党，1941 年入俄文大队学习。曾任八路军总部行政处科长、中央军委作战部行政科科长、北京通信兵部后勤部军需处处长、总参谋部通信部研究室研究员等职。1988 年荣获二级红星功勋荣誉章。

Liang Kechang (1918-2004), born in Jiexiu, Shanxi, joined the Eighth Route Army in 1937, became a member of the CPC in 1940, and enrolled in the Russian Department at Kangda in 1941. He served as a section chief in the Administration Department of the Eighth Route Army General Headquarters, Chief of the Administration Section of the Operations Department at the Central Military Commission, Head of the Military Supplies Office under the Logistics Department of Beijing Signals Corps, and member of the Research Office of the Communications Corps at the General Staff Department. He received the Red Star Medal 2nd Class in 1988.

凌祖佑

1923 年生于上海。1938 年加入中国共产党，1941 年进入俄文大队学习。历任中长铁路局首任军事代表、翻译处处长，铁道部财务局局长，全国审计学会秘书长等职务。

Ling Zuyou, born in Shanghai in 1923, joined the CPC in 1938 and enrolled in the Russian Department at Kangda in 1941. He served successively as the first Army Representative and Chief of the Translation Office at the Changchun Railways Bureau, Director of the Finance Department at the Ministry of Railways, and Secretary General of the National Audit Society.

刘永诚

（1919—2011），四川万县人。1938年
参加八路军，1940年加入中国共产党，
1941年入俄文大队学习。曾任装甲兵司
令部作战处处长、研究室主任等职务。

Liu Yongcheng (1919-2011), born in Wan County, Sichuan, joined the Eighth Route Army in 1938, became a member of the CPC in 1940, and enrolled in the Russian Department at Kangda in 1941. He served as Head of the Operations Department and Head of the Research Office at the Armoured Forces Headquarters.

刘玉堤

（1923—2015），河北沧县人。
1938年10月参加八路军，1941
年入俄文大队学习。历任空军第四
混成旅飞行中队长、副大队长，空
军团长、副师长、师长、军长，军
区空军司令员，北京军区副司令员
兼军区空军司令员。荣获三级独立
自由勋章和三级解放勋章。1988年
被授予空军中将军衔。荣获独立功
勋荣誉章。荣获"中国人民志愿军
一级战斗英雄"称号。中共十一大
代表。第三、四、六、七届全国人
民代表大会代表。第七、八届全国
政协委员。第七届全国政协常委。

Liu Yudi (1923-2015), born in Cang County, Hebei, joined the Eighth Route Army in October 1938 and enrolled in the Russian Department at Kangda in 1941. He served as a squadron leader and deputy wing commander of the 4th Mixed Flying Corps, a regiment commander, deputy division commander, division commander, army corps commander of the Chinese Air Force; air force commander of a military region command; Deputy Commander of the Beijing Military Region and concurrent Commander of its Air Force. He was awarded the Medal of Independence and Freedom 3rd Class, and the Medal of Liberation 3rd Class. In 1988 he was promoted to Air Force Lieutenant General. He was awarded the Honorary Medal of Independence and received the title of First-Class Combat Hero of the Chinese Volunteer Army. He was a delegate to the 11th CPC National Congress;a delegate to the 3rd, 4th, 6th and 7th NPC; a member of the National Committee of the 7th and 8th CPPCC.

卢振中

（1918—1996），河南鲁山人。1941年
入俄文大队学习。1956年被派往苏联学
习，获副博士学位。历任武汉大学外文系
主任、校党委常委，华中科技大学副校长
等职务。

Lu Zhenzhong (1918-1996), born in Lushan, Henan, enrolled in the Russian Department at Kangda in 1941. He was sent to study in the Soviet Union in 1956, where he received a doctorate degree. He served successively as Head of the Foreign Languages Department and member of the CPC Standing Committee at Wuhan University, and Vice President of Huazhong University of Science and Technology.

罗 焚

1921 年生于四川重庆。1938 年入延安陕北公学学习，同年加入中国共产党，1941年入俄文大队学习。1945 年赴张家口华北联合大学俄语系工作。1949 年后先后任职于中国驻苏联大使馆、中共中央编译局及中国文联。

Luo Fen, born in 1921 in Chongqing, Sichuan, became a student at North Shaanxi College in Yan'an in 1938, joined the CPC in the same year, and enrolled in the Russian Department at Kangda in 1941. He moved to Zhangjiakou to work in the Russian Department at North China Union University in 1945. After 1949, he worked at the Chinese Embassy to the Soviet Union, CPC Central Compilation and Translation Bureau, and China Federation of Literary and Art Circles.

罗俊才

1919 年生于山西太原。1940 年加入中国共产党，1941 年入俄文大队学习。1946年调入华北联合大学外语学院俄语系任政治助理员。历任中国人民大学俄语系主任、北京俄语学院教务处处长、北京外国语学院教务长等职务。

Luo Juncai, born in Taiyuan, Shanxi in 1919, joined the CPC in 1940, and enrolled in the Russian Department at Kangda in 1941. He was transferred to the Russian Department at North China Union University to become a Political Assistant in 1946. He served as Head of the Russian Department at Renmin University of China, Director of Teaching Affairs at Beijing Russian Institute and Teaching Affairs Officer at Beijing Foreign Languages Institute.

马杰三

1924 年生于河北曲周。1941 年入俄文大队学习，后在一大队航空工程队工作。1945 年在延安机场任参谋，其间参与组织毛泽东赴重庆谈判的专机安全保障工作。1945 年 10 月赴东北参加老航校创建工作。1949 年后历任空军混成第四旅大队长、空五师十五团团长、空五师师长、昆明军区空军指挥所主任。

Ma Jiesan, born in Quzhou, Hebei in 1924, enrolled in the Third Campus at the Military and Political University of War of Resistance Against Japan in 1941, and later worked in the Aeronautical Engineering Programme of Department One. He became a staff officer at Yan'an Airport in 1945, and was involved in the safety and security work on the plane taking Chairman Mao to the Chongqing for negotiations with Chiang Kai-shek. In October 1945 he went to Northeast China to setup a flight school. After 1949, he served as awing commander of the 4th Mixed Flying Corps, Commander of the 15th Regiment and then Division Commander of the 5th Air Division, and Director of the Air Force Command Centre of the Kunming Military Region Command.

马 列

1923年生于辽宁沈阳。1941年参加八路军，1941年入俄文大队学习，1945年参加中国共产党。历任政务院（后改为国务院）周恩来总理办公室外事秘书、国务院外办副秘书长、驻苏联大使馆政务参赞、外交部综合研究室主任、中国驻匈牙利大使等职务。

Ma Lie, born in Shenyang, Liaoning in 1923, joined the Eighth Route Army in 1941, enrolled in the Russian Department at Kangda in 1941 and joined the CPC in 1945. He served successively as the Foreign Affairs Secretary in the Office of Premier Zhou Enlai under the Government Administration Council, which was later renamed the State Council, Deputy Chief Secretary of the Foreign Affairs Office of the State Council, Administrative Counsellor at the Chinese Embassy to the Soviet Union, Director of the General Research Office at the Ministry of Foreign Affairs, and Chinese Ambassador to Hungary.

司马慧

（1916—2001），山西夏县人。1936年加入中国共产党，1941年入俄文大队学习。曾任中国人民志愿军第66军、第64军炮兵团政委，华北军区第14师炮兵政治部主任，军委北京炮兵学校副政委，炮兵第二研究所政委等职务。1988年被授予中华人民共和国二级红星荣誉章。

Sima Hui (1916-2001), born in Xia County, Shanxi, joined the CPC in 1936, and enrolled in the Russian Department at Kangda in 1941. He served as the political commissar of an artillery regiment of the 66th Army and then the 64th Army, Director of the Political Department at the 14th Division Artillery Corps in the North China Military Region Command, Deputy Political Commissar at the Military Commission Artillery School in Beijing, and Political Commissar of No.2 Research Institute at the Artillery Corps. He was awarded the Red Star Honorary Medal 2nd Class of the People's Republic of China in 1988.

苏 英

1922年生于山西稷山。1941入俄文大队学习，同年加入中国共产党。历任哈尔滨外专教务处副处长、大连解放军俄专训练部副部长、解放军军事科学院研究员等职务。获独立功勋章并被授予中国翻译协会"资深翻译家"称号。

Su Ying, born in Jishan, Shanxi in 1922, enrolled in the Russian Department at Kangda in 1941 and joined the CPC in the same year. He served successively as Deputy Director of Teaching Affairs at Harbin School of Foreign Language, Deputy Head of the Training Department at the People's Liberation Army Russian Language School in Dalian, and Research fellow at the PLA Academy of Military Science. He was awarded the Medal of Independence and received the title of Senior Translator from Translators Association of China.

王 诚

（1917—2013），山西原平人。1941 年入俄文大队学习。历任北京军区空军司令部修建处副处长、北京钢厂副厂长、第三钢厂副厂长等职务。1955 年荣获三级独立自由勋章和三级解放勋章。

Wang Cheng (1917-2013), born in Yuanping, Shanxi, enrolled in the Russian Department at Kangda in 1941. He served successively as Deputy Director of the Construction Department for the Air Force Headquarters of Beijing Military Region Command, Deputy General Manager of Beijing Steel Factory, and Deputy General Manager of No.3 Steel Factory. He was awarded the Medal of Independence and Freedom 3rd Class, and the Medal of Liberation 3rd Class in 1955.

王麦林

1925 年生于福建福州。1938 年加入中国共产党，1941 年入俄文大队学习。1945 年赴东北参加东北航校创建工作。1956—1958 年北京俄语学院进修学习。1949 年后历任空军司令部翻译科科长、科学大众杂志社第一主编、科普出版社党委书记兼社长、中国科协党组成员等职务。1955 年荣获自由独立勋章和三级解放勋章。

Wang Mailin, born in Fuzhou, Fujian in 1925, joined the CPC in 1938, enrolled in the Russian Department at Kangda in 1941, and went to Northeast China in 1945 to participate in the establishment of Northeast Flight School. She received further training at Beijing Russian Institute between 1956 and 1958. Her appointments after 1949 include Chief of the Translation Section at the Air Force Headquarters, First Chief Editor of Popular Science Magazine, Party Secretary and President of Popular Science Publishing House, and a member of CPC Leading Members' Group at China Association for Science and Technology. She was awarded the Medal of Freedom and Independence and the Medal of Liberation 3rd Class in 1955.

谢家彬

（1923—2011），山东茌平人。1938 年参加八路军，1939 年加入中国共产党，1941 年入俄文大队学习。1946 年参加筹建东北民主联军总司令部所属外国语学校，并任俄文教员、教育科科长。1949 年后历任东风（酒泉）基地司令部资料情报处处长、中央工艺美术学院图书馆馆长等职务。1955 年荣获三级独立自由勋章和三级解放勋章。

Xie Jiabin (1923-2011), born in Chiping, Shandong, joined the Eighth Route Army in 1938, became a member of the CPC in 1939, and enrolled in the Russian Department at Kangda in 1941. He helped to establish the School of Foreign Language Affiliated to General Headquarters of Northeast Democratic Coalition in 1946 and became a Russian language teacher at the School and Head of its Education Office. After 1949, he served as the Director of the Intelligence Department at Dongfeng (later known as Jiuquan) Military Base Headquarters, and Head Librarian at the Central Academy of Art and Design. He was awarded the Medal of Independence and Freedom 3rd Class and the Medal of Liberation 3rd Class in 1955.

张开帙

1918 年生于安徽阜南。1937 年考入国民党空军机械学校，1939 年加入中国共产党，1940 年入陕北公学学习、任教，1941 年入俄文大队学习。1945 年随军赴东北创建东北民主联军航空学校并任训练处机械科科长。其后历任南苑航空修理厂厂长、空军司令部机务部部长等职位。1955 年荣获三级独立自由勋章及独立功勋荣誉章。

Zhang Kaizhi, born in Funan, Anhui in 1918, was admitted into Kuomintang's Air Force Machinery School in 1937, but joined the CPC in 1939, went to study and teach at North Shaanxi College in 1940, and enrolled in the Russian Department at Kangda in 1941. He accompanied the army to Northeast China and helped establish the Northeast Democratic Coalition Flight School, and became Head of the Machinery Section in the School's Training Department. He then served as General Manager of Nanyuan Aviation Service Works and Director of the Maintenance Department for Air Force Headquarters. He was awarded the Medal of Independence and Freedom 3rd Class and the Honorary Medal of Independence in 1955.

张天恩

（1923—2010），山西汾阳人。1938 年参加八路军，同年加入中国共产党，1941 年入俄文大队学习。历任黑龙江大学党委副书记、副校长，北京第二外国语学院党委副书记、副院长、党委书记，中央教科所党委书记、常务副所长，教育科学出版社总编辑等职务。

Zhang Tianen (1923-2010), born in Fenyang, Shanxi, joined the Eighth Route Army in 1938, became a member of the CPC in the same year, and enrolled in the Russian Department at Kangda in 1941. He served successively as Deputy Party Secretary and Vice President of Heilongjiang University, Deputy Party Secretary and Vice President of Beijing No.2 Foreign Languages Institute, Party Secretary and Executive Director of the National Institute of Education Science, and Managing Editor of Education and Science Publishing House.

张铁民

（1918—1990），又名张西民，山东夏津人。1938 年加入中国共产党，1941 年入俄文大队学习。曾任中共第一任吉林省丹东火车站军代表、站长。1949 年以后，历任郑州铁路局汉口火车站军代表及站长、郑州铁路局副局长、武汉铁路局常务副局长、武汉钢铁公司和冶金部第一冶金建设公司副经理等职务。

Zhang Tiemin (1918-1990),alias Zhang Ximin, born in Xiajin, Shandong, joined the CPC in 1938, and enrolled in the Russian Department at Kangda in 1941. He was the first Army Representative and Station Manager at Dandong Train Station in Jinlin Province. After 1949, he served successively as the Army Representative and Station Manager of Hankou Train Station for the Zhengzhou Railways Bureau, Deputy Director of Zhengzhou Railways Bureau, Executive Deputy Director of Wuhan Railways Bureau, and Assistant General Manager of Wuhan Steel Company and No. 1 Metallurgical Construction Company under the Ministry of Metallurgical Industry.

部分担任领导职务的校友

Alumni in leadership positions (incomplete)

姓名	Name	毕业院系	School/Dept.	曾（现）任职务	Positions held
艾 平	Ai Ping	英语学院	School of English	中国人民政治协商会议第十二届全国委员会外事委员会委员、中共中央对外联络部副部长、驻埃塞俄比亚大使	Member of the Foreign Affairs Subcommittee of the National Committee of the 12th CPPCC; Vice Minister of the International Department of the CPC Central Committee; Ambassador to Ethiopia
蔡方柏	Cai Fangbai	法语系	Dept. of French	驻法国、瑞士大使，第九届全国人大外事委员会主任委员	Ambassador to France; Ambassador to Switzerland; Chairman of the Foreign Affairs Committee of the 9th NPC
陈 辞	Chen Ci	英语学院	School of English	中共海南省委常委、海口市委书记	Member of the Standing Committee of the CPC Hainan Provincial Committee; Secretary of the CPC Haikou Municipal Committee
陈昊苏	Chen Haosu	英语学院	School of English	第十一届全国政协外事委员会副主任、中俄友好协会会长、中国人民对外友好协会会长	Vice Chairman of the Foreign Affairs Subcommittee of the 11th CPPCC National Committee; President of the China-Russia Friendship Association; President of the Chinese People's Association for Friendship with Foreign Countries
陈 健	Chen Jian	英语学院	School of English	商务部副部长、联合国副秘书长、驻日本大使	Vice Minister of Commerce; UN Deputy Secretary-General; Ambassador to Japan
程幼东	Cheng Youdong	英语学院	School of English	黑龙江省政协副主席、黑龙江省副省长	Vice Chairman of the CPPCC Heilongjiang Provincial Committee; Deputy Governor of Heilongjiang Province
崔天凯	Cui Tiankai	高级翻译学院	Graduate School of Translation & Interpretation	驻美国大使、驻日本大使、外交部新闻发言人、外交部副部长	Ambassador to the US; Ambassador to Japan; Ministry of Foreign Affairs' spokesman; Vice Minister of Foreign Affairs
丁 伟	Ding Wei	英语学院	School of English	驻意大利大使兼驻圣马力诺大使、文化部部长助理	Ambassador to Italy and concurrent Ambassador to San Marino; Assistant Minister of Culture
杜起文	Du Qiwen	英语学院	School of English	驻希腊大使、中央外事办公室副主任	Ambassador to Greece; Deputy Director of the Foreign Affairs Office of the CPC Central Committee
段 津	Duan Jin	英语学院	School of English	中国人民外交学会副会长、外交部新闻发言人、驻英国大使	Vice President of the Chinese People's Institute of Foreign Affairs; Ministry of Foreign Affairs' spokesman; Ambassador to the UK
冯佐库	Feng Zuoku	阿拉伯语系	Dept. of Arabic	中国人民对外友好协会副会长、党组成员	Vice President of the Chinese People's Association for Friendship with Foreign Countries and a member of its leading Party members' group
傅 莹	Fu Ying	英语学院	School of English	全国人大常委会委员、全国人大外事委员会主任委员、驻英国大使、外交部副部长	Member of the NPC Standing Committee; Chairman of the NPC Foreign Affairs Committee; Ambassador to the UK; Vice Minister of Foreign Affairs
傅志寰	Fu Zhihuan	留苏预备部	Training Division for Studying in the Soviet Union	铁道部部长、中国工程院院士、中共第十五届中央委员	Minister of Railways; Academician of Chinese Academy of Engineering; a member of the 15th CPC Central Committee
郭业洲	Guo Yezhou	德语系	Dept. of German	中共中央对外联络部副部长、驻保加利亚大使	Vice Minister of the International Department of the CPC Central Committee; Ambassador to Bulgaria

姓名	Name	毕业院系	School/Dept.	曾（现）任职务	Positions held
何亚非	He Yafei	高级翻译学院	Graduate School of Translation & Interpretation	国务院侨务办公室副主任、外交部副部长、中国驻联合国日内瓦办事处和瑞士其他国际组织代表	Deputy Director of Overseas Chinese Affairs Office of the State Council; Vice Minister of Foreign Affairs; Representative of China to the UN Office in Geneva and other international organizations in Switzerland
胡正跃	Hu Zhengyue	亚非学院	School of Asian & African Studies	外交部驻澳门特别行政区特派员公署特派员、驻马来西亚大使、外交部部长助理	Commissioner of the Ministry of Foreign Affairs for the Macao Special Administrative Region; Ambassador to Malaysia; Assistant Minister of Foreign Affairs
宦国英	Huan Guoying	英语学院	School of English	中共中央对外联络部副部长	Vice Minister of the International Department of the CPC Central Committee
姜恩柱	Jiang Enzhu	英语学院	School of English	外交部副部长、人大外事委员会主任委员、驻英国大使	Vice Minister of Foreign Affairs; Chairman of the NPC Foreign Affairs Committee; Ambassador to the UK
姜　颖	Jiang Ying	俄语学院	School of Russian	国家知识产权局局长、党组书记，第九届全国政协委员	Commissioner of the State Intellectual Property Office and Secretary of its leading Party members' group; a member of the National Committee of 9th CPPCC
金立群	Jin Liqun	英语学院	School of English	世界银行中国副执行董事、财政部副部长、亚洲开发银行副行长、中国国际金融有限公司董事长、亚投行多边临时秘书处秘书长	Deputy Executive Director for China at the World Bank; Vice Minister of Finance; Vice President of the Asian Development Bank; Chairman of China International Capital Corporation; Secretary-General of the Multilateral Interim Secretariat for Establishing Asian Infrastructure Investment Bank
金永健	Jin Yongjian	英语学院	School of English	联合国副秘书长，中国联合国协会会长，常驻联合国副代表、大使	UN Deputy Secretary-General; President of the UN Association of China; Deputy Permanent Representative and Ambassador to the UN
井顿泉	Jing Dunquan	日语系	Dept. of Japanese	中国宋庆龄基金会副主席、中国人民对外友好协会副会长	Vice Chairman of China Soong Ching Ling Foundation; Vice President of the Chinese People's Association for Friendship with Foreign Countries
孔　泉	Kong Quan	附属学校	Affiliated School	中央外办副主任、驻法国兼驻摩纳哥公国大使、外交部部长助理、外交部新闻发言人	Deputy Director of the Foreign Affairs Office of the CPC Central Committee; Ambassador to France and concurrent Ambassador to the Principality of Monaco; Assistant Minister of Foreign Affairs; Ministry of Foreign Affairs' spokesman
李保东	Li Baodong	英语学院	School of English	外交部副部长，常驻联合国代表、大使，驻联合国日内瓦办事处和瑞士其他国际组织代表、大使，驻赞比亚大使	Vice Minister of Foreign Affairs; Permanent Representative and Ambassador to the UN; Representative and Ambassador to the UN Office in Geneva and other international organizations in Switzerland; Ambassador to Zambia
李北海	Li Beihai	西葡语系	Dept. of Spanish & Portuguese	中共中央对外联络部副部长、第十届全国政协外事委员会副主任	Vice Minister of the International Department of the CPC Central Committee; Deputy Director of the Foreign Affairs Subcommittee of the National Committee of the 10th CPPCC
李成仁	Li Chengren	俄语学院	School of Russian	中共中央对外联络部副部长、驻阿拉伯也门共和国大使	Vice Minister of the International Department of the CPC Central Committee; Ambassador to the Yemen Arab Republic
李东生	Li Dongsheng	法语系	Dept. of French	国家工商行政管理总局副局长	Deputy Minister of the State Administration for Industry and Commerce

姓名	Name	毕业院系	School/Dept.	曾（现）任职务	Positions held
李贵鲜	Li Guixian	留苏预备部	Training Division for Studying in the Soviet Union	中共第十二届、十三届、十四届、十五届、十六届中央委员，第九届全国政协副主席	Member of the 12th, 13th, 14th, 15th, and 16th CPC Central Committee; Vice Chairman of the National Committee of the 9th CPPCC
李 辉	Li Hui	俄语学院	School of Russian	驻俄罗斯大使、外交部副部长	Ambassador to Russia; Vice Minister of Foreign Affairs
李金章	Li Jinzhang	附属学校	Affiliated School	外交部副部长、驻巴西大使、第十七届中共中央纪律检查委员会委员	Vice Minister of Foreign Affairs ; Ambassador to Brazil; a member of the Discipline Inspection Commission of the 17th CPC Central Committee
李其庆	Li Qiqing	法语系	Dept. of French	中央编译局副局长	Deputy Director of the Central Compilation and Translation Bureau
李铁映	Li Tieying	留苏预备部	Training Division for Studying in the Soviet Union	中共第十二届中央候补委员、委员，第十三届、十四届、十五届中央委员，中央政治局委员，第十届全国人大常委会副委员长	Alternate member and then full member of the 12th CPC Central Committee; a member of the 13th, 14th, and 15th CPC Central Committee and Politburo; Vice Chairman of 10th NPC
李肇星	Li Zhaoxing	英语翻译班	English Translation Class	外交部部长，第十一届全国人大外事委员会主任委员，常驻联合国代表、大使，驻美国大使	Minister of Foreign Affairs; Chairman of the 11th NPC Foreign Affairs Committee; Permanent Representative and Ambassador to the UN; Ambassador to the US
凌 志	Ling Zhi	英语学院	School of English	中国银行副行长	Vice President of the Bank of China
刘古昌	Liu Guchang	欧语学院	School of European Languages & Cultures	外交部副部长、驻罗马尼亚大使、驻俄罗斯大使	Vice Minister of Foreign Affairs; Ambassador to Romania; Ambassador to Russia
刘建超	Liu Jianchao	英语学院	School of English	外交部部长助理、驻印度尼西亚大使、外交部新闻发言人、驻菲律宾大使	Assistant minister of Foreign Affairs; Ambassador to Indonesia; Ministry of Foreign Affairs' spokesman; Ambassador to the Philippines
刘结一	Liu Jieyi	高级翻译学院	Graduate School of Translation & Interpretation	中国常驻联合国代表、大使，中共中央对外联络部副部长	Permanent Representative and Ambassador to the UN; Vice Minister of the International Department of the CPC Central Committee
刘敬钦	Liu Jingqin	德语系	Dept. of German	中共中央对外联络部副部长	Vice Minister of the International Department of the CPC Central Committee
刘习良	Liu Xiliang	西葡语系	Dept. of Spanish & Portuguese	中国广播电视学会常务副会长、广电部副部长	Executive Vice President of the China Radio and Television Association; Vice Minister of Radio, Film and Television
吕国增	Lü Guozeng	法语系	Dept. of French	外交部副部长，驻突尼斯大使、后兼任驻巴勒斯坦大使	Vice Minister of Foreign Affairs; Ambassador to Tunisia, later concurrent Ambassador to the State of Palestine
马灿荣	Ma Canrong	德语系	Dept. of German	外交部部长助理、驻德国大使	Assistant Minister of Foreign Affairs; Ambassador to Germany
马胜荣	Ma Shengrong	英语学院	School of English	新华社副社长	Vice President of Xinhua News Agency
马毓真	Ma Yuzhen	英语学院	School of English	外交部新闻发言人、驻香港特别行政区特派员公署特派员、驻英国大使	Ministry of Foreign Affairs' spokesman; Commissioner of the Ministry of Foreign Affairs for the Hong Kong Special Administrative Region; Ambassador to the UK

姓名	Name	毕业院系	School/Dept.	曾（现）任职务	Positions held
马振岗	**Ma Zhen'gang**	英语学院	School of English	中国国际问题研究所所长、驻英国大使、第十届全国政协外事委员会副主任委员	Director of China Institute of International Studies; Ambassador to the UK; Deputy Director of the Foreign Affairs Subcommittee of the National Committee of the 10th CPPCC
梅兆荣	**Mei Zhaorong**	英语学院	School of English	中国人民外交学会会长、驻德国大使、国务院发展研究中心世界发展研究所所长	President of the Chinese People's Institute of Foreign Affairs; Ambassador to Germany; Director of the Institute of World Development, the Development Research Centre of the State Council
庞炳庵	**Pang Bing'an**	英语学院	School of English	新华社副社长	Vice President of Xinhua News Agency
钱洪山	**Qian Hongshan**	德语系	Dept. of German	外交部部长助理、北京外交人员服务局局长、驻格林纳达大使	Assistant Minister of Foreign Affairs; Director of the Beijing Service Bureau for Diplomatic Missions; Ambassador to Grenada
仇 鸿	**Qiu Hong**	英语学院	School of English	中央人民政府驻澳门特别行政区联络办公室副主任	Deputy Director of the Liaison Office of the Central People's Government in the Macao Special Administrative Region
裘援平	**Qiu Yuanping**	西葡语系	Dept. of Spanish & Portuguese	国务院侨办主任、党组书记，中央外事办副主任	Director of the Overseas Chinese Affairs Office of the State Council and Secretary of its leading Party members' group; Deputy Director of the Foreign Affairs Office of the CPC Central Committee
沈国放	**Shen Guofang**	英语学院	School of English	世界知识出版社总编辑，外交部部长助理，外交部新闻发言人，联合国副秘书长，中国常驻联合国代表、大使	General Managing Editor of the World Knowledge Publishing House; Assistant Minister of Foreign Affairs; Ministry of Foreign Affairs' spokesman; UN Deputy Secretary-General; Permanent Representative and Ambassador of China to the UN
宋 健	**Song Jian**	留苏预备部	Training Division for Studying in the Soviet Union	中共第十二届中央候补委员、委员，第十三届、十四届、十五届中央委员，全国政协副主席	Alternate member of the 12th CPC Central Committee; a member of the 13th, 14th, and 15th CPC Central Committee; Vice Chairman of the National Committee of the CPPCC
宋明江	**Song Mingjiang**	英语学院	School of English	驻欧盟大使、中国国际问题研究所所长	Ambassador to the EU; Director of the China Institute of International Studies
孙振宇	**Sun Zhenyu**	英语学院	School of English	世贸组织研究会会长、对外贸易经济合作部副部长、中国首任驻世贸组织大使	Chairman of China Society for World Trade Organization Studies; Vice Minister of Foreign Trade and Economic Cooperation; China's first Ambassador to the WTO
唐龙彬	**Tang Longbin**	英语学院	School of English	外交部部长助理、全国政协外事委员会副主任委员、驻瑞典大使兼驻拉脱维亚大使	Assistant Minister of Foreign Affairs; Vice Director of the Foreign Affairs Subcommittee of the National Committee of the CPPCC; Ambassador to the Kingdom of Sweden and concurrent Ambassador to the Republic of Latvia
唐闻生	**Tang Wensheng**	英语学院	School of English	中国宋庆龄基金会副主席、中华全国归国华侨联合会副主席	Vice Chairperson of the Soong Ching Ling Foundation; Vice Chairperson of the All-China Federation of Returned Overseas Chinese
田润之	**Tian Runzhi**	英语学院	School of English	海关总署副署长、国家出入境检验检疫局局长	Deputy Minister of the General Administration of Customs; Minister of the General Administration of Quality Supervision, Inspection and Quarantine

姓名	Name	毕业院系	School/Dept.	曾（现）任职务	Positions held
王海容	Wang Hairong	英语学院	School of English	外交部副部长	Vice Minister of Foreign Affairs
王锦珍	Wang Jinzhen	英语学院	School of English	中国贸促会副会长	Vice Chairman of China Council for the Promotion of International Trade (CCPIT)
王英凡	Wang Yingfan	英语学院	School of English	外交部亚洲事务特使、外交部副部长、中国常驻联合国代表、驻菲律宾大使	Special Envoy for Asian Affairs of the Ministry of Foreign Affairs; Vice Minister of Foreign Affairs; Permanent Representative of China to the UN; Ambassador to the Philippines
王运泽	Wang Yunze	阿拉伯语系	Dept. of Arabic	中国人民对外友好协会副会长、中韩友好协会副会长	Vice President of the Chinese People's Association for Friendship with Foreign Countries; Vice President of China-Republic of Korea Friendship Association
吴常康	Wu Changkang	英语学院	School of English	中国红十字会总会常务副会长	Executive Vice President of the Red Cross Society of China
吴海龙	Wu Hailong	英语学院	School of English	中国驻联合国日内瓦办事处和瑞士其他国际组织代表、大使，中国驻欧盟使团大使，外交部部长助理	Representative and Ambassador of China to the UN Office in Geneva and other international organizations in Switzerland; Head of the Chinese Mission to the EU; Assistant Minister of Foreign Affairs
吴红波	Wu Hongbo	英语学院	School of English	联合国副秘书长、驻德国大使、驻菲律宾大使	UN Deputy Secretary-General; Ambassador to Germany; Ambassador to the Philippines
吴建民	Wu Jianmin	法语系	Dept. of French	外交部新闻发言人、全国政协副秘书长兼新闻发言人、驻法国大使、外交学院院长、国际展览局主席	Ministry of Foreign Affairs' spokesman; Deputy Secretary-General and spokesman of the National Committee of the CPPCC; Ambassador to France; President of China Foreign Affairs University; President of the International Exhibitions Bureau
武大伟	Wu Dawei	亚非学院	School of Asian & African Studies	中国政府朝鲜半岛事务特别代表、外交部副部长、第十一届全国政协常委、外事委员会副主任委员	China's Special Representative for Korean Peninsula Affairs; Vice Minister of Foreign Affairs; a member of the 11th CPPCC National Committee and Deputy Chairman of its Foreign Affairs Subcommittee
武东和	Wu Donghe	法语系	Dept. of French	驻朝鲜大使、外交部部长助理、驻尼日尔大使、驻马里大使	Ambassador to the DPRK (North Korea); Assistant Minister of Foreign Affairs; Ambassador to Niger; Ambassador to Mali
夏道生	Xia Daosheng	英语学院	School of English	国务院外事办公室副主任、驻比利时大使兼驻欧共体使团团长	Deputy Director of the Foreign Affairs Office of the State Council; Ambassador to Belgium and Head of the Chinese Mission to the European Community
阎明复	Yan Mingfu	俄语学院	School of Russian	民政部副部长、中华慈善总会会长	Vice Minister of Civil Affairs; President of China Charity Federation
杨文昌	Yang Wenchang	英语学院	School of English	中国人民外交学会会长、外交部副部长、驻新加坡大使、香港特别行政区特派员	President of the Chinese People's Institute of Foreign Affairs; Vice Minister of Foreign Affairs; Ambassador to Singapore; Commissioner of the Ministry of Foreign Affairs for the Hong Kong Special Administrative Region
杨燕怡	Yang Yanyi	英语学院	School of English	驻欧盟使团团长、大使、中共中央对外联络部部长助理、驻文莱大使	Head and Ambassador of the Chinese Mission to the EU; Assistant Minister of the International Department of the CPC Central Committee; Ambassador to Brunei

姓名	Name	毕业院系	School/Dept.	曾（现）任职务	Positions held
查培新	**Zha Peixin**	英语学院	School of English	第十一届全国人大外事委员会副主任委员、第十一届全国人大常委会委员、中央外事办公室副主任、驻英国大使	Deputy Director of the Foreign Affairs Committee of the 11th NPC; a member of the 11th NPC Standing Committee; Deputy Director of the Foreign Affairs Office of the CPC Central Committee; Ambassador to the UK
张保庆	**Zhang Baoqing**	法语系	Dept. of French	教育部党组副书记、副部长，中国教育发展基金会会长	Deputy Secretary of the leading Party members' group of the Ministry of Education and Vice Minister of Education; Chairman of the China Education Development Foundation
张德广	**Zhang Deguang**	俄语学院	School of Russian	外交部副部长、上海合作组织秘书长、驻哈萨克斯坦大使、驻俄罗斯大使	Vice Minister of Foreign Affairs; Secretary-General of the Shanghai Cooperation Organization; Ambassador to the Republic of Kazakhstan; Ambassador to Russia
张　明	**Zhang Ming**	阿拉伯语系	Dept. of Arabic	外交部副部长、驻肯尼亚大使	Vice Minister of Foreign Affairs; Ambassador to Kenya
张伟超	**Zhang Weichao**	俄语学院	School of Russian	驻美国纽约大使衔总领事、国务院侨办副主任、全国政协港澳台侨委员会副主任委员	Consul General (ambassadorial level) of the Chinese Consulate in New York City, US; Deputy Director of the Overseas Chinese Affairs Office of the State Council; Deputy Chairman of the CPPCC Subcommittee for Hong Kong, Macao, Taiwan and Overseas Chinese
张业遂	**Zhang Yesui**	英语学院	School of English	外交部党委书记、常务副部长，中国常驻联合国代表、大使，驻美国大使	Party Secretary of the Ministry of Foreign Affairs; Executive Vice Minister of Foreign Affairs; Permanent Representative and Ambassador to the UN; Ambassador to the US
张志勇	**Zhang Zhiyong**	英语学院	School of English	国家税务总局党组成员、副局长	Member of the leading Party members' group and Deputy Director of the State Administration of Taxation
赵进军	**Zhao Jinjun**	法语系	Dept. of French	外交学院院长、全国政协外委会副主任、驻法国大使	President of China Foreign Affairs University; Deputy Director of the Foreign Affairs Sub-Committee of the National Committee of the CPPCC; Ambassador to France
周　南	**Zhou Nan**	英语学院	School of English	外交部副部长、新华社香港分社社长、常驻联合国副代表（大使衔）	Vice Minister of Foreign Affairs; Hong Kong Bureau Chief of the Xinhua News Agency; Deputy Permanent Representative and Ambassador to the UN

部分担任高级外交官的校友

Alumni serving as senior diplomats (incomplete)

姓名	Name	毕业院系	School/Dept.	曾（现）任职务	Positions held
安惠侯	An Huihou	法语系	Dept. of French	驻阿尔及利亚、突尼斯兼巴勒斯坦、黎巴嫩、埃及大使	Ambassador to Algeria; Ambassador to Tunisia and concurrent Ambassador to Palestine; Ambassador to Lebanon; Ambassador to Egypt
安永玉	An Yongyu	亚非学院	School of Asian & African Studies	外交学院党委书记、副院长，驻肯尼亚大使	Party Secretary and Vice President of China Foreign Affairs University; Ambassador to Kenya
鲍树生	Bao Shusheng	英语学院	School of English	驻博茨瓦纳、瓦努阿图大使	Ambassador to Botswana; Ambassador to Vanuatu
蔡润国	Cai Runguo	西葡语系	Dept. of Spanish & Portuguese	驻厄瓜多尔大使	Ambassador to Ecuador
柴玺	Chai Xi	英语学院	School of English	驻马来西亚、孟加拉、马耳他大使	Ambassador to Malaysia; Ambassador to Bangladesh; Ambassador to Malta
常华	Chang Hua	阿拉伯语系	Dept. of Arabic	驻阿联酋、也门大使	Ambassador to the United Arab Emirates; Ambassador to Yemen
常毅	Chang Yi	阿拉伯语系	Dept. of Arabic	驻伊拉克大使	Ambassador to Iraq
陈德来	Chen Delai	欧语学院	School of European Languages & Cultures	驻保加利亚、罗马尼亚大使	Ambassador to Bulgaria; Ambassador to Romania
陈棣	Chen Di	俄语学院	School of Russian	驻立陶宛、哈萨克斯坦、波兰大使	Ambassador to Lithuania; Ambassador to Kazakhstan; Ambassador to Poland
陈建福	Chen Jianfu	德语系	Dept. of German	驻格鲁吉亚、斯洛伐克大使	Ambassador to Georgia; Ambassador to Slovakia
陈京华	Chen Jinghua	英语学院	School of English	驻牙买加、斐济、苏里南大使	Ambassador to Jamaica; Ambassador to Fiji; Ambassador to Suriname
陈立钢	Chen Ligang	英语学院	School of English	驻加拿大多伦多总领馆总领事、驻安提瓜和巴布达大使	Consul General in Toronto, Canada; Ambassador to Antigua and Barbuda
陈明明	Chen Mingming	英语学院	School of English	驻新西兰、瑞典大使，外交部翻译室主任	Ambassador to New Zealand; Ambassador to Sweden; Director of the Translation and Interpreting Department, the Ministry of Foreign Affairs
陈平初	Chen Pingchu	英语学院	School of English	驻肯尼亚大使兼常驻联合国环境规划署代表、常驻联合国人居中心代表	Ambassador to Kenya and Permanent Representative to the UN Environment Programme (UNEP) and the UN Human Settlements Programme (UN-Habitat)
陈世泽	Chen Shize	欧语学院	School of European Languages & Cultures	驻波兰、意大利兼驻圣马力诺、印度、阿富汗大使	Ambassador to Poland; Ambassador to Italy and concurrent Ambassador to the Republic of San Marino; Ambassador to India and Afghanistan
陈文照	Chen Wenzhao	英语学院	School of English	驻新西兰大使	Ambassador to New Zealand
程瑞声	Cheng Ruisheng	英语学院	School of English	驻缅甸、印度大使	Ambassador to Myanmar; Ambassador to India
程涛	Cheng Tao	法语系	Dept. of French	中国人民外交学会副会长、驻摩洛哥大使	Vice President of the Chinese People's Institute of Foreign Affairs; Ambassador to Morocco
程文栋	Cheng Wendong	欧语学院	School of European Languages & Cultures	驻意大利兼驻圣马力诺大使	Ambassador to Italy and concurrent Ambassador to San Marino
崔惠欣	Cui Huixin	英语学院	School of English	驻瑞典哥德堡总领事（大使衔）、驻瑙鲁大使	Consul General(ambassadorial level) in Gothenburg, Sweden; Ambassador to Nauru

姓名	Name	毕业院系	School/Dept.	曾（现）任职务	Positions held
崔 杰	Cui Jie	阿拉伯语系	Dept. of Arabic	驻毛里坦尼亚大使	Ambassador to Mauritania
崔永乾	Cui Yongqian	法语系	Dept. of French	驻中非、刚果民主共和国大使	Ambassador to the Central African Republic; Ambassador to the Democratic Republic of Congo
邓洪波	Deng Hongbo	英语学院	School of English	驻美国使馆公使、馆长，驻肯尼亚大使兼常驻联合国环境署、人居署代表	Minister to the United States and Chief of Mission; Ambassador to Kenya and Permanent Representative to the UNEP and the UN-HABITAT
邓绍勤	Deng Shaoqin	阿拉伯语系	Dept. of Arabic	驻阿曼大使	Ambassador to the Oman
杜钟瀛	Du Zhongying	英语学院	School of English	驻意大利公使参赞、驻基里巴斯兼瓦努阿图大使	Minister Counsellor to Italy; Ambassador to Kiribati and concurrent Ambassador to Vanuatu
樊桂金	Fan Guijin	英语学院	School of English	驻塞拉利昂、乌干达、汤加大使	Ambassador to Sierra Leone; Ambassador to Uganda; Ambassador to Tonga
范承祚	Fan Chengzuo	俄语学院	School of Russian	驻阿尔巴尼亚大使	Ambassador to Albania
范先荣	Fan Xianrong	俄语学院	School of Russian	驻塔吉克斯坦大使	Ambassador to Tajikistan
房 利	Fang Li	英语学院	School of English	驻多伦多总领事、驻摩尔多瓦大使	Consul General in Toronto, Canada; Ambassador to Moldova
冯志军	Feng Zhijun	法语系	Dept. of French	驻布隆迪大使	Ambassador to Burundi
傅全章	Fu Quanzhang	俄语学院	School of Russian	驻塔吉克斯坦大使	Ambassador to Tajikistan
高 建	Gao Jian	英语学院	School of English	驻匈牙利、挪威大使	Ambassador to Hungary; Ambassador to Norway
高克祥	Gao Kexiang	西葡语系	Dept. of Spanish & Portuguese	驻安哥拉、几内亚比绍、葡萄牙大使	Ambassador to Angola; Ambassador to Guinea-Bissau; Ambassador to Portugal
高如铭	Gao Ruming	法语系	Dept. of French	驻乍得、喀麦隆大使	Ambassador to Chad; Ambassador to Cameroon
高文献	Gao Wenxian	阿拉伯语系	Dept. of Arabic	驻卡塔尔大使	Ambassador to Qatar
高玉琛	Gao Yuchen	法语系	Dept. of French	驻香港特别行政区特派员公署副特派员、驻毛里求斯大使	Deputy Commissioner of the Ministry of Foreign Affairs for the Hong Kong Special Administrative Region; Ambassador to Mauritius
高正月	Gao Zhengyue	西葡语系	Dept. of Spanish & Portuguese	驻秘鲁、哥伦比亚大使	Ambassador to Peru; Ambassador to Colombia
耿文兵	Geng Wenbin	法语系	Dept. of French	外交部驻部监察局局长，驻贝宁、塞舌尔大使	Director of the Department of Supervision, Ministry of Foreign Affairs; Ambassador to Benin; Ambassador to Seychelles
龚建忠	Gong Jianzhong	英语学院	School of English	驻加纳大使	Ambassador to Ghana
龚猎夫	Gong Liefu	俄语学院	School of Russian	驻土库曼斯坦大使	Ambassador to Turkmenistan
宫小生	Gong Xiaosheng	阿拉伯语系	Dept. of Arabic	驻土耳其大使	Ambassador to Turkey
顾懋萱	Gu Maoxuan	欧语学院	School of European Languages & Cultures	驻阿尔巴尼亚大使	Ambassador to Albania
顾欣尔	Gu Xiner	英语学院	School of English	驻加纳、津巴布韦、南非大使	Ambassador to Ghana; Ambassador to Zimbabwe; Ambassador to South Africa
关呈远	Guan Chengyuan	法语系	Dept. of French	驻欧盟大使	Ambassador to the EU

姓名	Name	毕业院系	School/Dept.	曾（现）任职务	Positions held
郭邦彦	Guo Bangyan	法语系	Dept. of French	驻吉布提大使	Ambassador to Djibouti
郭靖安	Guo Jing'an	英语学院	School of English	驻加纳大使	Ambassador to Ghana
何泗记	He Siji	法语系	Dept. of French	驻中非大使	Ambassador to the Central African Republic
洪　虹	Hong Hong	西葡语系	Dept. of Spanish & Portuguese	驻几内亚比绍、佛得角、莫桑比克大使	Ambassador to Guinea-Bissau; Ambassador to Cape Verde; Ambassador to Mozambique
侯贵信	Hou Guixin	法语系	Dept. of French	驻塞舌尔大使	Ambassador to Seychelles
侯清儒	Hou Qingru	英语学院	School of English	驻斐济、津巴布韦大使	Ambassador to Fiji; Ambassador to Zimbabwe
胡本耀	Hu Benyao	德语系	Dept. of German	驻奥地利大使	Ambassador to Austria
胡洪范	Hu Hongfan	英语学院	School of English	驻巴布亚新几内亚、委内瑞拉、玻利维亚大使	Ambassador to Papua New Guinea; Ambassador to Venezuela; Ambassador to Bolivia
胡小笛	Hu Xiaodi	英语学院	School of English	外交部军控司大使，驻联合国维也纳办事处和瑞士其他国际组织代表、大使	Ambassador to the Department of Arms Control, Ministry of Foreign Affairs; Representative and Ambassador to the UN Office in Vienna and other international organizations in Switzerland
胡业顺	Hu Yeshun	英语学院	School of English	驻拉脱维亚大使	Ambassador to Latvia
华黎明	Hua Liming	英语学院	School of English	驻伊朗、阿联酋、荷兰大使，兼中国常驻禁止化学武器组织代表团代表	Ambassador to Iran; Ambassador to the UAE; Ambassador to the Netherlands and Representative of the Permanent Mission of China to the Organisation for the Prohibition of Chemical Weapons (OPCW)
黄长庆	Huang Changqing	法语系	Dept. of French	驻喀麦隆大使	Ambassador to Cameroon
黄杰民	Huang Jiemin	阿拉伯语系	Dept. of Arabic	驻阿联酋、科威特大使	Ambassador to the United Arab Emirates; Ambassador to Kuwait
黄士康	Huang Shikang	西葡语系	Dept. of Spanish & Portuguese	驻智利、墨西哥、哥伦比亚大使	Ambassador to Chile; Ambassador to Mexico; Ambassador to Colombia
黄松甫	Huang Songfu	西葡语系	Dept. of Spanish & Portuguese	驻葡萄牙、莫桑比克大使	Ambassador to Portugal; Ambassador to Mozambique
黄　兴	Huang Xing	英语学院	School of English	驻芬兰、特立尼达和多巴哥大使	Ambassador to Finland; Ambassador to Trinidad and Tobago
黄志良	Huang Zhiliang	西葡语系	Dept. of Spanish & Portuguese	驻尼加拉瓜、委内瑞拉大使	Ambassador to Nicaragua; Ambassador to Venezuela
黄忠坡	Huang Zhongpo	欧语学院	School of European Languages & Cultures	驻爱沙尼亚大使	Ambassador to Estonia
霍淑珍	Huo Shuzhen	西葡语系	Dept. of Spanish & Portuguese	驻乌拉圭大使	Ambassador to Uruguay
火正德	Huo Zhengde	法语系	Dept. of French	驻突尼斯、几内亚大使	Ambassador to Tunisia; Ambassador to Guinea
冀敬义	Ji Jingyi	俄语学院	School of Russian	驻尼日尔大使	Ambassador to Niger
江承宗	Jiang Chengzong	英语学院	School of English	驻巴巴多斯兼驻安提瓜和巴布达大使	Ambassador to Barbados and concurrent Ambassador to Antigua and Barbuda
江勤政	Jiang Qinzheng	亚非学院	School of Asian & African Studies	驻斯里兰卡兼驻马尔代夫大使	Ambassador to Sri Lanka and concurrent Ambassador to the Maldives

姓名	Name	毕业院系	School/Dept.	曾（现）任职务	Positions held
江 翔	Jiang Xiang	法语系	Dept. of French	驻布基纳法索、几内亚大使	Ambassador to Burkina Faso; Ambassador to Guinea
蒋元德	Jiang Yuande	西葡语系	Dept. of Spanish & Portuguese	驻佛得角、安哥拉、巴西大使	Ambassador to Cape Verde; Ambassador to Angola; Ambassador to Brazil
焦东村	Jiao Dongcun	英语学院	School of English	驻巴哈马大使	Ambassador to the Bahamas
金伯雄	Jin Boxiong	英语学院	School of English	驻乌干达、尼日利亚大使	Ambassador to Uganda; Ambassador to Nigeria
金桂华	Jin Guihua	英语学院	School of English	外交部新闻发言人，驻泰国、马来西亚、文莱大使	Ministry of Foreign Affairs' spokesman; Ambassador to Thailand; Ambassador to Malaysia; Ambassador to Brunei
金 森	Jin Sen	法语系	Dept. of French	驻阿尔及利亚、埃塞俄比亚大使	Ambassador to Algeria; Ambassador to Ethiopia
居一杰	Ju Yijie	西葡语系	Dept. of Spanish & Portuguese	驻哥伦比亚、委内瑞拉、玻利维亚大使	Ambassador to Colombia; Ambassador to Venezuela; Ambassador to Bolivia
兰立俊	Lan Lijun	英语学院	School of English	驻瑞典、印度尼西亚、加拿大大使	Ambassador to Sweden; Ambassador to Indonesia; Ambassador to Canada
雷荫成	Lei Yincheng	英语学院	School of English	驻阿塞拜疆大使	Ambassador to Azerbaijan
李宝钧	Li Baojun	西葡语系	Dept. of Spanish & Portuguese	驻几内亚比绍大使	Ambassador to Guinea-Bissau
李长和	Li Changhe	英语学院	School of English	驻捷克大使	Ambassador to Czech
李长华	Li Changhua	西葡语系	Dept. of Spanish & Portuguese	驻哥斯达黎加、智利、哥伦比亚大使	Ambassador to Costa Rica; Ambassador to Chile; Ambassador to Colombia
李 琛	Li Chen	亚非学院	School of Asian & African Studies	驻巴林大使	Ambassador to Bahrain
李成文	Li Chengwen	阿拉伯语系	Dept. of Arabic	驻沙特阿拉伯、苏丹大使	Ambassador to Saudi Arabia; Ambassador to Sudan
李春华	Li Chunhua	西葡语系	Dept. of Spanish & Portuguese	驻莫桑比克、佛得角大使	Ambassador to Mozambique; Ambassador to Cape Verde
李德标	Li Debiao	俄语学院	School of Russian	驻尼泊尔大使	Ambassador to Nepal
李凤林	Li Fenglin	俄语学院	School of Russian	国务院发展研究中心欧亚社会发展研究所所长、驻俄罗斯大使	Director of the Euro-Asian Social Development Research Institute, the Development Research Centre of the State Council; Ambassador to Russia
李福顺	Li Fushun	法语系	Dept. of French	驻加蓬大使	Ambassador to Gabon
李国邦	Li Guobang	欧语学院	School of European Languages & Cultures	驻塞浦路斯大使	Ambassador to Cyprus
李国新	Li Guoxin	西葡语系	Dept. of Spanish & Portuguese	驻哥伦比亚、阿根廷、巴西大使	Ambassador to Colombia; Ambassador to Argentina; Ambassador to Brazil
李华新	Li Huaxin	阿拉伯语系	Dept. of Arabic	驻澳大利亚总领事、驻叙利亚大使	Consul General to Australia; Ambassador to Syria
李慧来	Li Huilai	俄语学院	School of Russian	外交部办公厅主任、驻俄罗斯公使	Director of the General Office, Ministry of Foreign Affairs; Ambassador to Russia
李家忠	Li Jiazhong	法语系	Dept. of French	驻老挝、越南大使	Ambassador to Laos; Ambassador to Vietnam

姓名	Name	毕业院系	School/Dept.	曾（现）任职务	Positions held
李景贤	Li Jingxian	俄语学院	School of Russian	驻俄罗斯使馆公使，驻格鲁吉亚、乌兹别克斯坦大使	Minister of the Chinese Embassy to Russia; Ambassador to Georgia; Ambassador to Uzbekistan
李举卿	Li Juqing	俄语学院	School of Russian	驻蒙古大使	Ambassador to Mongolia
李 立	Li Li	法语系	Dept. of French	驻毛里求斯大使	Ambassador to Mauritius
李满长	Li Manchang	欧语学院	School of European Languages & Culture	驻塞尔维亚、黑山大使	Ambassador to Serbia; Ambassador to Montenegro
李培宜	Li Peiyi	法语系	Dept. of French	驻多哥、扎伊尔（现为"刚果民主共和国"）大使	Ambassador to Togo; Ambassador to Zaire (Now the Democratic Republic of Congo)
李清玉	Li Qingyu	法语系	Dept. of French	驻叙利亚、阿尔及利亚大使	Ambassador to Syria; Ambassador to Algeria
李瑞宇	Li Ruiyu	英语学院	School of English	驻意大利兼驻圣马力诺大使、文化部部长助理	Ambassador to Italy and concurrent Ambassador to San Marino; Assistant Minister of Culture
李树立	Li Shuli	法语系	Dept. of French	驻刚果共和国、马达加斯加大使	Ambassador to the Republic of Congo; Ambassador to Madagascar
李燕端	Li Yanduan	俄语学院	School of Russian	驻萨摩亚大使	Ambassador to Samoa
李志国	Li Zhiguo	阿拉伯语系	Dept. of Arabic	驻利比亚、南苏丹、巴林大使	Ambassador to Libya; Ambassador to the Republic of South Sudan; Ambassador to Bahrain
李仲良	Li Zhongliang	西葡语系	Dept. of Spanish & Portuguese	驻乌拉圭、赤道几内亚大使	Ambassador to Uruguay; Ambassador to Equatorial Guinea
梁 栋	Liang Dong	英语学院	School of English	驻缅甸大使	Ambassador to Myanmar
梁健明	Liang Jianming	高级翻译学院	Graduate School of Translation & Interpretation	驻墨尔本总领事、驻圣卢西亚大使	Consul General in Melbourne, Australia; Ambassador to St. Lucia
林贞龙	Lin Zhenlong	欧语学院	School of European Languages & Cultures	驻摩尔多瓦大使	Ambassador to Moldova
刘宝莱	Liu Baolai	阿拉伯语系	Dept. of Arabic	驻阿联酋、约旦大使	Ambassador to the United Arab Emirates Ambassador to Jordan
刘碧伟	Liu Biwei	亚非学院	School of Asian & African Studies	驻丹麦、爱尔兰大使	Ambassador to Denmark; Ambassador to Ireland
刘昌业	Liu Changye	德语系	Dept. of German	驻奥地利大使	Ambassador to Austria
刘大群	Liu Daqun	英语学院	School of English	驻牙买加大使兼常驻国际海底管理局代表、联合国前南国际刑事法庭法官	Ambassador to Jamaica and Permanent Representative to the International Seabed Authority; Judge of the UN International Criminal Tribunal for the former Yugoslavia
刘 菲	Liu Fei	西葡语系	Dept. of Spanish & Portuguese	驻加拿大温哥华总领事、驻密克罗尼西亚大使	Consul General in Vancouver, the Canada; Ambassador to Micronesia
刘贵今	Liu Guijin	英语学院	School of English	中国政府非洲事务特别代表，驻津巴布韦、南非大使	Chinese Government's Special Representative for African Affairs; Ambassador to Zimbabwe; Ambassador to South Africa
刘焕兴	Liu Huanxing	英语学院	School of English	驻博茨瓦纳、巴巴多斯大使	Ambassador to Botswana; Ambassador to Barbados
刘 健	Liu Jian	英语学院	School of English	驻洛杉矶总领事、驻巴基斯坦大使	Consul General in Los Angeles, the US; Ambassador to Pakistan

姓名	Name	毕业院系	School/Dept.	曾（现）任职务	Positions held
刘峻岫	Liu Junxiu	西葡语系	Dept. of Spanish & Portuguese	驻厄瓜多尔大使	Ambassador to Ecuador
刘立德	Liu Lide	法语系	Dept. of French	驻马里、科特迪瓦大使	Ambassador to Mali; Ambassador to Cote d'Ivoire
刘培根	Liu Peigen	俄语学院	School of Russian	驻古巴大使、中联部拉美局局长	Ambassador to Cuba; Director of the Bureau of Latin America, the International Department of the CPC Central Committee
刘文信	Liu Wenxin	俄语学院	School of Russian	驻波黑大使	Ambassador to Bosnia
刘向华	Liu Xianghua	阿拉伯语系	Dept. of Arabic	驻黎巴嫩大使	Ambassador to Lebanon
刘新生	Liu Xinsheng	英语学院	School of English	驻文莱大使	Ambassador to Brunei
刘永兴	Liu Yongxing	亚非学院	School of Asian & African Studies	驻老挝大使	Ambassador to Laos
刘玉坤	Liu Yukun	法语系	Dept. of French	驻几内亚大使	Ambassador to Guinea
刘玉琴	Liu Yuqin	西葡语系	Dept. of Spanish & Portuguese	驻古巴、厄瓜多尔、智利大使	Ambassador to Cuba; Ambassador to Ecuador; Ambassador to Chile
刘增文	Liu Zengwen	欧语学院	School of European Languages & Cultures	驻立陶宛、罗马尼亚大使	Ambassador to Lithuania; Ambassador to Romania
鲁桂成	Lu Guicheng	俄语学院	School of Russian	外交部档案馆馆长、驻白俄罗斯大使	Director of the Department of Archive's of the Ministry of Foreign Affairs; Ambassador to Belarus
陆树林	Lu Shulin	英语学院	School of English	驻特立尼达和多巴哥、巴基斯坦大使	Ambassador to Trinidad and Tobago; Ambassador to Pakistan
陆宗卿	Lu Zongqing	英语学院	School of English	驻巴巴多斯大使兼驻安提瓜和巴布达大使	Ambassador to Barbados and concurrent Ambassador to Antigua and Barbuda
罗林泉	Luo Linquan	英语学院	School of English	驻爱尔兰、希腊大使	Ambassador to Ireland; Ambassador to Greece
罗小光	Luo Xiaoguang	阿拉伯语系	Dept. of Arabic	驻苏丹、也门大使	Ambassador to Sudan; Ambassador to Yemen
吕凤鼎	Lü Fengding	英语学院	School of English	中国公共外交协会副会长，第十一届全国政协委员、外事委员会委员，驻尼日利亚、瑞典大使	Vice Chairman of China Association for Public Diplomacy; member of the National Committee of 11th CPPCC and member of its Foreign Affairs Subcommittee; Ambassador to Nigeria; Ambassador to Sweden
马福林	Ma Fulin	法语系	Dept. of French	驻中非大使	Ambassador to the Central African Republic
马书学	Ma Shuxue	英语学院	School of English	驻巴哈马、基里巴斯大使	Ambassador to the Bahamas; Ambassador to Kiribati
梅 平	Mei Ping	英语学院	School of English	驻加拿大大使、外交部太平洋经济合作全国委员会会长	Ambassador to Canada; President of the National Committee for Pacific Economic Cooperation Council, Ministry of Foreign Affairs
宓世衡	Mi Shiheng	西葡语系	Dept. of Spanish & Portuguese	驻佛得角、莫桑比克大使	Ambassador to Cape Verde; Ambassador to Mozambique
闵永年	Min Yongnian	亚非学院	School of Asian & African Studies	世界知识出版社社长、驻文莱大使	President of World Knowledge Publishing House; Ambassador to Brunei
倪政建	Ni Zhengjian	英语学院	School of English	驻圭亚那、新西兰大使	Ambassador to Guyana; Ambassador to New Zealand

姓名	Name	毕业院系	School/Dept.	曾（现）任职务	Positions held
潘广学	Pan Guangxue	亚非学院	School of Asian & African Studies	驻柬埔寨、老挝大使	Ambassador to the Kingdom of Cambodia; Ambassador to the Lao People's Democratic Republic
潘祥康	Pan Xiangkang	阿拉伯语系	Dept. of Arabic	驻巴林大使	Ambassador to Bahrain
潘占林	Pan Zhanlin	俄语学院	School of Russian	政协第十届全国委员会委员，驻吉尔吉斯斯坦、乌克兰、南斯拉夫和以色列等国大使	Member of the 10th CPPCC National Committee; Ambassador to Kyrgyzstan; Ambassador to Ukraine; Ambassador to Yugoslavia; Ambassador to Israel
戚德恩	Qi Deen	法语系	Dept. of French	驻卢旺达大使	Ambassador to Rwanda
齐建国	Qi Jianguo	亚非学院	School of Asian & African Studies	驻越南大使	Ambassador to Vietnam
齐治家	Qi Zhijia	英语学院	School of English	驻蒙古大使	Ambassador to Mongolia
钱永年	Qian Yongnian	英语学院	School of English	驻印度尼西亚大使	Ambassador to Indonesia
秦鸿国	Qin Hongguo	英语学院	School of English	驻利比亚大使	Ambassador to Libya
邱胜云	Qiu Shengyun	英语学院	School of English	外交学会副会长、驻约旦大使、驻纽约总领事	Vice President of the Institute of Foreign Affairs; Ambassador to Jordan; Consul General in New York, the US
邱小琪	Qiu Xiaoqi	西葡语系	Dept. of Spanish & Portuguese	驻墨西哥、玻利维亚、西班牙兼驻安道尔、巴西大使	Ambassador to Mexico; Ambassador to Bolivia; Ambassador to Spain and concurrent Ambassador to Andorra; Ambassador to Brazil
邱学军	Qiu Xuejun	高级翻译学院	Graduate School of Translation & Interpretation	驻厄立特里亚大使、驻旧金山总领馆副总领事、驻美大使馆参赞兼总领事	Ambassador to Eritrea; Deputy Consul General in San Francisco, the US; Counsellor and Consul General in the Chinese Embassy in the US
仇伯华	Qiu Bohua	亚非学院	School of Asian & African Studies	驻巴布亚新几内亚大使	Ambassador to Papua New Guinea
曲 星	Qu Xing	法语系	Dept. of French	驻比利时大使	Ambassador to Belgium
任景玉	Ren Jingyu	西葡语系	Dept. of Spanish & Portuguese	驻秘鲁、智利、墨西哥大使	Ambassador to Peru; Ambassador to Chile; Ambassador to Mexico
任小萍	Ren Xiaoping	英语学院	School of English	驻安提瓜和巴布达、纳米比亚大使	Ambassador to Antigua and Barbuda; Ambassador to Namibia
沈智焕	Shen Zhihuan	英语学院	School of English	驻苏里南大使	Ambassador to Suriname
施燕华	Shi Yanhua	英语学院	School of English	外交部翻译室主任、中国翻译协会常务副会长、驻卢森堡大使	Director of Translation Department, Ministry of Foreign Affairs; executive Vice President of the Translators Association of China; Ambassador to the Grand Duchy of Luxembourg
石 虎	Shi Hu	法语系	Dept. of French	驻尼日尔、中非大使	Ambassador to Niger; Ambassador to the Central African Republic
时延春	Shi Yanchun	阿拉伯语系	Dept. of Arabic	驻也门、叙利亚大使	Ambassador to Yemen; Ambassador to Syria
舒 展	Shu Zhan	英语学院	School of English	驻卢旺达、厄立特里亚大使	Ambassador to Rwanda; Ambassador to the State of Eritrea
宋爱国	Song Aiguo	英语学院	School of English	驻埃及大使	Ambassador to Egypt
宋增寿	Song Zengshou	英语学院	School of English	驻乌干达大使	Ambassador to Uganda

姓名	Name	毕业院系	School/Dept.	曾（现）任职务	Positions held
苏 格	Su Ge	英语学院	School of English	中国国际问题研究院院长、党委书记，驻冰岛、苏里南大使	President and Party Secretary of the China Institute of International Studies; Ambassador to the Iceland; Ambassador to Suriname
苏 健	Su Jian	西葡语系	Dept. of Spanish & Portuguese	驻佛得角、东帝汶大使	Ambassador to Cape Verde; Ambassador to East Timor
孙必干	Sun Bigan	阿拉伯语系	Dept. of Arabic	中东特使，驻沙特阿拉伯、伊拉克、伊朗大使	Envoy of Middle East; Ambassador to Saudi Arabia; Ambassador to Iraq; Ambassador to Iran
孙春业	Sun Chunye	亚非学院	School of Asian & African Studies	驻卡拉奇总领事馆总领事	Consul General of Consulate General to Karachi
孙国祥	Sun Guoxiang	亚非学院	School of Asian & African Studies	中国驻纽约总领事，驻斯里兰卡兼驻马尔代夫、土耳其、越南大使	Chinese Consul General in New York; Ambassador to Sri Lanka and concurrent Ambassador to the Maldives; Ambassador to Turkey; Ambassador to Vietnam
孙和平	Sun Heping	英语学院	School of English	驻尼泊尔、乌干达大使	Ambassador to Nepal; Ambassador to Uganda
孙荣茂	Sun Rongmao	英语学院	School of English	驻圣保罗（巴西）总领事、驻佛得角大使	Consul General in Sao Paulo, Brazil; Ambassador to Cape Verde
孙荣民	Sun Rongmin	德语系	Dept. of German	中国外交学会副会长，驻卢森堡、波兰、斯洛文尼亚大使	Vice President of China Institute of Foreign Affairs; Ambassador to Luxembourg; Ambassador to Poland; Ambassador to Slovenia
孙树忠	Sun Shuzhong	法语系	Dept. of French	驻摩洛哥、卢旺达大使	Ambassador to Morocco; Ambassador to Rwanda
孙玉玺	Sun Yuxi	英语学院	School of English	驻波兰、意大利兼驻圣马力诺、印度、阿富汗大使	Ambassador to Poland; Ambassador to Italy and concurrent Ambassador to San Marino; Ambassador to India; Ambassador to Afghanistan
孙兆通	Sun Zhaotong	法语系	Dept. of French	驻尼日尔大使	Ambassador to Niger
孙治荣	Sun Zhirong	法语系	Dept. of French	驻吉布提、加蓬兼驻圣多美和普林西比大使	Ambassador to Djibouti; Ambassador to Gabon and concurrent Ambassador to Sao Tome and Principe
汤柏生	Tang Baisheng	西葡语系	Dept. of Spanish & Portuguese	驻苏里南大使	Ambassador to Suriname
唐湛清	Tang Zhanqing	欧语学院	School of European Languages & Cultures	驻斯洛伐克大使	Ambassador to Slovakia
陶卫光	Tao Weiguang	法语系	Dept. of French	驻科摩罗、贝宁大使	Ambassador to Comoros; Ambassador to Benin
田二龙	Tian Erlong	俄语学院	School of Russian	驻亚美尼亚大使	Ambassador to Armenia
田广凤	Tian Guangfeng	西葡语系	Dept. of Spanish & Portuguese	驻东帝汶、几内亚比绍、莫桑比克大使	Ambassador to East Timor; Ambassador to Guinea-Bissau; Ambassador to Mozambique
佟明涛	Tong Mingtao	德语系	Dept. of German	驻摩尔多瓦、立陶宛大使	Ambassador to Moldova; Ambassador to Lithuania
王保民	Wang Baomin	俄语学院	School of Russian	驻圭亚那大使	Ambassador to Guyana
王成家	Wang Chengjia	西葡语系	Dept. of Spanish & Portuguese	驻智利、古巴大使	Ambassador to Chile; Ambassador to Cuba

姓名	Name	毕业院系	School/Dept.	曾（现）任职务	Positions held
王春贵	Wang Chungui	英语学院	School of English	驻孟加拉、菲律宾、马来西亚大使	Ambassador to Bangladesh; Ambassador to the Philippines; Ambassador to Malaysia
王凤祥	Wang Fengxiang	俄语学院	School of Russian	驻格鲁吉亚、拉脱维亚大使	Ambassador to Georgia; Ambassador to Latvia
王辅国	Wang Fuguo	欧语学院	School of European Languages & Cultures	驻意大利佛罗伦萨总领事，驻波黑大使	Consul General in Florence, Italy; Ambassador to Bosnia and Herzegovina
王富元	Wang Fuyuan	英语学院	School of English	驻圭亚那、毛里求斯、斯洛文尼亚大使	Ambassador to Guyana; Ambassador to Mauritius; Ambassador to Slovenia
王桂生	Wang Guisheng	英语学院	School of English	驻瑞典大使	Ambassador to Sweden
王俊岭	Wang Junling	欧语学院	School of European Languages & Cultures	驻阿尔巴尼亚大使	Ambassador to Albania
王乐友	Wang Leyou	法语系	Dept. of French	驻科摩罗大使	Ambassador to Comoros
王弄笙	Wang Nongsheng	英语学院	School of English	驻巴布亚新几内亚、萨摩亚大使	Ambassador to Papua New Guinea; Ambassador to Samoa
王 强	Wang Qiang	阿拉伯语系	Dept. of Arabic	驻巴勒斯坦民族权力机构办事处主任（大使衔）	Director (ambassadorial level) of the Office to the Palestinian National Authority
王士雄	Wang Shixiong	西葡语系	Dept. of Spanish & Portuguese	驻厄瓜多尔、赤道几内亚大使	Ambassador to Ecuador; Ambassador to Equatorial Guinea
王旺生	Wang Wangsheng	阿拉伯语系	Dept. of Arabic	驻利比亚大使	Ambassador to Libya
王卫国	Wang Weiguo	亚非学院	School of Asian & African Studies	驻塞舌尔大使	Ambassador to Seychelles
王晓渡	Wang Xiaodu	法语系	Dept. of French	外交部边界与海洋事务特别代表、驻吉布提大使	Special Representative of the Department of Boundary and Ocean Affairs, Ministry of Foreign Affairs; Ambassador to Djibouti
王小庄	Wang Xiaozhuang	阿拉伯语系	Dept. of Arabic	驻巴林、阿曼大使	Ambassador to Bahrain; Ambassador to the Oman
王新元	Wang Xinyuan	英语学院	School of English	驻萨摩亚大使	Ambassador to Samoa
王信石	Wang Xinshi	英语学院	School of English	驻塞舌尔、贝宁、冰岛大使	Ambassador to Seychelles; Ambassador to Benin; Ambassador to Iceland
王学贤	Wang Xuexian	英语学院	School of English	驻南非大使、驻美国洛杉矶总领事、常驻联合国副代表	Ambassador to South Africa; Consul General in Los Angeles, the US; Deputy Permanent Representative to the UN
王延义	Wang Yanyi	德语系	Dept. of German	驻奥地利大使	Ambassador to Austria
王义浩	Wang Yihao	英语学院	School of English	驻博茨瓦纳大使	Ambassador to Botswana
王嵎生	Wang Yusheng	英语学院	School of English	驻尼日利亚大使	Ambassador to Nigeria
王钊贤	Wang Zhaoxian	英语学院	School of English	驻立陶宛大使	Ambassador to Lithuania
王 珍	Wang Zhen	西葡语系	Dept. of Spanish & Portuguese	驻乌拉圭、委内瑞拉、玻利维亚大使	Ambassador to Uruguay; Ambassador to Venezuela; Ambassador to Bolivia
魏敬华	Wei Jinghua	欧语学院	School of European Languages & Cultures	驻保加利亚、塞尔维亚大使	Ambassador to Bulgaria; Ambassador to Serbia
魏瑞兴	Wei Ruixing	英语学院	School of English	驻立陶宛、纳米比亚、巴布亚新几内亚大使	Ambassador to Lithuania; Ambassador to Namibia; Ambassador to Papua New Guinea

姓名	Name	毕业院系	School/Dept.	曾（现）任职务	Positions held
温西贵	Wen Xigui	欧语学院	School of European Languages & Cultures	驻波黑、南斯拉夫大使	Ambassador to Bosnia and Herzegovina; Ambassador to Yugoslavia
沃瑞棣	Wo Ruidi	法语系	Dept. of French	驻喀麦隆、马达加斯加、刚果共和国大使	Ambassador to Cameroon; Ambassador to Madagascar; Ambassador to the Republic of Congo
吴从勇	Wu Congyong	日语系	Dept. of Japanese	驻尼泊尔、巴林大使	Ambassador to Nepal; Ambassador to Bahrain
吴虹滨	Wu Hongbin	俄语学院	School of Russian	驻土库曼斯坦、白俄罗斯大使	Ambassador to Turkmenistan; Ambassador to Belarus
吴家淦	Wu Jiagan	英语学院	School of English	驻瑞典、希腊大使	Ambassador to Sweden; Ambassador to Greece
吴嘉森	Wu Jiasen	法语系	Dept. of French	驻布基纳法索大使	Ambassador to Burkina Faso
吴甲选	Wu Jiaxuan	英语学院	School of English	驻牙买加大使	Ambassador to Jamaica
吴久洪	Wu Jiuhong	阿拉伯语系	Dept. of Arabic	驻阿曼大使	Ambassador to Oman
吴俊峰	Wu Junfeng	俄语学院	School of Russian	驻斯洛文尼亚大使	Ambassador to Slovenia
吴连起	Wu Lianqi	英语学院	School of English	驻克罗地亚大使	Ambassador to Croatia
吴筱秋	Wu Xiaoqiu	俄语学院	School of Russian	驻白俄罗斯大使	Ambassador to Belarus
吴泽献	Wu Zexian	法语系	Dept. of French	驻黎巴嫩、刚果民主共和国大使	Ambassador to Lebanon; Ambassador to the Democratic Republic of Congo
吴祖荣	Wu Zurong	英语学院	School of English	驻瓦努阿图大使	Ambassador to Vanuatu
武春华	Wu Chunhua	阿拉伯语系	Dept. of Arabic	驻埃及大使	Ambassador to Egypt
肖思晋	Xiao Sijin	西葡语系	Dept. of Spanish & Portuguese	驻莫桑比克、安哥拉大使	Ambassador to Mozambique; Ambassador to Angola
谢佑昆	Xie Youkun	亚非学院	School of Asian & African Studies	驻乌干达、坦桑尼亚大使	Ambassador to Uganda; Ambassador to Tanzania
邢耿	Xing Geng	法语系	Dept. of French	驻尼日尔大使	Ambassador to Niger
徐次农	Xu Cinong	英语学院	School of English	驻塞拉利昂大使	Ambassador to Sierra Leone
徐代杰	Xu Daijie	俄语学院	School of Russian	驻科摩罗大使	Ambassador to Comoros
徐贻聪	Xu Yicong	西葡语系	Dept. of Spanish & Portuguese	驻厄瓜多尔、古巴、阿根廷大使	Ambassador to Ecuador; Ambassador to Cuba; Ambassador to Argentina
徐中楷	Xu Zhongkai	欧语学院	School of European Languages & Cultures	驻摩尔多瓦大使	Ambassador to Moldova
许昌财	Xu Changcai	西葡语系	Dept. of Spanish & Portuguese	驻赤道几内亚大使	Ambassador to Equatorial Guinea
许镜湖	Xu Jinghu	法语系	Dept. of French	驻瑞士、马达加斯加、摩洛哥大使	Ambassador to Switzerland; Ambassador to Madagascar; Ambassador to Morocco
许士国	Xu Shiguo	英语学院	School of English	驻瑙鲁大使	Ambassador to Nauru
薛捍勤	Xue Hanqin	英语学院	School of English	联合国国际法委员会主席、国际法院法官，驻荷兰、东盟大使	Chairman of the UN International Law Commission; Judge of the International Court of Justice; Ambassador to the Netherlands; Ambassador to ASEAN
薛金维	Xue Jinwei	法语系	Dept. of French	驻加蓬、喀麦隆大使	Ambassador to Gabon; Ambassador to Cameroon

姓名	Name	毕业院系	School/Dept.	曾（现）任职务	Positions held
严邦华	Yan Banghua	西葡语系	Dept. of Spanish & Portuguese	驻乌拉圭大使，驻巴塞罗那（西班牙）总领事（大使衔），驻几内亚比绍大使	Ambassador to Uruguay; Consul General (ambassadorial level)in Barcelona, Spain; Ambassador to Guinea-Bissau
严小敏	Yan Xiaomin	英语学院	School of English	驻赤道几内亚大使	Ambassador to Equatorial Guinea
杨广胜	Yang Guangsheng	俄语学院	School of Russian	驻希腊大使	Ambassador to Greece
杨桂荣	Yang Guirong	法语系	Dept. of French	驻瑞典、马耳他、马达加斯加大使	Ambassador to Sweden; Ambassador to Malta; Ambassador to Madagascar
杨洪林	Yang Honglin	阿拉伯语系	Dept. of Arabic	驻沙特阿拉伯、伊拉克大使	Ambassador to Saudi Arabia; Ambassador to Iraq
杨 健	Yang Jian	英语学院	School of English	驻文莱大使	Ambassador to Brunei
杨克容	Yang Kerong	俄语学院	School of Russian	驻亚美尼亚大使	Ambassador to Armenia
杨伟国	Yang Weiguo	阿拉伯语系	Dept. of Arabic	驻巴林大使	Ambassador to Bahrain
杨秀萍	Yang Xiuping	英语学院	School of English	驻东盟使团团长、大使，驻斯里兰卡兼驻马尔代夫、立陶宛大使	Head of the Mission and Ambassador to ASEAN; Ambassador to Sri Lanka and concurrent Ambassador to the Maldives; Ambassador to Lithuania
杨永瑞	Yang Yongrui	欧语学院	School of European Languages & Cultures	驻乍得大使	Ambassador to Chad
杨优明	Yang Youming	英语学院	School of English	驻赞比亚、特立尼达和多巴哥大使	Ambassador to Zambia; Ambassador to Trinidad and Tobago
杨友勇	Yang Youyong	英语学院	School of English	驻巴巴多斯大使	Ambassador to Barbados
姚培生	Yao Peisheng	俄语学院	School of Russian	驻哈萨克斯坦、乌克兰大使	Ambassador to Kazakhstan; Ambassador to Ukraine
殷恒民	Yin Hengmin	西葡语系	Dept. of Spanish & Portuguese	驻阿根廷、秘鲁、墨西哥大使	Ambassador to Argentina; Ambassador to Peru; Ambassador to Mexico
殷立贤	Yin Lixian	法语系	Dept. of French	驻塞舌尔大使	Ambassador to Seychelles
殷松龄	Yin Songling	俄语学院	School of Russian	驻土库曼斯坦大使	Ambassador to Turkmenistan
尹玉福	Yin Yufu	英语学院	School of English	驻马耳他大使	Ambassador to Malta
俞成仁	Yu Chengren	西葡语系	Dept. of Spanish & Portuguese	驻尼加拉瓜、哥伦比亚大使	Ambassador to Nicaragua; Ambassador to Colombia
余洪耀	Yu Hongyao	亚非学院	School of Asian & African Studies	驻马尔代夫、蒙古大使	Ambassador to the Maldives; Ambassador to Mongolia
于文哲	Yu Wenzhe	英语学院	School of English	驻圭亚那、加纳大使	Ambassador to Guyana; Ambassador to Ghana
郁序忠	Yu Xuzhong	法语系	Dept. of French	驻布隆迪大使	Ambassador to Burundi
乐俊清	Yue Junqing	英语学院	School of English	驻萨摩亚大使	Ambassador to Samoa
曾宪桼	Zeng Xianqi	法语系	Dept. of French	驻卢森堡、布隆迪大使	Ambassador to Luxembourg; Ambassador to Burundi
张备三	Zhang Beisan	西葡语系	Dept. of Spanish & Portuguese	驻葡萄牙、安哥拉大使	Ambassador to Portugal; Ambassador to Angola
张滨华	Zhang Binhua	英语学院	School of English	驻汤加、密克罗尼西亚大使	Ambassador to Tonga; Ambassador to Micronesia

姓名	Name	毕业院系	School/Dept.	曾（现）任职务	Positions held
张伯伦	Zhang Bolun	西葡语系	Dept. of Spanish & Portuguese	驻安哥拉大使	Ambassador to Angola
张 栋	Zhang Dong	阿拉伯语系	Dept. of Arabic	驻苏丹大使	Ambassador to Sudan
张国强	Zhang Guoqiang	俄语学院	School of Russian	驻阿塞拜疆大使	Ambassador to Azerbaijan
张海舟	Zhang Haizhou	俄语学院	School of Russian	驻俄罗斯公使、驻阿塞拜疆大使	Minister to Russia; Ambassador to Azerbaijan
张鸿照	Zhang Hongzhao	西葡语系	Dept. of Spanish & Portuguese	驻厄瓜多尔大使	Ambassador to Ecuador
张金凤	Zhang Jinfeng	亚非学院	School of Asian & African Studies	外交部驻澳门公署副特派员，驻文莱、柬埔寨大使	Deputy Commissioner of the Ministry of Foreign Affairs for the Macao Special Administrative Region; Ambassador to Brunei; Ambassador to Cambodia
张九桓	Zhang Jiuhuan	亚非学院	School of Asian & African Studies	驻泰国大使	Ambassador to Thailand
张克远	Zhang Keyuan	英语学院	School of English	驻马耳他、加纳、冰岛大使	Ambassador to Malta; Ambassador to Ghana; Ambassador to Iceland
张利民	Zhang Limin	英语学院	School of English	驻塞浦路斯、拉脱维亚、新西兰兼驻库克群岛、纽埃大使	Ambassador to Cyprus; Ambassador to Latvia; Ambassador to New Zealand and concurrent Ambassador to the Cook Islands and Niue
张鹏翔	Zhang Pengxiang	英语学院	School of English	驻巴布亚新几内亚大使	Ambassador to Papua New Guinea
张沙鹰	Zhang Shaying	西葡语系	Dept. of Spanish & Portuguese	驻墨西哥、智利、阿根廷大使	Ambassador to Mexico; Ambassador to Chile; Ambassador to Argentina
张 拓	Zhang Tuo	西葡语系	Dept. of Spanish & Portuguese	驻古巴、玻利维亚、阿根廷、委内瑞拉、玻利瓦尔大使	Ambassador to Cuba; Ambassador to Bolivia; Ambassador to Argentina; Ambassador to Venezuela; Ambassador to Bolivar
张万海	Zhang Wanhai	英语学院	School of English	驻格林纳达大使	Ambassador to Grenada
张维秋	Zhang Weiqiu	阿拉伯语系	Dept. of Arabic	驻伊拉克大使	Ambassador to Iraq
张卫东	Zhang Weidong	西班牙语系	Dept. of Spanish	驻冰岛大使	Ambassador to Iceland
张 霄	Zhang Xiao	俄语学院	School of Russian	驻乌兹别克斯坦大使	Ambassador to Uzbekistan
张小康	Zhang Xiaokang	英语学院	School of English	驻新加坡、爱尔兰大使	Ambassador to Singapore; Ambassador to Ireland
张鑫森	Zhang Xinsen	英语学院	School of English	驻韩国大使	Ambassador to Republic of Korea
张 炎	Zhang Yan	英语学院	School of English	驻印度大使	Ambassador to India
张延年	Zhang Yannian	俄语学院	School of Russian	驻阿塞拜疆、吉尔吉斯斯坦大使	Ambassador to Azerbaijan; Ambassador to the Kyrghyzstan
张义山	Zhang Yishan	英语学院	School of English	常驻维也纳联合国和其他国际组织代表团大使、联合国副代表（大使衔）	Ambassador of the Permanent Mission to the UN and other international organizations in Vienna; Deputy Representative (ambassadorial level) to the UN
张咏荃	Zhang Yongquan	俄语学院	School of Russian	驻格鲁吉亚大使	Ambassador to Georgia
张直鉴	Zhang Zhijian	英语学院	School of English	驻芬兰大使	Ambassador to Finland
张志良	Zhang Zhiliang	英语学院	School of English	驻卡塔尔、新加坡、泰国大使	Ambassador to Qatar; Ambassador to Singapore; Ambassador to Thailand

姓名	Name	毕业院系	School/Dept.	曾（现）任职务	Positions held
章德良	Zhang Deliang	英语学院	School of English	驻约旦大使	Ambassador to Jordan
章均赛	Zhang Junsai	英语学院	School of English	驻加拿大、澳大利亚大使	Ambassador to Canada; Ambassador to Australia
章启月	Zhang Qiyue	英语学院	School of English	驻纽约总领事、外交部新闻发言人、驻印度尼西亚大使	Consul General in New York; Ministry of Foreign Affairs' spokesperson; Ambassador to Indonesia
赵彬	Zhao Bin	欧语学院	School of European Languages & Cultures	驻奥地利大使	Ambassador to Austria
赵惠民	Zhao Huimin	英语学院	School of English	驻中非、贝宁大使	Ambassador to the Central African Republic; Ambassador to Benin
赵稷华	Zhao Jihua	英语学院	School of English	中英联合联络小组中方首席代表（大使衔）、外交部驻香港公署副特派员	Chief Representative (ambassadorial level) of the Sino-British Joint Liaison Group (JLG); Deputy Commissioner of the Ministry of Foreign Affairs for the Hong Kong Special Administrative Region
赵家骅	Zhao Jiahua	法语系	Dept. of French	驻老挝大使	Ambassador to Laos
赵梁	Zhao Liang	英语学院	School of English	驻卢森堡大使	Ambassador to Luxembourg
赵荣宪	Zhao Rongxian	西葡语系	Dept. of Spanish & Portuguese	驻古巴、委内瑞拉、玻利维亚大使	Ambassador to Cuba; Ambassador to Venezuela; Ambassador to Bolivia
赵维	Zhao Wei	英语学院	School of English	驻巴布亚新几内亚大使	Ambassador to Papua New Guinea
赵五一	Zhao Wuyi	西葡语系	Dept. of Spanish & Portuguese	驻玻利维亚、秘鲁大使	Ambassador to Bolivia; Ambassador to Peru
赵希迪	Zhao Xidi	俄语学院	School of Russian	驻亚美尼亚、白俄罗斯、匈牙利大使	Ambassador to Armenia; Ambassador to Belarus; Ambassador to Hungary
郑耀文	Zheng Yaowen	英语学院	School of English	驻津巴布韦、丹麦兼驻冰岛大使	Ambassador to Zimbabwe; Ambassador to Denmark and concurrent Ambassador to Iceland
智昭林	Zhi Zhaolin	欧语学院	School of European Languages & Cultures	驻黑山、斯洛文尼亚大使	Ambassador to Montenegro; Ambassador to Slovenia
钟建华	Zhong Jianhua	英语学院	School of English	中华人民共和国政府非洲事务特别代表、驻南非大使	Special Envoy for African Affairs of the Government of the People's Republic of China; Ambassador to South Africa
周刚	Zhou Gang	俄语学院	School of Russian	驻马来西亚、巴基斯坦、印尼、印度大使	Ambassador to Malaysia; Ambassador to Pakistan; Ambassador to Indonesia; Ambassador to India
周国斌	Zhou Guobin	阿拉伯语系	Dept. of Arabic	驻也门大使	Ambassador to Yemen
周锦明	Zhou Jinming	英语学院	School of English	驻马绍尔群岛大使	Ambassador to Marshall Islands
周善延	Zhou Shanyan	英语学院	School of English	驻斯里兰卡兼马尔代夫大使	Ambassador to Sri Lanka and concurrent Ambassador to the Maldives
周贤觉	Zhou Xianjue	英语学院	School of English	驻中非大使	Ambassador to the Central African Republic
周晓沛	Zhou Xiaopei	俄语学院	School of Russian	驻乌克兰、波兰、哈萨克斯坦大使	Ambassador to Ukraine; Ambassador to Poland; Ambassador to Kazakhstan
周欲晓	Zhou Yuxiao	英语学院	School of English	驻赞比亚、利比里亚大使	Ambassador to Zambia; Ambassador to Liberia
周振东	Zhou Zhendong	英语学院	School of English	驻乍得大使	Ambassador to Chad

姓名	Name	毕业院系	School/Dept.	曾（现）任职务	Positions held
朱邦造	**Zhu Bangzao**	法语系	Dept. of French	驻西班牙兼驻安道尔大使、外交部新闻发言人	Ambassador to Spain and concurrent Ambassador to Andorra; Ministry of Foreign Affairs' spokesman
朱曼黎	**Zhu Manli**	英语学院	School of English	驻荷兰大使	Ambassador to the Netherlands
朱应鹿	**Zhu Yinglu**	法语系	Dept. of French	驻突尼斯、巴勒斯坦、埃及、挪威大使	Ambassador to Tunisia: Ambassador to Palestine; Ambassador to Egypt; Ambassador to Norway
朱祖寿	**Zhu Zushou**	英语学院	School of English	驻荷兰、匈牙利大使兼驻联合国禁化武组织首席代表	Ambassador to the Netherlands: Ambassador to Hungary and Chief Representative to the UN Organisation for the Prohibition of Chemical Weapons (OPCW)
邹明榕	**Zou Mingrong**	英语学院	School of English	驻瑞典大使	Ambassador to Sweden
左福荣	**Zuo Furong**	俄语学院	School of Russian	驻阿尔巴尼亚大使	Ambassador to Albania
左学良	**Zuo Xueliang**	俄语学院	School of Russian	驻亚美尼亚、塔吉克斯坦大使	Ambassador to Armenia; Ambassador to Tajikistan

文教经贸等领域的部分校友

Alumni in cultural, education, economic and trade sectors

姓名	Name	毕业院系	School/Dept.	曾（现）任职务	Positions held
毕淑敏	Bi Shumin	附属学校	Affiliated School	国家一级作家	National first-class writer
陈建平	Chen Jianping	英语学院	School of English	广东外语外贸大学党委副书记、副校长，中国英语教学研究会副会长	Deputy Secretary of the CPC Guangdong University of Foreign Studies Committee and the University's Vice President; Vice President of China English Language Education Association
谌 容	Chen Rong	俄语学院	School of Russian	中央人民广播电台音乐编辑和翻译、作协北京分会专业作家	Music editor and translator at China National Radio; professional writer of the Beijing Branch of the Writers' Association
陈向阳	Chen Xiangyang	英语系	School of English	山东大学党委副书记、纪委书记	Deputy Secretary of the CPC Shandong University Committee and Secretary of its Discipline Inspection Commission
崔 威	Cui Wei	日语系	Dept. of Japanese	东莞市新美诺数码印花技术有限公司董事长、2015 "全国五一品牌建设奖" 获得者	Chairman of Dongguan New Mellow Digital Printing Technology Co.; winner of the 2015 "National May Day Brand Building Award"
高志凯	Gao Zhikai	英语学院	School of English	大和资本市场香港有限公司驻中国区主席、北京耶鲁大学校友会会长	Chairman of China Operations at Daiwa Capital Markets Hong Kong Limited; President of the Beijing Yale Alumni Association
郭尚平	Guo Shangping	留苏预备部	Training Division for studying in Russia	中科院院士，流体力学、生物力学专家	Academician of Chinese Academy of Sciences; an expert in fluid mechanics and biomechanics
何 炅	He Jiong	阿拉伯语系	Dept. of Arabic	湖南卫视主持人	Hunan TV presenter
何世德	He Shide	法语系	Dept. of French	少将、驻法国大使馆武官、总参二部武官局局长	Major General, Military Attaché attached to the Chinese Embassy in France; Director of the Bureau of Military Attachés, the Second Department of the General Staff Headquarters
胡福印	Hu Fuyin	日本学研究中心	Japanese Studies Centre	对外经济贸易大学副校长	Vice President of the University of International Business and Economics
黄友义	Huang Youyi	英语学院	School of English	中国网总裁、外文局副局长	Chinanet President; Vice President of China International Publishing Group
孔 洁	Kong Jie	英语学院	School of English	北京电视台主持人	Beijing TV presenter
李朋义	Li Pengyi	英语学院	School of English	中国教育出版传媒集团有限公司党组书记、总经理，高教出版社社长	Secretary of the leading Party members' group and General Managing Director of China Education Publishing & Media Group; President of Higher Education Press
李向玉	Li Xiangyu	西葡语系	Dept. of Spanish & Portuguese	澳门理工学院院长	President of Macao Polytechnic Institute
廖学盛	Liao Xuesheng	俄语学院	School of Russian	中国社会科学院世界历史研究所所长	Director of the Institute of World History, Chinese Academy of Social Sciences
刘二飞	Liu Erfei	英语学院	School of English	美林（亚太）有限公司董事总经理兼中国地区主席	Chairman & Managing Director at Merrill Lynch Asia-Pacific Ltd and concurrent Chairman for Merrill Lynch's China Operations
刘 恒	Liu Heng	附属学校	Affiliated School	著名作家	Famous writer
刘太迟	Liu Taichi	英语学院	School of English	空军装备部副部长、少将	Deputy Director of the Air Force Armament Department; Major General
马晓霖	Ma Xiaolin	阿拉伯语系	Dept. of Arabic	博联社总裁	Bo Lian She's President
孟 怡	Meng Yi	英语学院	School of English	渣打银行中国区总裁兼董事总经理	Standard Chartered Bank-China's CEO and Managing Director

姓名	Name	毕业院系	School/Dept.	曾（现）任职务	Positions held
秦秀白	Qin Xiubai	英语学院	School of English	首届国家教学名师、华南理工学院教授	One of the first national renowned teachers; professor of South China Institute of Technology
秦亚青	Qin Yaqing	高级翻译学院	Graduate School of Translation & Interpretation	外交学院党委书记、常务副院长	Secretary of CPC China Foreign Affairs University Committee and Executive Vice President of the University
曲 维	Qu Wei	日本学研究中心	Japanese Studies Centre	辽宁师范大学副校长	Vice President of Liaoning Normal University
邵文光	Shao Wenguang	高级翻译学院	Graduate School of Translation & Interpretation	凤凰卫视欧洲台台长	Managing Director of Phoenix Chinese News and Entertainment Channel in Europe
谭晶华	Tan Jinghua	日本学研究中心	Japanese Studies Centre	上海外国语大学常务副校长	Executive Vice President of Shanghai International Studies University
王东明	Wang Dongming	法语系	Dept. of French	中信证券董事长	Chairman of CITIC Securities
王刚毅	Wang Gangyi	英语学院	School of English	北京周报社社长兼总编辑	President and General Managing Editor of Beijing Review
王建清	Wang Jianqing	西葡语系	Dept. of Spanish & Portuguese	江苏吴江平望中学高级教师、全国"三八"红旗手	Senior teacher at Wujiang Pingwang Secondary School in Jiangsu; a National "March the Eighth" Red Flag Bearer
吴国华	Wu Guohua	俄语学院	School of Russian	解放军外国语学院院长、教授，国务院学位委员会学科评议组成员	President and professor of the People's Liberation Army Institute of International Studies; member of the Academic Discipline Appraisal Board, the Degree Committee of the State Council
吴志良	Wu Zhiliang	西葡语系	Dept. of Spanish & Portuguese	澳门基金会主席	Chairman of the Macao Foundation
杨 澜	Yang Lan	英语学院	School of English	阳光文化影视公司董事局主席	Chairperson of the Sun Media Group and the Sun Culture Foundation
徐烈均	Xu Liejun	英语学院	School of English	中国轻工业品进出口公司总裁	CEO of China Light Industrial Products Import and Export Corporation
许戈辉	Xu Gehui	英语学院	School of English	凤凰卫视主持人	Phoenix TV Presenter
姚越灿	Yao Yuecan	英语学院	School of English	中国国际旅行社总社有限公司董事长	Chairman of China International Travel Service
尹 卓	Yin Zhuo	法语系	Dept. of French	海军信息化专家咨询委员会主任、少将	Chairman of the Navy Information Technology Expert Advisory Board, Major General
俞 渝	Yu Yu	英语学院	School of English	当当网总裁	CEO of E-commerce China Dangdang Inc
张建益	Zhang Jianyi	英语学院	School of English	江苏瀚康生物科技有限公司董事长	Chairman of Jiangsu Hankang Biological Technology Co.
张绍杰	Zhang Shaojie	中国外语教育研究中心	National Research Centre for Foreign Language Education	东北师范大学副校长	Vice President of Northeast Normal University
张 宇	Zhang Yu	西葡语系	Dept. of Spanish & Portuguese	中国对外文化集团公司董事长兼总经理	Chairman and General Managing Director of China Arts and Entertainment Group
周宝义	Zhou Baoyi	欧语学院	School of European Languages & Cultures	国际广播电台党组书记	Secretary of leading Party members' group of China Radio International
周伯荣	Zhou Borong	英语学院	School of English	驻香港部队副司令员，海军副参谋长、少将	Deputy Commander of troops stationed in Hong Kong; Deputy Chief of Staff of the Navy; Major General
周 烈	Zhou Lie	阿拉伯语系	Dept. of Arabic	第二外国语学院院长	President of Beijing International Studies University
朱 灵	Zhu Ling	英语学院	School of English	中国日报社社长、总编辑	President and General Managing Editor of the China Daily Group
朱 彤	Zhu Tong	高级翻译学院	Graduate School of Translation & Interpretation	德意志银行中国区总经理	General Manager of Deutsche Bank-China

北京外国语大学 图史

An Illustrated History of Beijing Foreign Studies University

第十一章
开放窗口　友谊桥梁

Chapter Eleven
Embracing the world through international exchanges

　　自改革开放以来，北京外国语大学因其自身特点及优势，一直是我国与世界各国发展友好关系、增进相互了解、促进文化交流的重要窗口与纽带。与此同时，与世界各国在文化教育等领域的交流与合作，有力推动了学校的学科建设、教育教学改革发展以及国际化水平的提高，在建设国际一流外国语大学的进程中起到了重要作用。

　　Since the start of China's reform and opening-up, Beijing Foreign Studies University, for its own unique character and advantage, has always been an important nexus facilitating the development of China's friendly relations with other countries, the deepening of mutual understanding between the Chinese people and the people of the world, and promoting cultural exchange. At the same time, the cultural and educational exchange and collaboration it has forged with partner universities around the world have provided the impetus to push forward the University's academic development, pedagogical reforms and level of internationalisation, playing a crucial role in the process of building an internationally recognised first-class foreign language university.

与我校建立交流合作关系的部分高校和学术机构

Some of the institutions of higher education and other academic institutions that have established exchange and collaboration with BSFU

澳大利亚
- 昆士兰大学
- 拉筹伯大学
- 格利菲斯大学
- 悉尼大学
- 堪培拉大学
- 阿德莱德大学

加拿大
- 魁北克拉瓦尔大学
- 加拿大纽芬兰纪念大学
- 多伦多大学
- 维多利亚大学
- 蒙特利尔大学
- 布鲁克大学
- 昆特兰理工大学
- 渥太华大学
- 阿尔伯塔大学

哥伦比亚
- 哈维利亚纳教廷大学
- 经管学院大学

朝鲜
- 平壤外国语大学

芬兰
- 坦佩雷大学
- 于韦斯曲莱大学
- 赫尔辛基大学
- 拉普兰大学

法国
- 蒙彼利埃大学
- 巴黎第一大学
- 巴黎第三大学
- 艾克斯—马塞大学
- 保罗·塞尚大学
- 巴黎高等师范学校
- 巴黎政治学院
- 巴黎第四大学

德国
- 海德堡大学
- 汉堡大学
- 康斯坦茨大学
- 哥廷根大学
- 海因里希·海涅大学
- 慕尼黑应用语言大学
- 曼海姆大学
- 弗赖堡大学

印度尼西亚
- 印度尼西亚教育大学

日本
- 早稻田大学
- 神户大学
- 大东文化大学
- 名古屋外国语大学
- 明海大学
- 大阪外国语大学
- 樱美林大学
- 关西大学
- 立教大学
- 杏林大学
- 法政大学

马来西亚
- 马来亚大学

墨西哥
- 墨西哥国立自治大学
- 韦拉克鲁斯大学
- 墨西哥学院

新西兰
- 奥克兰大学
- 惠灵顿维多利亚大学

波兰
- 华沙大学
- 罗兹大学
- 雅盖隆大学
- 格但斯克大学
- 西里西亚大学

韩国
- 高丽大学
- 仁济大学
- 江原大学
- 又松大学
- 汉阳大学
- 成均馆大学
- 梨花女子大学
- 韩国外国语大学
- 釜山外国语大学
- 庆熙大学

俄罗斯
- 普希金俄语学院
- 莫斯科大学
- 俄罗斯人民友谊大学
- 俄语世界基金会
- 莫斯科国立语言大学
- 莫斯科国立国际关系学院
- 圣彼得堡大学

沙特阿拉伯
- 沙特国王大学
- 吉赞大学
- 塔布克大学

南非
- 西开普大学
- 西北大学

西班牙
- 马德里自治大学
- 巴塞罗那自治大学
- 布尔戈斯大学
- 庞培法布拉大学
- 奥维耶多大学
- 塞维利亚大学
- 卡斯蒂利亚拉曼查大学
- 比戈大学

泰国
- 清迈皇家大学
- 朱拉隆功大学
- 皇太后大学

英国
- 剑桥大学
- 牛津大学
- 肯特大学
- 威斯敏斯特大学
- 普利茅斯大学
- 利兹大学
- 诺丁汉大学
- 兰卡斯特大学
- 华威大学
- 谢菲尔德大学
- 圣安德鲁斯大学
- 伦敦大学学院教育研究院
- 伦敦大学亚非学院
- 伦敦玛丽女王大学
- 博尔顿大学
- 阿尔斯特大学

美国
- 耶鲁大学
- 普渡大学
- 华盛顿大学
- 西北大学
- 加利福尼亚大学伯克利分校
- 密苏里大学
- 亚利桑那大学
- 马萨诸塞大学
- 夏威夷大学
- 新奥尔良大学
- 丹佛大学国际关系学院
- 巴纳德学院
- 德堡大学
- 莫瑞州立大学
- 中密执根大学

越南
- 河内外国语大学
- 胡志明市师范大学

Australia
- The University of Queensland
- La Trobe University
- Griffith University
- University of Sydney
- University of Canberra
- University of Adelaide

Canada
- Laval University, Quebec
- Memorial University of Newfoundland, Canada
- University of Toronto
- University of Victoria
- University of Montreal
- Brock University
- Kwantlen Polytechnic University
- University of Ottawa
- University of Alberta

Colombia
- The Pontifical Xavierian University
- EAN University

Democratic People's Republic of Korea
- Pyongyang University of Foreign Studies

Finland
- University of Tampere
- University of Jyvaskyla
- University of Helsinki
- University of Lapland

France
- University of Montpellier
- University of Paris I
- University of Paris III
- Aix-Marseille University
- Paul Cezanne University
- Normal College of Paris
- Paris Institute of Political Studies
- University of Paris IV

Germany
- University of Heidelberg
- University of Hamburg
- University of Konstanz
- University of Goettingen
- Heinrich Heine University Düsseldorf
- University of Applied Languages, Munich
- University of Mannheim
- University of Freiburg

Indonesia
- Indonesia University of Education

Japan
- Waseda University
- Kobe University
- Daito Bunka University
- Nagoya University of Foreign Studies
- Meikai University
- Osaka University of Foreign Studies
- J.F.Oberlin University
- Kansai University
- Rikkyo University
- Kyorin University
- Hosei University

Malaysia
- University of Malaya

Mexico
- National Autonomous University of Mexico
- University of Veracruz
- The College of Mexico

New Zealand
- The University of Auckland
- Victoria University of Wellington

Poland
- University of Warsaw
- University of Lodz
- Jagiellonian University
- University of Gdańsk
- University of Silesia

Republic of Korea
- Korea University
- Inje University
- Kangwon University
- Woosong University
- Hanyang University
- Sungkyunkwan University
- Ewha Womans University
- Hankuk University of Foreign Studies
- Busan University of Foreign Studies
- Kyung Hee University

Russia
- The Pushkin State Russian Language Institute
- Moscow State University
- People's Friendship University of Russia
- Russian World Foundation
- Moscow State Linguistic University
- Moscow State Institute of International Relations
- St Petersburg State University

Saudi Arabia
- King Saud University
- Jazan University
- University of Tabuk

South Africa
- University of Western Cape
- North-West University

Spain
- Autonomous University of Madrid
- Autonomous University of Barcelona
- University of Burgos
- Pompeu Fabra University
- University of Oviedo
- University of Seville
- University of Castilla-La Mancha
- University of Vigo

Thailand
- Chiang Mai Rajabhat University
- Chulalongkorn University
- Mae Fah Luang University

UK
- University of Cambridge
- University of Oxford
- University of Kent
- University of Westminster
- University of Plymouth
- University of Leeds
- University of Nottingham
- Lancaster University
- University of Warwick
- University of Sheffield
- University of St Andrews
- Institute of Education, University College London
- School of Oriental and African Studies, University of London
- Queen Mary University of London
- University of Bolton
- University of Ulster

USA
- Yale University
- Purdue University
- University of Washington
- Northwest University
- University of California, Berkeley
- University of Missouri
- The University of Arizona
- University of Massachusetts
- University of Hawaii at Manoa
- University of New Orleans
- Josef Korbel School of International Studies, the University of Denver
- Barnard College
- DePauw University
- Murray State University
- Central Michigan University

Vietnam
- University of Languages and International Studies, Hanoi
- Ho Chi Minh City University of Pedagogy

加强与国外大学及其他学术机构的交流与合作，是推动学科建设与师资队伍建设、拓宽人才培养渠道、提高学校国际化水平的重要途径。到2014年为止，学校与世界上72个国家的400余所高等学校及学术机构建立了合作与交流关系，其中包括耶鲁大学、牛津大学、剑桥大学、圣彼得堡大学、哥廷根大学、罗马大学、早稻田大学等著名院校。

Strengthening exchange and collaboration with overseas universities and other academic institutions is an important means for a university to promote its disciplinary development and teacher development, create new channels for student education and enhance its level of internationalization. By 2014, the University had established academic links for exchange and collaboration with over 400 institutions of higher education and other academic institutions in 72 countries across the world, including Yale University, University of Oxford, University of Cambridge, University of St Petersburg, University of Goettingen, University of Rome, Waseda University, etc.

1. 1998 年 9 月 16 日，华沙大学代表团访问我校。

2. 2002 年 6 月 26 日，泰国皇太后大学代表团来访。

3. 2005 年 6 月 30 日，与英国圣安德鲁斯大学签订
   交流协议。

1. A delegation from University of Warsaw visiting
   the University on 16th September 1998

2. A delegation from Mae Fah Luang University
   in Thailand visiting the University on 26th June
   2002

3. An exchange agreement was signed with the
   University of St Andrews on 30th June 2005

4. 2005 年 11 月 11 日，与爱尔兰国立大学梅努斯
分校签署合作协议仪式。

5. 2006 年 10 月，美国夏威夷大学代表团来访。

6. 2006 年 10 月 23 日，北京外国语大学与列日大
学、布鲁塞尔自由大学合作框架协议签字仪式。

4. Signing ceremony of a collaboration agreement with the National University of Ireland,
Maynooth, on 11th November 2005

5. A delegation from the University of Hawaii
visiting the University in October 2006

6. Signing ceremony of a collaborative
framework agreement between BFSU and the
University of Liege and the Free University of
Brussels, on 23th October 2006

1. 2008 年 9 月 22 日，北京外国语大学与海德
   堡大学校际交流 25 周年庆典。

2. 2011 年 12 月 8 日，丹佛大学国际关系学院
   院长希尔在我校演讲。

3. 2012 年 3 月 13 日，北京外国语大学与英国
   威斯敏斯特大学合作备忘录签署仪式。

1. Celebrating the 25th anniversary of inter-university
   exchange between the University of Heidelberg and
   BFSU on 22nd September 2008

2. Christopher Hill, Dean of Josef Korbel School of
   International Studies, the University of Denver, giving
   a talk at the University on 8th December 2011

3. Signing ceremony of the Memorandum of Collaboration between BFSU and Westminster University, UK,
   on 13th March 2012

4. 2013 年 3 月 4 日，北京外国语大学
   与日本大东文化大学协议签署仪式。

5. 2013 年 3 月 11 日，北京外国语大
   学与夏威夷大学协议签署仪式。

6. 2013 年 3 月 26 日，墨西哥国立自
   治大学代表团来访。

4. Signing ceremony of an agreement
   between BFSU and Daito Bunka University,
   Japan, on 4th March 2013

5. Signing ceremony of an agreement
   between BFSU and the University of Hawaii
   at Manoa on 11th March 2013

6. A delegation from National Autonomous
   University of Mexico visiting the University
   on 26th March 2013

1. 2013 年"汉语桥——美国校长访华之旅"代表团来访。

2. 2014 年 9 月 15 日，国际高校翻译学院联盟主席来访。

3. 2014 年彭龙校长访问英国皇家国际问题研究所。

1. A "Chinese Bridge"American Principals delegation visiting the University in 2013

2. The President Hannelore Lee-Jahnkeof CIUTI (Conférence Internationale Permanente d'Instituts Universitaires de Traducteurs et Interprètes) visiting the University on 15th September 2014

3. University President Peng Long visiting the Royal Institute of International Affairs in the UK in 2014

4

5

6

4. 2014 年彭龙校长访问牛津大学。

5. 2014 年彭龙校长与兰卡斯特大学
   校长马克·史密斯签署合作协议。

6. 2014 年彭龙校长与伦敦大学亚非
   学院签署交流协议。

4. President Peng Long visiting Oxford
   University in 2014

5. President Peng Long signing a
   collaboration agreement with Vice
   Chancellor Mark Smith of Lancaster
   University in 2014

6. President Peng Long signing an
   exchange agreement with SAAS
   (School of Asian and African
   Studies), University of London, in
   2014

北京外国语大学承办的孔子学院

Confucius Institutes run by BFSU

◆ 地拉那大学孔子学院 CIUT	◆ CI at the University of Tirana
◆ 维也纳大学孔子学院 CIUV	◆ CI at the University of Vienna
◆ 布鲁塞尔孔子学院 CIB	◆ CI in Brussels
◆ 列日孔子学院 CIL	◆ CI in Liege
◆ 索菲亚孔子学院 CIS	◆ CI in Sofia
◆ 帕拉茨基大学孔子学院 CIPU	◆ CI at Palacký University
◆ 杜塞尔多夫孔子学院 CID	◆ CI in Dusseldorf
◆ 哥廷根大学孔子学院 CIUG	◆ CI at the University of Goettingen
◆ 慕尼黑孔子学院 CIM	◆ CI in Munich
◆ 纽伦堡—埃尔兰根孔子学院 CEN	◆ CI in Erlangen-Nürnberg
◆ 罗兰大学孔子学院 CIELU	◆ CI at EötvösLoránd University
◆ 罗马大学孔子学院 CIURLS	◆ CI at the University of Rome La Sapienza
◆ 马来亚大学孔子汉语学院 CITCLUM	◆ CI for the Teaching of Chinese Language at the University of Malaya
◆ 克拉科夫孔子学院 CIK	◆ CI in Krakow
◆ 韩国外国语大学孔子学院 CIHUFS	◆ CI at Hankuk University of Foreign Studies
◆ 莫斯科国立语言大学孔子学院 CIMSLU	◆ CI at Moscow State Linguistic University
◆ 巴塞罗那孔子学院 CIB	◆ CI in Barcelona
◆ 科伦坡大学孔子学院 CIUC	◆ CI at the University of Colombo
◆ 扎耶德大学孔子学院 CIZU	◆ CI at Zayed University
◆ 伦敦孔子学院 LCI	◆ London Confucius Institute
◆ 夏威夷大学孔子学院 CIUHM	◆ CI at the University of Hawaii at Manoa

学校秉承"把世界介绍给中国，把中国介绍给世界"的使命，利用自身优势，主动参与国家"中国文化走出去"战略行动，积极推动中国语言文化在世界各国的传播。截至 2014 年底，学校承办了 21 所海外孔子学院，分布在亚、欧、美洲的 16 个国家。

To carry out its mission of "introducing the world to China and introducing China to the world", the University has actively participated in the government's strategic initiative of "letting Chinese culture go abroad". By making use of its advantages, the University has successfully propagated Chinese culture to various countries across the world. By the end of 2014 the number of Confucius Institutes (CI) run by the University in conjunction with oversea-partner institutions had reached 21, covering 16 countries across Asia, Europe and North and South America.

1. 2009年6月25日，教育部副部长郝平、国家汉语国际推广领导小组办公室主任许琳为我校"汉语国际推广多语种基地"揭牌。

2. 2013年7月21日，由孔子学院总部、国家汉语国际推广领导小组办公室主办，我校承办的"2013年欧盟官员来华研修班"开班。

1. Deputy Minister of Education Hao Ping and Director General Xu Lin of Hanban unveiling the plaque for the University's Multilingual Base for International Propagation of Chinese on 25th June 2009.

2. The 2013 Chinese Training Programme for EU Officials sponsored by Confucius Institute Head-quarters and Hanban and hosted by the University started on 21st July 2013

1. 1998 年 12 月 11 日，叙利亚副总统来访。

2. 1999 年 4 月 10 日，卢森堡副首相雅克·普斯来访，参观外语教学与研究出版社。

3. 1999 年 6 月 1 日，马来西亚外交部部长赛义德·哈米特在《马哈蒂尔演讲集》首发式上讲话。

1. Syrian Vice President visiting the University on 11th December 1998

2. Deputy Prime Minister Jacques F. Poos of Luxembourg visiting Foreign Language Teaching and Research Press on 10th April 1999

3. Malaysian Foreign Minister Syed Hamid Albar speaking at the launch of *Selected Speeches by Mahathir bin Mohamad*, Prime Minister of Malaysia on 1st June 1999

作为国家重点建设的外国语大学，多年来我校接待了大量外国政府代表团参观来访，承担国家在文化教育领域的重要国际合作项目，不断增强办学实力与活力。

As a key national university, BFSU has received a large number of foreign government delegations over the past decades and has undertaken some major international collaboration projects in the cultural and educational sectors, continuously enhancing its academic strengths and vitality.

4

5

4. 1999 年 10 月 11 日，斯洛伐克语班的学生为来访的斯洛伐克教育部部长一行表演小节目。

5. 2000 年 5 月 11 日，捷克教育部部长来访，与捷克语专业学生交流。

6. 2001 年 5 月 14 日，叙利亚副总统阿卜杜·哈利姆·哈达姆阁下访问我校。

4. Students of Slovak giving a performance in Slovak for the visiting Slovakian Foreign Minister and members of his delegation on 11th October 1999

5. Visiting Czech Minister of Education communicating with students of Czech on 11th May 2000

6. Syrian Vice President Abdul Halim Khaddam visiting the University on 14th May 2001

6

1. 2001 年 9 月 25 日，新西兰教育代表团来访。

2. 2001 年 10 月 22 日，古巴教育部副部长来访并向我校赠书。

3. 2002 年 6 月 28 日，罗马尼亚教育部副部长率团来访，与罗马尼亚语专业师生交流。

1. A New Zealand educational delegation visiting the University on 25th September 2001

2. Visiting Deputy Minister of Education of Cuba presenting books to the University on 22nd October 2001

3. Deputy Minister of Education of Romania exchanging thoughts with teachers and students of Romanian on 28th June 2002

4

5

4. 2003 年 10 月 29 日，俄罗斯文化部部长什
维德科伊来访并发表演讲。

5. 2004 年 3 月 1 日，葡萄牙外长特雷莎·戈
维亚女士来访。

6. 2004 年 3 月 4 日，保加利亚教育部部长来
访，与刘知白教授亲切握手交谈。

6

4. Visiting Russian Minister of Culture Mikhail Shvydkoy
making a speech at the University on 29th October 2003

5. Portuguese Foreign Minister Teresa Gouveia visiting the
University on 1st March 2004

6. Bulgarian Minister of Education visiting the University on
4th March 2004 and meeting with Professor Liu Zhibai

1. 2005 年 9 月 1 日，马来西亚副总理纳吉布来访，与马来语专业学生亲切交谈。
2. 2005 年 11 月 22 日，克罗地亚科学教育体育部副部长来校访问，与丁超教授握手交谈。
3. 2006 年 4 月 6 日，希腊教育部部长代表团一行访问我校。

1. Malaysian Deputy Prime Minister Najib visiting the University on 1st September 2005 and chatting with students of Malay
2. Vice Minister of Science, Education and Sports of Croatia visiting the University on 22nd November 2005 and meeting with Professor Ding Chao
3. A delegation led by the Greek Minister of Education visiting the University on 6th April 2006

4. 2006 年 9 月 14 日，冰岛教育科学文化部赠书仪式，部长托尔杰尔迪·卡特琳·贡纳尔斯多蒂尔致辞。

5. 2006 年 10 月 23 日，比利时教育与科学技术部部长（右一）来访，与郝平校长交谈。

6. 2007 年 4 月 10 日，阿联酋外长阿卜杜拉率团来访，与阿拉伯语系部分师生合影。

4. Thorgereur Katrin Gunnarsdottir, Minister of Education, Science and Culture of Iceland, speaking at a ceremony on 14th September 2006 to mark the Ministry's presentation of books to the University

5. Marie-Dominique Simonet (1st right), Minister of Education, Science and Technology of Belgium, visiting the University on 23rd October 2006 and talking with University President Hao Ping

6. A delegation led by UAE Foreign Minister Abdullah bin Zayed Al Nahyan visiting the University on 10th April 2007 and being photographed with some of the teachers and students of the Department of Arabic

1

2

1. 2008 年 11 月 7 日，保加利亚副总理兼教育科技部部长丹尼埃尔·沃尔切夫来校访问。

2. 2009 年 3 月 27 日，俄罗斯副总理茹科夫来访。

3. 郝平校长授予俄罗斯副总理茹科夫北京外国语大学名誉博士学位。

1. Daniel Mitov, Bulgarian Deputy Prime Minister and Minister of Education and Science, visiting the University on 7th November 2008

2. Russian Deputy Prime Minister Alexander Zhukov visiting the University on 27th March 2009

3. University President Hao Ping conferring an Honorary Doctorate on Russian Deputy Prime Minister Alexander Zhukov

3

4. 2011 年 10 月 12 日，亚非学院僧伽罗语专业学生欢迎来访的斯里兰卡教育部部长。

5. 2012 年 3 月 15 日，爱尔兰教育与技能部国务部长夏兰·卡农来访，参观爱尔兰研究中心。

6. 2012 年 4 月 10 日，阿尔巴尼亚教育和科学部部长米切雷姆·塔法伊率团来访，与阿尔巴尼亚语专业师生合影。

4. Students of Sinhala welcoming visiting Sri Lanka Minister of Education on 12th October 2011

5. Ciarán Cannon, Irish Minister of State for Training and Skills, visiting the University's Irish Studies Centre on 15th March 2012

6. A delegation led by Myqerem Tafaj, Minister of Education and Science of Albania, visiting the University on 10th April 2012, photographed with teachers and students of Albanian

1. 2012 年 6 月 12 日，缅甸外交部部长吴温纳貌伦（右侧左四）来访，与缅甸语专业师生交流。

2. 2012 年 6 月 19 日，意大利教育、大学和科研部部长弗朗西斯科·普罗夫莫在与北外中、意学生交流会上讲话。

3. 2012 年 6 月 19 日，意大利教育、大学和科研部部长弗朗西斯科·普罗夫莫与北外中、意学生合影。

1. Myanmar Foreign Minister Wunna Maung Lwin (4th left on the right side) exchanging thoughts with teachers and students of Burmese on 12th June 2012

2. Italian Minister for Education, Universities and Research, Francesco Profumo making a speech at BFSU's Chinese-Italian Student Exchange Conference on 19th June 2012

3. Italian Minister for Education, Universities and Research, Francesco Profumo photographed with Chinese and Italian students at BFSU on 19th June 2012

4. 2012 年 10 月 29 日，斯洛文尼亚教育代表团来访，与斯洛文尼亚语专业师生合影。

5. 2013 年 2 月 26 日，秘鲁外交部部长拉斐尔·龙卡利奥洛来访并发表演讲。

6. 2013 年 3 月 11 日，斯里兰卡青年部部长来访，参观亚非学院。

4. A Slovenian educational delegation photographed with teachers and students of Slovenian on 29th October 2012

5. Peruvian Foreign Minister Rafael Roncagliolo making a speech on Peru's foreign policy during his visit to the University on 26th February 2013

6. Dullas Alahapperuma, Minister of Youth Affairs and Skills Development of Sri Lanka, visiting the School of Asian and African Studies on 11th March 2013

1. 2013 年 5 月 27 日，马耳他教育与就业部部长艾伯里斯特·巴托罗来访。

2. 2013 年 6 月 25 日，波兰科学与高等教育部副部长达利亚·利平斯卡—纳文赤来访。

3. 2013 年 11 月 19 日，厄瓜多尔外交及移民部部长里卡多·帕蒂尼奥来访并发表演讲。

1. Maltese Minister of Education and Employment Evarist Bartolo visiting the University on 27th May 2013

2. Daria Lipińska-Nałęcz, Deputy Minister of Science and Higher Education of Poland, visiting the University on 25th June 2013

3. Ricardo Armando Patiño Aroca, Minister of Foreign Affairs, Trade and Integration of Ecuador, making a speech on Ecuador's foreign policy during his visit to the University on 19th November 2013

4

5

6

4. 2014 年 4 月 25 日，丹麦教育部部长（右二）来访，在欧语学院与丹麦语专业学生交流。

5. 2014 年 6 月 24 日，斯里兰卡经贸部部长来访。

6. 2014 年 7 月 9 日，俄罗斯总统办公厅主任来访，与俄语学院师生交流。

4. Danish Minister of Education (2nd right) visiting the University on 25th April 2014 and talking to students of Danish in School of European Languages and Cultures

5. Sri Lanka Minister of Industry and Commerce visiting the University on 24th June 2014

6. Sergei Ivanov, Chief of Staff of the Presidential Executive Office of Russia, talking to teachers and students of the School of Russian on 9th July 2014

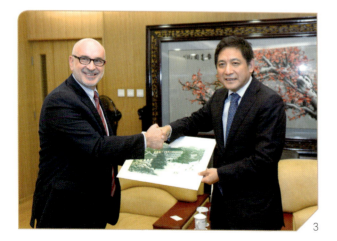

1. 2014 年 9 月 9 日, 立陶宛教育部部长来访, 与立陶宛语专业学生合影。

2. 2014 年 9 月 11 日, 坦桑尼亚代表团来访。

3. 2014 年 9 月 23 日, 克罗地亚科技教育部副部长来访。

1. Dainius Pavalkis (centre wearing a tie), Lithuanian Minister of Education, photographed with students of Lithuanian during his visit to the University on 9th September 2014

2. A Tanzanian delegation visiting the University on 11th September 2014

3. Roko Andričević, Deputy Minister of Science, Education and Sports of Croatia, visiting the University on 23rd September 2014

学校十分注重与各国社会著名人士的联系与交往，加强非官方合作，扩大学校国际影响力，增进相互之间的了解、友谊与信任。

The University attaches great importance to its relationships and connections with socially renowned figures from all over the world. By strengthening non-governmental cooperation with them, the University has enhanced its international influence, increased mutual understanding, friendship and trust.

4. 1996 年，俄罗斯总统叶利钦的夫人奈娜访问我校。

5. 2000 年 11 月 6 日，西班牙王储费利佩·德博尔冯-格雷西亚来访。

4. Nainalosifovna Yeltsina, wife of Russian President Boris Yeltsin, visiting the University in 1996

5. His Royal Highness Prince Felipe de Borbon y Grecia of Spain visiting the University on 6th November 2000

1. 2001 年 8 月 22 日，国际大学生体育联合会主席乔治·基里安博士受聘为北京外国语大学名誉教授。

2. 2001 年 11 月 29 日，前美国助理国务卿希尔来校做演讲。

3. 2003 年 3 月 7 日，西班牙王后索菲娅访问我校。

1. George Ernest Killian, President of the International University Sports Federation (FISU), was appointed an honorary professor of BFSU on 22nd August 2001.

2. Former US Assistant Secretary of State Christopher Hill giving a talk at the University on 29th November 2001

3. Queen Sofia of Spain visiting the University on 7th March 2003

4. 2004 年 4 月 19 日，阿联酋亲王来访并发表演讲。

5. 2005 年 9 月 1 日，西班牙东方研究专家塔西亚娜·费萨克女士受聘为北京外国语大学名誉教授。

6. 2005 年 9 月 27 日，瑞典公主来校访问。

4. His Highness Sheikh Hamdan bin Zayed Al Nahyan, Crown Prince of Dubai, Deputy Prime Minister and Minister of State for Foreign Affairs of UAE, making a speech during his visit to the University on 19th April 2004

5. Taciana Fisac, a Chinese studies expert from Spain, was appointed an honorary professor of BFSU on 1st September 2005

6. Her Royal Highness Princess Victoria of Sweden visiting the University on 27th September 2005

1. 2007 年 9 月 4 日，约旦王后拉尼亚访问我校。

2. 2009 年法国前总理拉法兰在我校演讲。

3. 2009 年 3 月 21 日，欧盟多语言事务委员受聘为北京外国语大学名誉教授。

1. Queen Rania of Jordan visiting the University on 4th September 2007

2. Former French Prime Minister Jean-Pierre Raffarin giving a speech at the University in 2009

3. Leonard Orban, European Commissioner for Multilingualism, was appointed as an honorary professor by BFSU on 21st March 2009.

4. 2011年6月23日，国际奥委会主席罗格受聘为北京外国语大学名誉教授。

5. 2011年12月8日，美国前助理国务卿希尔来校演讲，和梅仁毅教授交谈。

6. 2012年3月28日，阿联酋亲王来校访问。

4. IOC President Jacques Rogge was appointed as an honorary professor by BFSU on 23rd June 2011.

5. Former US Assistant Secretary of State Christopher Hill talking to Professor Mei Renyi after making a speech at the University on 8th December 2011

6. His Highness Sheikh Mohammed bin Zayed, Crown Prince of Abu Dhabi, UAE, visiting the University on 28th March 2012

1. 2012 年 6 月 1 日，波兰总统夫人安娜·科莫罗夫斯卡来访，与波兰语专业学生座谈。

2. 2012 年 8 月 31 日，马来西亚语文局局长阿旺·沙利延博士受聘为北京外国语大学名誉教授。

3. 2013 年 4 月 15 日，冰岛总理夫人约尼娜·莱兹多蒂来访，与冰岛语专业学生座谈并合影。

1. Polish First Lady Anna Komorowska talking with students of Polish during her visit to the University on 1st June 2012

2. Dr Awang Sariyan, Director of the Language and Literature Bureau, receiving his appointment as an honorary professor of BFSU on 31st August 2012

3. Jonina Leosdottir, wife of the Prime Minister of Iceland, visiting the University on 15th April 2013 and photographed with students of Icelandic after an informal discussion

4. 2014 年 8 月 22 日，日本前首相鸠山由纪夫（左二）偕夫人来访，并受聘为北京外国语大学荣誉教授。图为鸠山由纪夫参观北京日本学研究中心。

5. 日本前首相鸠山由纪夫与北京日本学研究中心研究生合影。

6. 2014 年 9 月 10 日，印尼国民民主党主席苏里亚·巴罗来访，并受聘为北京外国语大学名誉教授，彭龙校长为其颁发聘书。

4. Former Japanese Prime Minister Yukio Hatoyama (2nd left), accompanied by his wife, visiting Beijing Japanese Studies Centre at the University on 22nd August 2014. He was appointed as an honorary professor of the University.

5. Former Japanese Prime Minister Yukio Hatoyama photographed with students at Beijing Japanese Studies Centre

6. Surya Paloh, Chairman of the Indonesia's Nasdem Party, receiving his appointment as an honorary professor of BFSU from University President Peng Long on 10th September 2014

1995

▌ 1995 年，德国总理科尔访问北京外国语大学。

German Chancellor Helmut Kohl visiting BFSU on 14th November 1995

1996

▌ 1996 年 11 月，瑞典首相佩尔松来访，校长王福祥陪同参观校园。

Swedish Prime Minister Goran Persson, accompanied by University President Wang Fuxiang, visiting the University in November 1996

　　北京外国语大学作为国内历史最久，开设语种最多的外国语大学，是国家改革开放的一个重要窗口。自改革开放以来，我校接待了诸多外国政要的参观访问，在展示学校办学水平的同时，有力提升了学校的国际知名度与影响力。

　　As a foreign language university with the longest history in China and offering the largest number of foreign language programmes, Beijing Foreign Studies University is an important institution showcasing China's educational development. Since China's reform and opening-up in the late 1970s, the University has received a large number of foreign dignitaries during their visit of China. By demonstrating its teaching standard and academic achievements, the University has significantly enhanced its international reputation and influence.

1996

▌1996 年 6 月 12 日，澳大利亚议长斯蒂芬·马丁来访。

Stephen Paul Martin, Speaker of the Australian House of Representatives, visiting the University on 12th June 1996

2002

▌2002 年 4 月 5 日，卢森堡首相容克来访并发表演讲。

Prime Minister of Luxembourg Jean-Claude Juncker making a speech during his visit to the University on 5th April 2002

2003

▌2003 年 11 月 21 日，瑞士联邦主席帕斯卡尔·库什潘来访。

Swiss President Pascal Couchepin, visiting the French Department at the University on 21st November 2003

2004

■ 2004 年 5 月 29 日，马来西亚总理阿卜杜拉来访，并在我校举办的"中国—马来西亚友好关系研讨会"上演讲。

Malaysian Prime Minister Abdullah Ahmad Badawi speaking at the China-Malaysia Friendship Seminar on 29th May 2004

2008

■ 2008 年 1 月 10 日，阿联酋总统哈利法·本·扎耶德·阿勒纳哈扬来访。

University President Hao Ping photographed with United Arab Emirates President Abdullah bin Zayed Al Nahyan, during his visit to make a donation to the University on 10th January 2008

2009

■ 2009 年 6 月 3 日，教育部副部长、北京外国语大学校长郝平授予来访的马来西亚总理纳吉布北京外国语大学名誉博士学位。

Deputy Minister of Education and President of BFSU Hao Ping conferring an Honorary Doctorate on Malaysian Prime Minister Najib Razak on 3rd June 2009

2010

2010 年，俄罗斯总统梅德韦杰夫与
我校学生进行交流。

Russian President Dmitry Medvedev talking
with students at the University in 2010

2011 年 8 月 11 日，陈雨露校
长授予来访的斯里兰卡总统马欣
达·拉贾帕克萨名誉博士学位。

University President Chen Yulu
conferring an Honorary Doctorate
on Sri Lankan President Mahinda
Rajapaksa on 11th August 2011

2011

2012

2012 年 9 月 9 日，拉脱维亚总理瓦
尔蒂斯·东布罗夫斯基来访。

Latvian Prime Minister Valdis Dombrovskis
visiting the University on 9th September 2012

▌ 2013 年 3 月 25 日，阿联酋联邦国民议会议长
穆罕默德·穆尔来访，与阿拉伯语系师生合影。

UAE Federal National Council Speaker Mohammed
Ahmed Al Murr photographed with teachers and students
of the Arabic Department on 25th March 2013

▌ 2013 年 6 月 14 日，埃塞俄比亚总理海尔马里
亚姆·德萨莱尼来访并发表演讲。

Ethiopian Prime Minister Hailemariam Desalegn making
a speech at the University on 14th June 2013

2013

▌ 2013 年 5 月 27 日，韩震校长与来访的
乌拉圭总统何塞·穆希卡在校园内共同
栽下友谊树后合影。

University President Han Zhen photographed
with visiting Uruguayan President Jose Mujica
after planting a tree of friendship on campus on
27th May 2013

▌2014 年 5 月 16 日，葡萄牙总统卡瓦科·席尔瓦
出席"中葡语言文化合作交流联合体"成立仪式，
与彭龙校长相互祝贺联合体成立。

University President Peng Long and visiting Portuguese
President Cavaco Silva congratulating one another on the
establishment of China-Portugal Language and Culture
Collaboration and Exchange Union on 16th May 2014

▌2014 年 5 月 30 日，马来西亚总理纳吉布出席我校
承办的"2014 北京马来研究国际研讨会"开幕式。

Malaysian Prime Minister Datuk Seri Najib Tun Razak
attending the opening ceremony of the 7th International
Conference on Malay Studies, Beijing 2014, hosted by the
University on 30th May 2014

2014

▌葡萄牙总统卡瓦科·席尔瓦
发表演讲。

Portuguese President Cavaco
Silva making a speech

一九四一年，抗大三分校俄文队在陕北高原成立，播下中国共产党创办外语教育的火种。七十余年后的今天，经过几代人的努力奋斗，北京外国语大学已基本形成了以外国语言文学学科为主体，文、法、经、管多学科协调发展的专业格局，成为一所享誉海内外、具有鲜明特色和突出学科优势的大学。学校坚持"外、特、精"的办学理念，以建设国际一流、特色鲜明的高水平外国语大学为办学目标，以培养高层次国际化人才、研究和传播中外优秀文化、探索新知、推动世界文明多样性发展为办学宗旨，追求卓越，精益求精，致力于成为中国外语教育发展的引领者、服务国家全球战略的智库和中华文化向世界传播的重要基地。北京外国语大学将永远奋发图强，创造更加辉煌的明天！

Summary

1941 saw the founding of the Russian Programme at the Third Campus of Kangda, sowing the seeds for the CPC to start its own foreign language education programme. Seven decades later and through the efforts of several generations, Beijing Foreign Studies University has developed its own range of academic disciplines in which foreign languages and literature are its mainstay, and arts, law, economics and management subjects help to maintain the University's coordinated development. Today, it has grown into a university well-known both at home and abroad, with distinct characteristics and prominent disciplinary strengths. The University has upheld its guideline of development, namely, "Striving to be strong in foreign languages, unique in characteristics, and high in standards", and endeavoured to build itself into an internationally recognised first-class university with its own characteristics, cultivate high-calibre international professionals, study and propagate the cultures of China and other countries, explore new horizons of knowledge, and promote the diversified development of civilisations around the world. In the future it will continue to pursue academic excellence and perfection, endeavour to be the leader of China's foreign language education, a think tank serving the nation's global strategy, and an important centre for introducing Chinese culture to the world. Beijing Foreign Studies University will always strive to achieve its lofty ambitions in order to create a more glorious future.

图书在版编目（CIP）数据

北京外国语大学图史：1941~2014：汉英对照 / 《北京外国语大学图史》编撰委员会编. —
北京：外语教学与研究出版社，2015.12
ISBN 978-7-5135-6973-6

I. ①北… II. ①北… III. ①北京外国语大学－校史－1941~2014－图集 IV. ①G649.281-64

中国版本图书馆CIP数据核字(2015)第319707号

出 版 人　蔡剑峰
责任编辑　李　鑫　李潇洒
封面设计　孙　力
出版发行　外语教学与研究出版社
社　　址　北京市西三环北路19号（100089）
网　　址　http://www.fltrp.com
印　　刷　北京华联印刷有限公司
开　　本　889×1194　1/16
印　　张　22
版　　次　2016年2月第1版 2016年2月第1次印刷
书　　号　ISBN 978-7-5135-6973-6
定　　价　98.00元

购书咨询：（010）88819926　电子邮箱：club@fltrp.com
外研书店：https://waiyants.tmall.com
凡印刷、装订质量问题，请联系我社印制部
联系电话：（010）61207896　电子邮箱：zhijian@fltrp.com
凡侵权、盗版书籍线索，请联系我社法律事务部
举报电话：（010）88817519　电子邮箱：banquan@fltrp.com
法律顾问：立方律师事务所　刘旭东律师
　　　　　中咨律师事务所　殷　斌律师
物料号：269730001